ETHICS WITHOUT PRINCIPLES

Jonathan Dancy presents a long-awai
particularism in ethics, a view with wh
twenty years. He argues that the traditio
principles, or between being moral and havii
a mistake. The possibility of moral thought a   .y
way depend on an adequate supply of princip   ...s claim
on a form of reasons-holism, holding that wha   ...son in one case need
not be any reason in another, and maintaining that moral reasons are no
different in this respect from others. He puts forward a distinctive form of
value-holism to go with the holism of reasons, and he gives a detailed
discussion of the currently popular topic of 'contributory' reasons.
Opposing positions of all sorts are summarized and criticized.

   Ethics Without Principles is the definitive statement of particularist ethical
theory, and will be required reading for all those working on moral
philosophy.

Jonathan Dancy is Professor of Philosophy at the University of Reading.

ETHICS WITHOUT PRINCIPLES

JONATHAN DANCY

CLARENDON PRESS • OXFORD

OXFORD

UNIVERSITY PRESS

Great Clarendon Street, Oxford OX2 6DP

Oxford University Press is a department of the University of Oxford.
It furthers the University's objective of excellence in research, scholarship,
and education by publishing worldwide in

Oxford New York

Auckland Cape Town Dar es Salaam Hong Kong Karachi
Kuala Lumpur Madrid Melbourne Mexico City Nairobi
New Delhi Shanghai Taipei Toronto
With offices in
Argentina Austria Brazil Chile Czech Republic France Greece
Guatemala Hungary Italy Japan South Korea Poland Portugal
Singapore Switzerland Thailand Turkey Ukraine Vietnam

Oxford is a registered trade mark of Oxford University Press
in the UK and in certain other countries

Published in the United States
by Oxford University Press Inc., New York

© Jonathan Dancy 2004

The moral rights of the author have been asserted

Database right Oxford University Press (maker)

Reprinted 2009

ISBN 978-0-19-929768-9

Printed in the United Kingdom by
Lightning Source UK Ltd., Milton Keynes

For Sarah, once again

PREFACE

I have been thinking about the matters with which this book is concerned off and on for more than twenty years. I remember when I was a graduate at Oxford wondering why causation was held to be so obviously impossible in the absence of causal laws. It was only later that I extended this bemusement to ethics, where, in trying to turn mere puzzlement into something more like a philosophical position, I took myself to be building on the work of John McDowell and David Wiggins. During that period I spent many hours in discussion with David McNaughton. Later we were joined at Keele by Eve Garrard, another kindred spirit who has kept me on the straight and narrow in more than one sense over the years. Apart from them, and in the main more recently, I am grateful to a whole host of friends and colleagues, conversations with whom (in some cases many conversations) have made differences to this book in all sorts of ways. I am thinking here particularly of David Bakhurst, Bill Blattner, John Broome, Larry Cahoone, Roger Crisp, Stephen Gardiner, Jay Garfield, Peter Hacker, Richard Holton, Brad Hooker, Tom Hurka, Frank Jackson, Mark Lance, Rae Langton, Margaret Little, Jonathan Lowe, Stephen Mulhall, Derek Parfit, Joseph Raz, Michael Ridge, Toni Rønnow-Rasmussen, Michael Smith, Philip Stratton-Lake, Christine Swanton, Charles Travis, Heath White, and Tim Williamson.

Gratitude to institutions is less personal but can still be keenly felt. The existence of this book can be ascribed to (or blamed on) the generosity of the British Academy, which gave me the extraordinary privilege of a Research Readership (1999–2001) to write it. I owe the Academy an apology for not producing the promised object quite on time. I am almost equally grateful to All Souls College, Oxford, for a Visiting Fellowship in 1993–4, which was given to enable me to continue working on the themes of my earlier *Moral Reasons* (1993). Chapters 9, 10, and 12 of the present book were initially drafted during that period, although I was then sidetracked into work that became my *Practical Reality* (2000). I owe thanks to the Philosophy Department at Georgetown University, Washington, DC (primarily in the person of Wayne Davis) for giving me a research position in early 2000, which enabled me to spend three happy months reading what others had said about the topics that I was interested in. I am also grateful to the University of Canterbury (NZ) for the award of an Erskine Fellowship in early 2002, in which I started writing the second and final draft of this book. Finally, I owe thanks to the University of Reading for its provision of sabbatical leave, and to my colleagues at Reading in general for their charitable attitude to the way in which I used my research time. But this last debt is more personal than institutional.

Simon Kirchin, Maggie Little, Sean McKeever, and Michael Ridge read an entire first draft, as did Geoffrey Sayre-McCord and groups of graduate students at Georgetown and Chapel Hill. My second draft was read by Bart Streumer and Roger Crisp, in addition to Maggie Little (again!) and Richard Holton, who acted as OUP's referees. All of these kind folk gave me detailed comments to which I have tried to respond appropriately, and I am much in their debt.

Some material in Chapter 7 is taken from my 'Scanlon's Principles'. Some of the material in Chapter 12 appeared in my 'The Particularist's Progress'. A version of Chapter 10 has appeared in *Ethics* under the title 'Are there Organic Unities?'. Some material from Chapters 2, 3, and 4 has appeared under the title 'What do reasons do?' in the proceedings of a Spindel conference in the *Southern Journal of Philosophy*.

Ethics without Principles is the culmination of twenty-five years' work— effectively my philosophical lifetime. Throughout, I have been sustained by the love and friendship of my wife Sarah. She has, I fear, seen through me; but she has also seen me through. This book is dedicated to her.

CONTENTS

1

What are the Options?

1. INTRODUCTION

In this book I try to elaborate and to defend a particularist conception of morality, or of ethics more generally. A particularist conception is one which sees little if any role for moral principles. Particularists think that moral judgement can get along perfectly well without any appeal to principles, indeed that there is no essential link between being a full moral agent and having principles. So there are plenty of attacks on principles in this book. It is for this sort of reason that particularism is often mistakenly thought of as an attack on morality—as a form of moral scepticism. That would be quite wrong. Particularists, if they are anything like myself, think that morality is in perfectly good shape and functioning quite happily, and that abandoning the mistaken link between morality and principles is if anything a defence of morality rather than an attack on it.

This can seem rather startling. We are accustomed to think that the moral person is the person of principle. We have learnt that an unprincipled person is one not to be trusted (especially our political leaders, who are supposed to have principles—political ones—even if nobody else does). We take it that the right way to think morally is to bring moral principles to bear on each new situation, and that it is only if one has a full set of principles in one's grasp that one is in the best possible position to decide what to do in the tricky situations that life throws up. In a more theoretical vein, we have also come to think that without principles there could be no such thing as morality at all—no difference between the right and the wrong. So we have inherited a complex picture of the ethical which puts principles right at the centre, in ways that are worth distinguishing. There are three distinct questions, the answer to each of which is thought to make important appeal to principles. These questions are: what is it to be a moral person? how ought one to make moral decisions? and how is it possible for an action to be right or wrong? The supposed answers are that a moral person is a person of principle, that one should make decisions by relating one's principles to the facts of the case before one, and that an action can only be right if there is a principle that somehow says so.

Particularists think all this is wrong. They face an uphill struggle, because principled conceptions of the ethical are culturally dominant and have been for centuries, at least in the West. And it is not as if nobody acts in accordance with such conceptions. People do 'have' principles, and they do (sometimes, at least) appeal to them in making their own decisions and in judging the actions of others. They condemn anyone who fails to act on his own principles, or whose principles they take not to be the right ones. And they try to act 'consistently', where this means making their decisions in such a way that they can all be fitted in under the same set of principles. So it is not as if all this talk of principles is mere theory. People actually order their lives (and the lives of others) according to their principles, and it is not very surprising that they are reluctant to admit that there is any chance that the whole thing is a mistake.

There are two sorts of approach that a particularist can take in trying to make a persuasive case against any essential link between morality and principles. The first is to try to show that no suggested principles are anything like flexible enough to cover the ground and do the job we require of them. Moral life, it can be said, is just too messy, and the situations we encounter differ from each other in subtle ways that no panoply of principles could ever manage to capture. Principles deal in samenesses, and there just aren't enough samenesses to go round.

I think that this is true, but it is not the way in which I tend to argue, and it is not the strategy of this book. To write such a book, one would presumably have to give more and more subtle and delicate descriptions of complex moral situations, and show that no matter how carefully one tries to frame one's principles, there will always be a situation about which those principles would generate the wrong answer. But you will find very little of that sort in this book—which is rather a shame, since it would be an interesting thing to try to do. Instead, I argue that there is no reason whatever to suppose that morality stands or falls with a supply of principles capable of doing the job required of them. I suggest that morality can get along perfectly well without principles, and that the imposition of principles on an area that doesn't need them is likely to lead to some sort of distortion.

The book I have not written would really be an investigation of the subtleties of our moral thought and the actual complexities of life. The book I have written is about how to understand the way in which reasons work, and deals largely with *theories* about reasons rather than with life. As you can see, I would like to have been able to write the other book, the one about life, but this one is all I could manage.

I think, however, that if you come to be persuaded of the truth of particularism, and even if you only recognize some strength in particularist arguments of the sort that I will be putting forward, you will come to make your own moral decisions in rather different ways from the ones you have used in the past. So even if the issues discussed in this book are theoretical, the book does have a practical purpose, which is to change the ways in which we think about what to do, and thereby to change what we do. I don't mean that everything that principled people do is wrong, of course; only that they often come to do the right thing in the wrong sort of way, and that sometimes mistakes in their approach can result in mistakes in action.

2. A RANGE OF OPTIONS

In this section I will be offering readers a range of options, and the remainder of the book is intended to persuade you that the most extreme of these options is in the end the most defensible. The different options are different ways of understanding the relation between morality and moral principles. By morality I mean moral thought and judgement, and more generally moral distinctions such as that between right and wrong. I offer no account of the distinction between the moral and the non-moral—between moral judgement and non-moral judgement, for instance. I simply rely on the reader's intuitive grasp of this distinction; in fact, I think that there is no known theoretical way of characterizing it, and we had better not put too much stress on it.

I start with an option which I take to be largely discredited. We can call this the subsumptive option. It thinks of moral thought and judgement as the subsumption of the particular case under some universal principle. The idea is that, if we are doing our moral thinking properly, we approach a new case with a set of principles, and that we look to see which of those principles the case falls under. If this *alone* sufficed for moral judgement, the principles we are dealing with would have to be of a certain sort. It would, that is, either have to be impossible for a given case to fall under more than one principle or, if more than one principle does apply, they must all recommend the same thing. For otherwise, once we had done our subsuming, we would not have finished our work; we would then have to decide which principle, of all those that apply, is the dominant one in the case, and this would require more than subsumption. So the subsumptive option thinks of its principles in the following way. For each case, all principles that apply to it must recommend the same action, and each such principle must be *decisive* in the sense that it decides the issue; however things are in other ways, *any* principle that applies gives you *the* answer to the question what you should (morally speaking) do.

I said that the subsumptive option is now largely discredited. If it is discredited, this is for three reasons. It gives the wrong sense to the notion of moral conflict, it can make no sense of the relevant notion of moral regret, and it lacks a persuasive epistemology.

The subsumptive option gives the wrong sense to the notion of moral conflict because it is forced to say that anyone who thinks that there are conflicting reasons in a given case, some in favour and some against, is confused. There can be no such thing as conflicting reasons, because reasons are keyed into principles, and if there is only one principle that applies to the case, all the available reasons must be keyed into that principle, and so all speak on the same side. So if you think that there are conflicting reasons in the case, you must be wrong. There may be a conflict in you (which will probably be about what the relevant principle is) but there can be no conflict between reasons. All that I want to say about this position is that we would need a very strong argument before accepting any such thing.

Given that all the reasons in the case will be on the same side, it is going to be very hard to give any decent sense to the notion of regret. The sort of regret I am thinking of here is the regret we feel when, though what we did was the right thing to do, still there were strong reasons to do something else. The standard example here is that of someone who is forced to break a significant engagement in order to help someone knocked down in the street. Suppose, for instance, that I represent some large body of opinion in the community, and that I am on my way to meet our local Member of Parliament (or of Congress, or whatever) to press our case on a key issue such as whether there should or should not be a second ring road built around the town; and this is the only chance of meeting her. If I stop to help the person knocked down in front of me in the street by a passing car, I will miss my appointment and let my constituency down. If I walk on past, I will (rightly) feel dreadful. In fact, I will feel dreadful, and rightly so, whatever I do. The world has conspired against me. But the subsumptive option says that, whichever I ought to do, there can be no reason to feel bad about not having done the other thing. It is not just that it would have been wrong to do that thing. There was no reason to do the other thing at all, since only one principle applied to the case, and it was decisive, and the only reasons around were those which depend for their existence on that principle. If I suppose that I did the right thing, then, I should suppose that there was no reason to take the alternative course, and so I should not have anything to regret. One might perhaps think that I could reasonably regret the fact that fate had put me in such a difficult position. But the position is not itself difficult, according to the subsumptive option. Any difficulty lies in working out what to do in it. But this is an epistemological difficulty, not a moral one. And regretting an epistemological difficulty makes little sense, since there is no ground for expecting the world always to provide us with simple answers. The sort of regret we were after was the sort that goes with having to let someone down, not the sort that goes with having to make a difficult decision.

Let us suppose, though, that the subsumptive option can somehow manoeuvre so as to avoid the difficulties mentioned so far.[1] There remains the question how we are to know which principles are the right ones and which

---

[1] It might, for instance, hope to do better by introducing a new set of principles, second-level ones whose business it is to tell us which of two conflicting basic principles is to win. But this manoeuvre would have to explain why a 'defeated' principle is not thereby refuted. If the basic principles continue to say the sorts of thing we originally thought of them as saying, it is not clear how a conflict between them can fail to be a test case which only one basic principle can survive.

are mere pretenders. We certainly cannot hope to extract principles from our judgements about particular cases, because that sort of judgement is supposed to be based on principles. If judgement is subsumptive, it needs principles to start from, which cannot be got from further judgement on pain of a regress. But how else are we to distinguish true principles from false ones? It is not attractive to suppose that the true principles will somehow bear truth on their face, so that one only has to contemplate them long enough to tell that they are true. Nor is it attractive to suppose, as the subsumptive option does, that particular cases can never be tests for principles. If we have in mind two possible principles, under either of which the present case could be subsumed, and which give different (i.e. conflicting) answers to the question what to do, we are in no position (as the subsumptive option sees things) to decide which principle is the sound one by checking its results against the facts. We cannot say, 'this principle says we should not do it, and indeed we should not do it, and so the principle is sound'—this would be too much like asking the principle to validate itself; for the judgement that we should not do it must itself be principle-based, on this option, and the only available principle is the one we were supposed to be checking.

These points could all be elaborated in fancy ways, but their role in my overall argument is merely to give us reason to look for a different account of moral judgement and its relation to principles. But the alternative account that I will be arguing for is very extreme. It claims that morality has no need for principles at all. Moral thought, moral judgement, and the possibility of moral distinctions—none of these depends in any way on the provision of a suitable supply of moral principles. This claim is what I call particularism. And it is certainly quite a step from the rejection of the subsumptive option to accepting particularism. After all, the subsumptive option was rejected, not because it involved an appeal to principles, but because the sort of appeal to principles that it made failed to deliver on several fronts. What is needed, we might think, must therefore be a different sort of appeal to principles, not no appeal to principles at all.

Things went wrong because the principles we were dealing with were decisive, which meant that even if more than one principle could apply to a given case, they must all recommend the same action. This was the feature that made conflict and regret unintelligible. What we want, therefore, is an account under which several principles can apply to one and the same case, some recommending one action and others recommending another, in a way that somehow yields an overall verdict as to how to act. We could call such principles contributory principles. W. D. Ross (1930, ch. 2) constructed the classic theory of contributory principles, which he called principles of prima facie duty.[2]

---

[2] It is important not to be misled by this term. In Ross's usage, it does not mean 'at first sight', as it does, for instance, in the law, where a prima facie case is one which may turn out to be no case at all. For Ross, a prima facie duty is *not* one which may turn out to be a mere appearance of a duty. His notion of a prima facie duty is a technical one which means what he defines it as meaning.

The leading idea here is that a single action can have several features, some of which count in favour of the action and others of which count against; where we have several options to choose between, the same will be true of each. We are capable of recognizing which features are operating in this way and which are not, and we are capable of bringing together the features that count in favour of and against each option, and thus eventually of coming to an overall judgement about which action is the one that overall we should do. For each such morally relevant feature, there is a principle of prima facie duty, which specifies the feature and says whether it counts in favour or against. So: one should not lie, one should save life, one should be kind, one should be fair, one should not break a promise, and so on. These are all principles of prima facie duty, since they specify morally relevant features along with what we might call their valence or polarity (positive or negative as the case may be). None of these principles is decisive, since each is such that it may apply in a case where overall one should not behave as it says. And the theory is not subsumptive, or rather not merely subsumptive, since it maintains that once we have recognized which principles apply to the case (that is, which prima facie duties are in play here), we still have something to do which is not subsumption, namely determine where the balance of duty lies, and so what we ought overall to do (which Ross calls our duty proper). Ross maintains that there are no principles telling us where the balance of duty lies, and leaves the matter up to unaided judgement.

I will later lay this theory out in much greater detail, and try to show why I don't think it can be got to work. For the moment all I want to do is to point out that the theory avoids the problems we found with the subsumptive option. First, it can easily make sense of moral conflict, since it allows that there can be reasons both for and against one and the same action. Maybe to save a life I will have to lie. If so, I have a duty proper to do something which I have a prima facie duty not to do. Moral reasons and prima facie duties go together for Ross, though he did not tend to talk in terms of reasons. So there can be conflict between prima facie duties. Second, the theory can for that reason make sense of moral regret as the rational response to the fact that a defeated prima facie duty was still exactly that, namely a reason not to do the action which overall one had (morally speaking) to do. The reason not to do the action does not go away; it remains in play, in Ross's theory, and regret consists in an appropriate recognition of that fact. Finally, Ross is able to provide something in the way of an epistemology for his prima facie duties. He suggests that we are able to discern, in a given case, that a given feature is here counting in favour of action. This is an instance of empirical moral knowledge whose relevance is restricted to the case before us. But we can immediately infer from this, by a process which Ross calls intuitive induction, that the same feature will count in favour of action wherever else it is to be found. Knowledge of this universal fact is knowledge of a general prima facie duty, and in knowing this universal fact we know a moral principle. But we don't know that principle directly; since we infer it from what we discern in a particular case, particular cases can act as tests for principles.

So Ross's theory is much more healthy than the subsumptive option with which we started. (To be sure, as I have presented it so far it is not much of a theory, since it has very little structure; but there is really a lot more in it, as will be revealed later.) We will be needing to take Ross's position very seriously. But suppose that we reject his position as a general account of moral thought. The main reason for rejecting it is that Ross asserts without hesitation that if a feature counts in favour of action in one case, then necessarily it counts in favour in any case in which it appears. This is what takes him from the recognition that this feature matters here (which is what is epistemically basic, for him) to knowledge of a general principle. The particularist will challenge the crucial assumption that what is relevant in one case is necessarily similarly relevant elsewhere. This is the moment to introduce some more terminology, in addition to what we have so far:

Particularism: the possibility of moral thought and judgement does not depend on the provision of a suitable supply of moral principles.
Generalism: the very possibility of moral thought and judgement depends on the provision of a suitable supply of moral principles.

Particularists and generalists, as I define them, disagree about the relation between moral thought and moral judgement. Officially, they hold no views on topics outside morality. But of course that is unrealistic. The debate between them tends to turn on the rights and wrongs of two other views, which have nothing especially to do with morality at all:

Holism in the theory of reasons: a feature that is a reason in one case may be no reason at all, or an opposite reason, in another.
Atomism in the theory of reasons: a feature that is a reason in one case must remain a reason, and retain the same polarity, in any other.

The atomist holds that features carry their practical relevance around from place to place; the holist thinks that context can affect the ability of a feature to make a difference in a new case. (Here, making a difference means being a reason for acting one way rather than another.)

Normally, particularists are holists and generalists are atomists (though we will later see all sorts of ways in which one can locate oneself with respect to the four positions above). Ross, anyway, is a generalist and he is an atomist (though the principles he has in mind are prima facie ones, not decisive ones), and these facts are not unconnected. The particularists that I have in mind will be holists. And it is their holism that underlies their rejection of Ross's form of generalism.

But there are forms of holism that do not go so far as particularism. That is, we can accept the context-sensitivity, the variability, of reasons, but still suppose that there are the sorts of general truths about how reasons behave that might be expressed by moral principles. So even if we do reject Ross's position, there remains some distance to go before we get to particularism. Consider the following series of conditionals offered by Robert Brandom (2000: 88):

1. If I strike this dry, well-made match, then it will light. ($p \rightarrow q$)
2. If p and the match is in a very strong electromagnetic field, then it will *not* light. ((p & r) $\rightarrow -q$)
3. If p and r and the match is in a Faraday cage, then it will light. ((p & r & s) $\rightarrow q$)
4. If p and r and s and the room is evacuated of oxygen, then it will *not* light. ((p & r & s & t) $\rightarrow -q$)

Someone might believe all these conditionals at once, and the same would be true of a similar series whose right-hand side (the constant 'q' in Brandom's example) is not 'it will light', but something like 'I ought not to do this'. In either case the sort of reasoning we are involved in, symbolized by the arrow in the formulations above, is what is technically called 'non-monotonic'. An inference is monotonic if additions to the premises cannot make a good or cogent inference less good or cogent. Deductive reasoning is like this; an inference, once logically valid, remains so no matter what one adds as a premise (even if it be the negation of one of the original premises). Brandom's example is non-monotonic, since the cogent inference in (1) is reversed by the addition of the further consideration that the match is in a strong electromagnetic field.

If one allows that this sort of thing can happen, is one therefore a holist in my sense? One would be if the fact that I am striking a dry, well-made match is functioning as a reason for believing that it will light in the first case, but not in the second or the fourth. But Brandom is not trying to allude to that sort of possibility by his example. His point is rather the sort of phenomenon we find in chemistry: a feature may have a certain effect when alone, even though its combination with another feature will have the opposite effect. One could call this a 'holistic' point perfectly sensibly, but it is not holistic in my sense of that term. Holism in my sense is the claim that a feature which has a certain effect when alone can have the opposite effect in a combination. It is one thing to say, as Brandom does, that though a alone speaks in favour of action, $a + b$ speaks as a whole against it; it is another to say that though a speaks in favour of action when alone, *it* speaks against action when in combination. The difference lies in what is doing the speaking against in cases where features are combined. In the former case (Brandom's) it is the combination; in the latter case (mine) it is the feature that originally spoke in favour. For an example of the difference between Brandom and me, consider the relation between the following three 'principles':

1. If you are causing someone pain, you are doing something wrong. ($p \rightarrow q$)
2. If p and the pain is a statutory punishment for a recognized offence, you are not doing something wrong. ((p & r) $\rightarrow -q$)

3. If p & r and the punishee was unjustly convicted, you are doing something wrong. $((p \text{ \& } r \text{ \& } s) \rightarrow q)$

If we say these things, are we therefore holists? That depends on whether we think that, in the second case, the fact that we are causing someone pain ceases to be a reason not to do what we are doing. Holists in my sense would be open to such a suggestion, even if they decided that it is not how things in fact work in this case. But Brandom's approach doesn't really ask about the role of any particular part of the combination.

In what way, then, would a Brandom-style approach to ethics differ from Ross? The answer to this question is not entirely simple. The first point is that Ross would not offer any principles like (1)–(3) above, for these look as if they are offered as decisive principles with increasingly complex left-hand sides. Ross would say that no such principles could be correct, because even where things are as the left-hand side of one of these principles has it, there might be a stronger duty to act in some other way. On the other hand, if we understand (1)–(3) above as expressions of contributory principles, they would not make sense to Ross at all. The idea that a feature such as causing pain could be the ground of a prima facie duty not to act and part of the ground of a prima facie duty to act does not fit Ross's general approach at all. The only way in which Ross could come to agree with (1)–(3) above is if (2) is understood as specifying one feature that is a reason against acting and another that is a stronger reason in favour of acting, and (3) is understood as introducing a second reason against acting which, together with the reason specified by (1), is sufficient to turn the tables back again. But that is not Brandom's picture. So if we find that Brandom's picture offers a suggestive possibility for understanding the way in which moral reasoning might work, we have moved away from what Ross is offering in favour of something that could be called holistic—but it is not the sort of holism that takes one to particularism. We will want to know, therefore, what takes us any further away from Ross's picture than Brandom is willing to go.

What is more, one can move beyond Brandom without yet being a particularist. Brandom did not look inside combinations of reasons, and so was unable to say that a feature that is a reason in favour in one case is a reason against in another. Shelly Kagan (1988) does look inside combinations of reasons, and as a result denies what he calls 'The Additive Fallacy', which is the fallacy of treating moral deliberation on what I think of as a kitchen scales model. In a kitchen, everything we weigh has an independent weight which remains the same whatever we weigh it with—whatever it is present with on the weighing pan. Similarly, as the Additive Fallacy has it, reasons for and against an action have each a certain weight, and one can tell whether to do the action by weighing the reasons for and the reasons against, and seeing which combination is the weightier. Crucially, the weight of all the reasons against is identical with the sum of the independent weights of each reason against, and the same is true of the reasons in favour. The whole matter is additive, and the only question is which side adds up to more than the other.

Kagan suggests that an additive model like this is too simple, and that we need to entertain something more like a multiplicative model: one under which the result of combining two reasons is not the sum of their independent weights, as on the kitchen scales model, but their product. On the additive model, if one reason has a weight of 1 and another a weight of 2, the weight of the combination is $1 + 2 = 3$. On a simple multiplicative model, it will be $1 \times 2 = 2$. More dramatically, if one has a weight of 1 and another a weight of 0, then on the multiplicative model the weight of the combination will be $1 \times 0 = 0$.

This multiplicative model does not go as far as particularism does in its denial of invariability. The form of holism it enshrines is quite limited. Each feature that has weight, as it sees things, has the same weight in every case; so far, the position is invariabilist. The trick is that though a feature always has the same weight, that weight does not always make the same difference to how one should act. Whether that weight is, as it were, passed on in the calculation depends on what it is multiplied by. A feature may, in this sense, have its normal weight but pass on more than that weight (as it would when multiplied by anything more than 1) or less (as it would when multiplied by anything between 1 and 0) or even nothing at all (as it would be if multiplied by 0 or a negative number).

So what we get is a picture under which features with constant weight make variable contributions to how one should act; the effect of the presence of a feature varies case by case, but the weight it has does not. This position is different from particularism, and the holism it expresses is less extreme, because the particularist sees no need to think that every feature has a constant weight; indeed, particularists can be expected to suggest that there is something incoherent in Kagan's mix of variability and invariability—an unholy marriage. For the particularist, it is going to be variability all the way down. (I criticize Kagan's views in detail in Chapter 10.3.)

What we have seen here is a sort of spectrum of options. From the subsumptive option we moved to Ross's theory of prima facie principles. From that, under pressure from holism in the theory of reasons, we moved to a conception of moral reasoning that we built on an example of Brandom's. From that, influenced by the weakness of Brandom's rejection of atomism, we moved to Kagan's picture under which the contribution of an individual feature, though in some sense it remains the same from case to case, can be increased, reduced, or even reversed by the presence of another feature (which was more than anything that Brandom was in a position to say). From that we moved to particularism proper, which denies that there need be anything at all that remains the same from case to case.

Which of these views is appropriate to ethics will be debated later. My purpose at this stage is merely to show that there are various conceptions of the ways in which moral reasons function, some more and some less 'variabilist', as one might put it. Our first two options (subsumption and Ross) were fully invariabilist in their conception of the way in which reasons work. The other three became more and more variabilist until we reached the extreme of particularism.

Before leaving these cartographical considerations, I want to introduce a different spectrum, that of the codifiability of moral principles. Here again the particularist is out at one end, and it may be helpful to see just how this works. Let us start at the other end, where codifiability reigns supreme. Welfarism is the view that there is only one moral principle: one's duty on any and all occasions is to do that action whose performance will maximize the general welfare. This principle is fully codifiable; I have just codified it.

Ross's view is that there are many codifiable principles. Unlike the Welfarist's Sole Principle they are all principles of prima facie duty, not of duty proper. But like the Welfarist's Principle, they are all simple, in a way that is made possible by Ross's atomism; they don't have to be very complex, because each specifies a single feature and tells us what difference it makes wherever it appears.

Next in line are positions which I will label 'expansionist'. Suppose that we find a feature F that has counted in favour of action on every occasion we have yet come across, and we formulate a principle, 'Actions with feature F are right'. Think of this as a principle of prima facie duty. Now we come across an awkward case in which, because of the presence of a different feature G, F does not count in favour of action at all. So we complicate our principle. It now reads, 'Actions with feature F are prima facie right, unless they also have G'. Then we realize that having G only has this effect if the action does not also have another feature H. Now our principle has to read, 'Actions with feature F are prima facie right, unless they also have G—except when they have H as well'. Our original simple formulations will become more and more complex in this sort of way, if the intuitions that underlie holism in the theory of reasons are at all sound. But that doesn't matter, we may say. The crucial point is that we still have some codified principles, even if they are rather more unwieldy than the ones we started from.

Expansionism of this sort takes us from simple principles of prima facie duty to more complex ones; but each complex principle is still thought of as specifying something contributory. And there is another sort of expansionism, which offers principles that are complex but decisive. We find a view of this sort in Scanlon (1998; 2000: 309). Scanlon rejects all contributory conceptions of the way in which appeal to principles works; properly understood, principles cannot conflict, and so we do not need to appeal to balancing case by case or to a lexical ordering established in advance, or any other such device, in order to show how conflict can be resolved. What looks like a conflict between principles is really a relation between inadequately understood and incompletely specified principles, and the matter is resolved by a more complete specification of at least one of them. For instance, if I start with two principles, or rather formulations, 'Do not lie' and 'Save life', I may come across a case where one of them has to give. But what in fact happens then is that I complicate one of them so as to remove the conflict; I end up, perhaps, with 'Do not lie except to save life' and 'Save life'—and all is well, at least for a while. Moral progress, then, seems to require more and more elaborately codified principles, with each so expressed that it is impossible for it to require of us actions forbidden by other principles. Properly understood, it seems, the duty to save life is incapable of conflicting with the duty not to lie. This kind of internal complexity takes us further away from the simple formulations with which we began, and, of course, adopts a less respectful attitude to the formulations that we are currently using.

At the end of this spectrum is the particularist, who is likely to be fairly sceptical about a process whose presumed end point will be one in which all principles contain complex reference to any other principle with which they might otherwise conflict. It is not hard to wonder what the point of such a process is and whether the complexities of its eventual product are ones that we could hope to grasp and operate. For the particularist, if principles have got to be like this, we would be better off without any such things at all.

PART I

Catching the Contributory

2

Contributory Reasons

Particularism is supposed to be a doctrine about how moral reasons work, and what is required or not required for them to operate as they do. As I understand things and will try to present them, undistorted views about how reasons work lead naturally to a particularist account of moral thought and judgement. This part of the book, therefore, offers what is in a way an independent enquiry into the nature of reasons. This may surprise some; but I offer no apology. My underlying view is that the errors of generalism can mostly be traced back to errors in the theory of reasons. There is a pervasive tendency to think that all reasons are grounded in principles of reason, or that if not all, still all the moral ones must be. There are, however, some philosophers who think that the need for moral principles is more practical than theoretical, and I try to respond to them in Chapter 7.5.

In the present chapter, I argue in favour of a certain explanation of what reasons do, and against other explanations which I take to be prejudicial to the prospects of particularism.

1. REASON AND REASONS

When I talk in this book about reasons for action, I mean to be talking of what I call contributory reasons. A contributory reason for action is a feature whose presence makes something of a case for acting, but in such a way that the overall case for doing that action can be improved or strengthened by the addition of a second feature playing a similar role. Also, a contributory reason on one side is not necessarily destroyed by the presence of a reason on the other side. This does happen sometimes, I agree, but it is far from the standard case. Contributory reasons are officially reasons capable of doing what they do either alone or in combination with others. But they can combine in peculiar and irregular ways, as we will see. There is no guarantee that the case for doing an action, already made to some extent by the presence of one reason, will be improved by adding a second reason to it. Reasons are like rats, at least to the extent that two rats that are supposedly on the same side may in fact turn and fight among themselves; similarly, the addition of the second reason may make things worse rather than better. Remember the joke about a New York restaurant: there are two things wrong with this restaurant—the food is terrible and the portions are too small.[1]

Much of our talk of reasons is about contributory reasons in this sense, reasons on one side or on the other, reasons that stack up with others to make a better or worse case for an action. But as well as talking about reasons in this way, we also speak of what there is overall reason to do. There is nothing wrong with that, of course, but it should not delude us into thinking that there are such things as overall reasons in addition to the contributory ones. To talk of what there is overall reason to do (and note that 'reason' in this phrase is not a count noun) is to talk about where the contributory reasons come down—on this side or on that. We can say we have more reason to do this than to do that, but most reason to do some third thing. These verdicts[2] do not themselves specify further reasons (of an overall sort), on pain of changing the very situation on which they pass verdict. So there are no overall reasons. All reasons, then, are contributory, unless we can find a further sort of reason that is neither contributory nor overall. (Which may not be so hard; we might think that there are such things as decisive reasons, which are neither verdictive, since they don't pass verdict on other reasons, nor contributory, since they would be destroyed (as decisive, at least) by the presence of an opposing decisive reason.)

En passant: the point that verdictive judgements do not contribute to the situations on which they pass judgement is only one application of the more general truth that thin concepts cannot be used to add to the store of reasons. That an action is good, or right, is no reason to do it. It is the features that make the action good or right that are the reasons for doing it, and to say that it is good or right is merely to express a judgement about the way in which other considerations go to determine how we should act. At least, this is true if we identify these thin judgements with judgements about overall reason. We might follow Thomas Scanlon (1998: 95–7) and earlier intuitionists before him such as Ewing (1947: 148–9) in identifying the judgement that an act is good with the judgement that it has features that give us overall reason to admire, respect, imitate it, etc. We might follow Stratton-Lake (2000: 14–15) in identifying the judgement that an act is right with the judgement that it has features that give us overall reason to do it, to approve of it, and so on. But even if we do not accept these 'buck-passing' accounts of the thin properties, and suppose instead that the relevant judgements about what we have overall reason to do are consequences of the thin judgements about rightness and goodness, we will get the same result. It will be the features that make the action good or right that stand as the reasons for doing it, approving of it, or

---

[1] Thanks to Jerry Dworkin for this and other jokes.

[2] I get this term from Philip Stratton-Lake (2000: 14), who in turn owes it to Philippa Foot. Stratton-Lake also accepts Foot's contrast between the verdictive and the evidential. But I prefer the term 'contributory' to their 'evidential', since I do not identify reasons for doing an action with evidence that the action ought to be done.

whatever. That it is good or right will not add to those reasons. The action's being good or right merely passes on whatever normative pressure is coming from below, without increasing that pressure. In this respect the thin properties differ from the thick ones. There is some temptation to think that the relation between thick and thin is similar to the relation between the thick and whatever lies below it; but whatever the similarities, there will be this difference: that the applicability of a thick concept is capable of altering, or adding to, the reasons thrown up from below. That an action is obscene makes a difference to how we should act (though not always the same difference) beyond any made by the features that make the action obscene.

2. THE CONTRIBUTORY AND THE OVERALL

Returning now to the main theme: how are we to understand the role played by a contributory reason? This question is not often asked, and when it has been asked the answers given have tended to be a bit incautious. Those who have addressed the issue have mostly tried to explain the role of the contributory in terms of what happens at the overall level. Jean Hampton, for instance, knows perfectly well that there are contributory reasons; she makes reference, for instance, to Ross's notion of the prima facie (1998: 51n). But when she talks about reasons, she constantly uses terms that are, one would have thought, quite inappropriate for the merely contributory. She says that reasons are 'directive' (pp. 51, 85), have 'obligatory force' (p. 99), have 'compelling rightness' (pp. 93, 99), are 'prescriptive' (p. 87), are or express commands (p. 88), concern the 'ought to be' (p. 92), 'feel like orders' (p. 106), and have a 'compelling quality' (pp. 91–2). All these remarks seem to be more appropriate at the overall level. An overall 'ought' (that is, the answer to the question what we ought to do, all things considered) is indeed a directive; in a perfectly clear sense (at least for present purposes), it tells us what to do—what we should do. It expresses a command, maybe, it has a compelling quality, it has 'obligatory force' in some sense or other, it feels like an order and directs us to do this rather than that. The question then is whether contributory reasons do the same as the overall 'ought' does. And the answer is surely that they don't. If an overall 'ought' commands, it cannot be that contributory reasons command as well; there is no such thing as a *pro tanto*[3] command. We have reasons on both sides of the question, often enough. Is it that each reason on either side commands, and then that somehow the sum

---

[3] This is the first occurrence of this term in this book. '*Pro tanto*' means 'as far as that goes'. It has become common to prefer this term to Ross's term 'prima facie', because the latter looks as if it means 'at first glance'—which, in Ross's usage, it most definitely does not. In this book I try to avoid both of them in favour of 'contributory reason'. But all these terms are trying to capture the same phenomenon.

total of them commands as well? I don't think this is a coherent scenario; there are too many commands floating about.

Hampton may have made a mistake in offering a rather direct explication of what reasons do which really applies only at the overall level. But this does not show that with a bit more subtlety we could not do better, while still appealing to some relation to an overall ought. (From now on I will drop the inverted commas around 'ought' and talk of oughts rather than of 'ought's.) In what follows I consider a long list of suggestions of this sort, and reject them all. But they are rejected not because there is reason in advance to say that no attempt of this sort can succeed. Each will be rejected for specific failings rather than for being of that general style. I will, however, eventually suggest a general reason for thinking that we have been looking in the wrong place.

The first and most common suggestion about the relation between contributory reasons and oughts is that to be a contributory reason is to be a consideration that would decide the issue (i.e. ground an overall ought) if it were the only relevant consideration. My own favourite version of this idea is in Ross, who wrote:

> I suggest 'prima facie' duty or 'conditional duty' as a brief way of referring to the characteristic (quite distinct from that of being a duty proper) which an act has, in virtue of being of a certain kind (e.g. the keeping of a promise), of being an act which would be a duty proper if it were not at the same time of another kind which is morally significant. (1930: 19–20)

We can think of this as a functional definition or characterization of the role played by a reason: the characterization runs by appeal to something that such a thing would do in a certain circumstance. And this is supposed not just to get it right about which things are reasons and which are not, but to capture what is going on when a consideration is not alone, or is defeated, but still making a contribution of the style that we are trying to understand. Now there can be no objection to functional definitions of this sort, I think, but there can be objections to instances—and there are to this one. I have three objections, in what I think of as increasing strength.[4] The first is that the supposed definition makes essential appeal to the very concept it is trying to explicate. It does this because of the presence of the word 'significant' at the end, for this sort of significance is exactly what we are trying to understand, and the account appeals to that concept in a way that certainly looks viciously circular. It would be just the same if Ross had spoken of what is morally 'relevant'; what we are trying to understand is what it is to be 'relevant' to how to act, in the sort of way that a contributory reason is. So an answer which makes essential use of any such notion does not seem able to advance us very far.

---

[4] I have been offering objections to Ross's account for twenty years, but a recent conversation with Richard Holton has caused me to make significant adjustments to them.

My understanding of functional explanations, however, is not good enough to tell me whether this first objection is really important. Perhaps we should be thinking of Ross's definition as non-explicit; we could understand him as saying something like this:

To say that an act is a prima facie duty is to say that, in virtue of being of a certain kind, it is an act which would be a duty proper if it had no other property that functions in this same sort of way.

This gives no explicit account of the 'sort of way' at issue, but still one might feel that something has been achieved. So I pass to my second objection. This is that the definition is trying to characterize something that a feature can do in concert with others by appeal to something that can only be done in isolation, and this is a peculiar procedure. I think of it as no better than trying to characterize the contribution made by a football player to his side's victory by talking only about how things would have been had he been the only player on the field. This is no better than trying to give an account of what it is to contribute to a conversation in terms of the nature of a monologue.

Third, and perhaps most forcibly, the definition assumes that each relevant feature could be the only relevant feature. But this assumption seems not to be true. There can be, and are, some reasons that are only reasons if there is another reason present as well. The most direct example I know of this, which is contrived but still effective, I owe to Michael Ridge. Suppose that I promise to do something for you only if I have some other reason to do it. If I have no other reason to do it, my having promised gives me no reason either. The promise only comes into play as a reason if there is a second reason present. The definition we are considering fails to capture reasons of this sort. But such reasons are as much reasons as any other, and so the definition is defective. John Tasioulas offered me some less artificial examples of reasons depending on other reasons: reasons of forgiveness, mercy, tolerance, and forbearance. 'Perhaps the best example is mercy', he wrote.[5] 'It depends on seeing mercy as the foil of justice. Reasons to be merciful with respect to the administration of punishment presuppose reasons (of justice) to punish in the first place. It makes no sense to say of someone that they showed "mercy" to another, when in fact there was no reason to punish them to begin with. Another example is reasons to tolerate some activity. They only exist where there are other reasons: reasons to condemn, curtail, interfere with, that activity. That's why the Scottish legal philosopher who reassured his gay colleague by saying "I tolerate you", intending to imply that he thought there was nothing wrong with being gay, was betraying a misunderstanding of the concept of toleration.' Tasioulas's examples are of reasons which require the presence of other reasons, not necessarily on the same side; Ridge's example was special because the reason required was on the same side as the

---

[5] In a private communication.

reason that required it. But these are just different ways of falsifying isolation-based approaches.

It is important to be clear about what is going on here. There is something apparently undeniable in the offing, namely that if there is a reason to ϕ, and no reason for doing anything else, and no reason not to ϕ, one ought to ϕ. The plausibility of this claim is surely part of what explains the attraction of Ross's approach. Now I do not suppose it to be in fact undeniable, since I will shortly deny it myself.[6] But whether it is true or not, it should be distinguished from the falsehood that I exposed in the previous paragraph, namely that to be a reason to ϕ is to be such that if there is no other reason in the case, the agent ought to ϕ. The latter is false because there are some reasons of which the antecedent and the consequent of this conditional explication cannot both be true at once. The example of the promise to act only if there is some other reason is exactly of this sort. This being so, what we have here is not a full characterization of what it is to be a reason.

I now leave that attempt to capture the role of a reason, which we could call the 'isolation approach', for another equally down-to-earth attempt. Perhaps a contributory reason is a consideration in whose absence the relevant action would be less obligatory, or even not obligatory at all. This version requires us to make sense of the notion that obligatoriness can be a matter of degree. But I let that pass, for reasons that will emerge later. The problem, as I see it, with this definition is that sometimes a consideration is a reason, even though in its absence we would have more reason, not less. To see what I mean by this, consider a case in which I am thinking of doing something for a friend. My action, were I to do it, would be good, and partly good because it is an expression of our friendship. But now, if I were to be doing the action and not doing it for a friend, I would presumably be doing it for someone who is not a friend, and it might be that doing it for someone who is not a friend is even better than doing it for a friend would be. It might even be that the only other potential recipients are people I don't know at all, and that if I were to do the action for one of them, it would be best of all. Now one does not have to accept this actual example in order to accept the point it is trying to make. The point is that the sort of support we are trying to capture is not easily capturable in subjunctive conditional terms. The relevant counterfactual is that if the person for whom I am doing it were not a friend, the action would be worse, and this counterfactual seems to be false. However we are to understand the matter, our friendship seems to be a reason to do the action even though if we were not friends I would have even more reason to do it. The contribution of a reason seems to be non-comparative, in this sense. (This is all very contentious, but there is more on the point in Chapter 4.1.)

---

[6] John Broome (2004) denies it implicitly, I think, because he thinks that there can be some oughts that are not grounded in reasons. If so, there might be a reason around, and that the only reason, without that reason grounding an ought, because there is an opposing ought of the special Broomean sort already in play.

A further objection to this definition will emerge at the end of the next chapter, but I pass on to the idea that a contributory reason is a consideration on which we ought to act if it is stronger than other reasons. This suggestion is not a form of isolation test, and it is therefore not vulnerable to the same sort of attack. I could content myself with saying that its appeal to the notion of strength is viciously circular (and I think the charge of vicious circularity is this time more obviously effective than it was in the case of the isolation approach). But I have another suggestion to make at this point. This is that as well as the sort of 'peremptory' reasons I have so far been discussing, which certainly do stand in some close relation to oughts (even if we are finding it hard to characterize them in terms of that relation), there are reasons of another style, which I call enticing reasons, and these do not stand in the same relation to oughts at all. Enticing reasons are to do with what would be fun, amusing, attractive, exciting, pleasant, and so on. They can be stronger and weaker, and they are often strong enough for action. But (as I understand the matter) they never take us to an ought; it is not true of an enticing reason that if one has one of them and no reason of any other sort, one ought to do what the reason entices one to do. One can do that; but one has the right not to. With peremptory reasons we could not say any such thing.[7]

Of course, if there were enticing reasons, no attempt to define the general notion of a reason in terms of some relation to oughts could hope to succeed. So perhaps I should have mentioned the possibility of enticing reasons earlier.[8] But if there are such things, we could simply restrict ourselves to the claim that peremptory reasons can be understood in terms of their relation to oughts. And this itself would not be insignificant. Note that Ross, at least, was thinking in the first instance only of moral reasons, which are indeed peremptory; it would have been irrelevant to raise the possibility of enticing reasons against him. So it is worth continuing the chase, leaving the possibility of enticing reasons to one side.

My next suggestion is that a contributory reason is a consideration that ought to motivate one. This suggestion has an interesting structure. The ought involved is of course an overall ought, as it needs to be if we are to make any progress at all. The notion of motivation involved, however, is in a sense contributory; for it allows that there may be contrary motivations, only one of which can win. 'Motivate' here is not the success-term which means 'get to act' but the attempt-term which means 'incline to act'. This affects the way in which previous arguments apply to the present suggestion. There is no isolation test involved, but might there be an appeal to the comparative idea that with this reason one ought to be more motivated than one would be

---

[7] One might allow that there is a weak sense of 'ought' in which one ought to choose the most enjoyable way of spending the afternoon, where no considerations other than pleasure are at issue. But in this weak sense of 'ought', it might be both that one ought overall to choose this and that one is permitted not to choose it. And this is hardly a sense of 'ought' at all.

[8] For much more detail about enticing reasons, see my (2004a).

without it? I think any such appeal would be optional. So far, then, we are in good shape. The main new difficulty that I see is that it is hard to believe that the structure of motivation *should* match the profile of reasons in the way suggested. It is not as if for every reason one ought to have a little bit of motivation (whatever that might mean); am I somehow in the wrong if I am not motivated at all by a reason which I am well aware is defeated in the present case? In similar vein, one could ask whether one's overall motivation to do the action ought somehow to match the extent to which the reasons for doing it are stronger than the reasons against, or the reasons for doing something else. The answer to this question seems to me to be no.[9]

A somewhat similar idea is that a reason is a consideration that ought to affect how one deliberates. The main defect of this suggestion is that it attempts to understand a reason for action by identifying it with a reason for deliberating in one way rather than another, and this seems to subvert the focus of the reason.[10] The reason, we might say, is trying to get us to act in the way it wants; it would not be satisfied if we told it that we had fully recognized it by deliberating in the way it told us to. (Apologies for the anthropomorphism here.) Admittedly, the proposal at issue is not that a reason for action is a reason for deliberating in a certain way, but that it is a consideration that *ought* to affect how one deliberates—and again this ought needs to be an overall ought, for otherwise we are merely using the notion of a contributory reason to explain itself. But even so the focus of the reason still seems to be subverted. A second problem is that there may be reasons (even overall reason) to deliberate in a certain way that are not matched by reasons for action. For instance, suppose that there is a feature that is very commonly a reason but is not a reason in the present case. We should, perhaps, bear the presence of this feature in mind when deliberating, here as elsewhere, but only so as to determine whether it is a reason—which it is not here. So being a reason for action is not the same as being a consideration that one ought to bear in mind when deliberating.

Finally, consider a remark by Jean Hampton: 'we speak of reasons using the language of obligation, as in "you ought not to drink that stuff because it is petrol"' (1998: 80). The best way to take what Hampton is saying here, I think, if it is to be different from anything we have seen before and rejected, is that to be a reason is to be the sort of thing that leads to an ought. Now this is plausible, but there is a subtle problem with it. There is a presumption here that reasons are essentially 'ought-makers'. But it seems to me that we are in fact dealing with two normative relations rather than one. The first is the relation between reasons and ought-judgements; we specify the reasons, and pass to the judgement that we ought to act. The second is a relation between

---

[9] Bart Streumer pointed out that the suggested link between reasons and motivation does not seem to fit reasons for belief.

[10] This point about subversion of focus might also apply to the previous suggestion, about motivation.

reasons and action which is not necessarily mediated by any ought at all; it is the one that is in play when we engage in the sort of practical reasoning whose 'conclusion' is an action. I don't always think, 'There is this reason for jumping; so I ought to jump'; sometimes I just think, 'There is this reason for jumping; so I'll jump'. Crucially, the relation between reason and ought-judgement is different from the relation between reason and action. And it is really the latter that we are after when we try to understand the notion of a reason for action—a practical reason. Ought-judgements are judgements, and reasoning to those judgements, however practical its purpose, is theoretical rather than practical, since it is reasoning to something that is accepted as true. It is compatible with this to suppose that people often reason to action by passing from reasons to ought-judgements, and only then to action. The point is only that the relation between the reasons and the action is different from the relation between the reasons and the ought-judgement. And we should also avoid supposing that the relation between the reasons and the action is the same as the relation between the ought-judgement and the action. For, as we said earlier on, an overall ought is not a reason. This, I think, is evidence (should any still be needed) that the attempt generally to capture what a reason does in terms of some relation to an ought is looking in the wrong place. The relation that lies between reason and action is not going to be captured in ways that discuss only the different relation that lies between reason and ought-judgement.

We can test this view by considering a promising suggestion which I owe to Judith Thomson. This is, in my terms, that we should understand a contributory reason for action as a contributory reason for believing that one ought to act. And we should then understand a contributory reason to believe that one ought to act as a feature that increases the probability that one ought. In this way the whole thing is brought under control. The two normative relations, favouring and right-making, become one again. This is a very attractive simplification. But there seems to be something left out. The focus of a reason to act is action; it is *acting* that the reason is aiming at. If one were merely to believe that one ought to act, one would not have done what the reason is a reason to do. Could we sidestep this difficulty by missing out Thomson's intermediate stage and understanding a reason for action directly as a feature that increases the probability that one ought to act? Well, not if there are such things as enticing reasons. And what if the probability that one ought to act is already so high that this further reason does not increase it significantly, even though it is a significant reason? Further, is it not possible for the addition of one good reason to another not actually to increase in the slightest the probability that one ought to act? Remember the joke about the restaurant: each reason for not going there is fine in its own terms, but the combination is no better than either separately. We could try thinking in subjunctive conditional terms now: a reason is a feature that would increase the probability that one ought to act if there were no other such feature present. But this runs foul of the objection to Ross's isolation test, that some reasons cannot be the only reason present in the case.

I have been arguing that there is no known way of understanding what a contributory reason does by appeal to some relation in which the contributory stands to the overall ought. Every suggestion we have come up with has fallen to one objection or another. It is worth confessing, however, that this deprives us of two considerable advantages. If we had been able to understand contributory reasons in terms of some relation to the overall ought, we would have been handed on a plate answers to two important questions:

1. What makes the notion of a reason normative?
2. What makes the notion of a reason deontic?

We take it that the notion of an ought is both normative and deontic. It is deontic by definition, more or less. The normative realm is divided into two halves, the evaluative and the deontic, the former being concerned with what is good and bad, the latter with what is right or wrong, with what one ought to do, with duty and obligation, and so on. The idea is that one can sense a sort of family resemblance between the different deontic concepts, even if one cannot do much to explicate that resemblance. Now which side of the divide would the notion of a reason fall on? Traditionally, it is shown to be both deontic and normative because of its definability in terms of an overall ought. However, we have now decided that we cannot define a reason in that way, and I think we have also seen the possibility of non-deontic reasons. For enticing reasons, if indeed there are any such things, do not seem to be concerned with what we ought to do; they are more concerned with what it would be pleasant to do, without any suggestion that somehow one *ought* to take the most pleasant course (at least, not in any sense that is incompatible with one's being permitted not to). If so, these reasons don't take us to oughts, and it looks as if we are going to have to think of them as lying on the evaluative side of the evaluative/deontic distinction. They are more to do with what is best than with what one ought to do. This leaves us groping for some way of capturing the sense in which they are normative. But that issue also now arises for the non-enticing reasons, the peremptory ones, once we have accepted that they cannot be shown to be normative by simple appeal to the sort of definition we have rejected. If we want still to think of the notion of a reason as normative (or even as *the* basic normative notion, as I will be urging later), we will have to think of it not as extrinsically normative (that is, as normative in virtue of some relation it bears to an intrinsically normative ought) but as intrinsically normative. We will, it seems, have to appeal directly to the notion of favouring and maintain that it is itself normative, normative in its own nature. Perhaps this can be done, but there is a struggle ahead. We may find ourselves saddled with two styles of favouring, the more deontic style that is appropriate for the peremptory, and the more evaluative style that is suited to enticers.

3. DOING WITHOUT THE CONTRIBUTORY

Having now abandoned all attempts to explicate the contributory in terms of the overall, we seem to have only two alternatives. The first is to abandon the conception of a contributory reason altogether. The second is to run an independent account of what contributory reasons do.

Scanlon (1998: 197–201; also 2000) takes the first line. As I said in the previous chapter, he rejects familiar models of the way in which the appeal to principles works, under which principles can conflict. If they can conflict, there seem to be two ways of resolving the issue, that is, of getting a determinate answer to the question what to do. The more strategic way is to rank our principles lexically; once we have done this, we have a simple decision procedure, namely that of taking the answer given us by the higher-ranked principle. The less strategic way is simply to think of principles as having some sort of weight; the decision procedure is again simple, since we adopt the course of action enjoined by the most weighty principles. (This is Ross, effectively.) These two ways are different. On the first, a lexically superior principle can never be defeated, no matter how many subordinate principles are lined up on the other side. On the second, a weightier principle can be defeated by a combination of individually less weighty ones. But Scanlon's view, as I said before, seems to be that conflict is not to be resolved in either of these two ways. In fact, there are no actual conflicts, only appearances of conflict. If two of our principles seem to get in each other's way, what this shows is that at least one of them is incompletely specified, and the matter is resolved by a more complete specification.[11] Suppose we face a choice between killing one person and helping another. The idea here is that in a proper understanding of the principle that requires us to help those in need, there would probably be included an exception to that duty for all cases where to help one we have to kill another. Properly understood, therefore, the duty to help cannot conflict with the duty not to kill. And Scanlon adopts this model across the board.[12]

---

[11] This idea of 'specification' was first properly characterized by Henry Richardson (1990); see also his (2000).

[12] That he does so is, I think, not entirely clear in his (1998); but the language of his (2000) is explicit, most notably at pp. 310–11 where the rhetoric of 'counting decisively' is very strong. In his (1998) there is one place where Scanlon says that a moral principle ruling out killing specifies what is 'normally a conclusive reason'; but he does not generalize this. There is one point, however, where he seems to opt for a ranking of principles, in the discussion of what he calls the Rescue Principle and the Principle of Helpfulness: 'The Rescue Principle . . . presumably takes precedence in cases of conflict' (1998: 225). I think this remark must be a slip.

   The friends of principles should, I think, be happy with this suggestion that
at least some apparent conflicts are really not conflicts at all, and that the
matter is resolved by a better determination of one of the principles. They
may not be so happy with the idea that *all* apparent conflicts are like this.
They might think that there is no reason to go so far as that; indeed, that to
do so is to distort a good idea by trying to make it do too much work.[13] One
thing we seem to have lost, if we apply Scanlon's model across the board, is
any conception of contributory reasons. For by abandoning the idea that
there can be genuine conflict, I think we also abandon the idea that two
principles can combine. If each principle, when properly understood, specifies a 'decisive' or a 'conclusive' reason, how can we make sense of the view
that the claims of friendship and those of the profession may *combine* to give
us sufficient reason to act (e.g. to read a colleague's paper over the weekend
when we would rather be dozing in the shade), even though neither would
have been decisive on its own?[14]
   So Scanlon's conception of the role of principles leads him to deny any role
for contributory reasons (or contributory principles, come to that). This
seems to me a pretty drastic move. Quite apart from the fact that it seems
fairly easy to offer examples in which the idea of a contribution seems to be
required if we are to make sense of what is going on, it would seem that
Scanlon has also deprived himself of the idea of a defeated reason, and
thereby prevented himself even from addressing the question what the
appropriate response is to such a thing. Normally we would speak of regret
and residual duties, but if all conflict is, as Scanlon suggests, merely
apparent, there are no defeated considerations capable of demanding regret,
and nothing to generate a residual duty. So Scanlon's position involves some
dramatic surgery (by which I mean amputation).
   There is a further question about whether we really want an overall
structure of Scanlon's kind. It is all very well to suppose that whenever one
has to choose between saving a life and telling a lie, mendacity will be
required of us. In such a case, the answer is pretty obvious, and there is
nothing wrong with supposing that 'implicitly' the principle against lying has
a get-out clause, so that properly understood it reads 'Do not lie except to
save a life'. It is quite another thing to maintain that for every potential
conflict it is going to be possible to specify in advance which of the
(potentially) competing considerations should dominate. But this seems to
be the ideal for Scanlon. For him, properly formulated principles cannot

---

   [13] This would, I think, be Henry Richardson's position.
   [14] There is of course considerable incentive for Scanlon to think of principles as specifying conclusive reasons, derived from his contractualist claim that an act is wrong iff it is ruled out by
principles that nobody could reasonably reject. (I owe this suggestion to Derek Parfit.) This claim, and
the general picture in which it is placed, requires principles to *rule things out* rather than just to specify
a consideration that counts against them. The idea of objecting to a principle because it specifies a
feature that favours an action to which one can reasonably reject is much less compelling than the idea
of objecting to a principle because it permits, or even requires such an action.

conflict; so a proper understanding of principles would cut off any possible conflict before it even gets going. For this to work, there must be a 'final' understanding under which each principle is internally related to every other principle with which it could conceivably 'conflict'. But though this may be Scanlon's ideal, for me it is not even desirable. Ross, for instance, held that ordinarily considerations of promising should take precedence over those of beneficence (it being more important ordinarily to keep one's promise than to do good); but he also supposed that there could be such a thing as a trivial breach of promise and a very large good to be done, in which case, he thought, the promise should be broken. This seems just common sense to me, but it looks as if Scanlon's general approach will require him at least to see some point in trying to decide, of any two considerations, which in general dominates the other, and then to alter one of them to enshrine this decision, in a way that determines one's judgement in advance for all possible future cases.

I take the main point in the previous paragraph to be a general objection to theories that require some sort of lexical ordering; a particularist will say that sometimes one consideration matters more than another, and sometimes the other matters more than the one, without there needing to be any way of writing the rules for which way it goes when. Scanlon is opposed to lexical ordering, but his position seems to share its defect in this respect.

Perhaps the reply to this would be to have a sort of disaster clause, to the effect that one ought to keep one's promises unless doing so would lead to disaster. Myself, however, I am deeply suspicious of such clauses, for two reasons. The first is that they seem to introduce a step when what we really want is a matter of degree. The second is that they seem to be a sort of camouflage for the idea that Scanlon is trying to get away from. What underlies the idea that it is more important to keep a promise than to do good, but that occasionally things go the other way around? It seems to me that what is being said is that the requirement to keep a promise is generally weightier than the requirement to do good, though not always; and this looks very like the sort of thing that the friend of contributory reasons wants to say. To assess whether in this case it should be promise-keeping or benevolence that wins, we would need to 'weigh' the pressure put on us here by each consideration. And this really takes us back to a situation in which there are opposing contributory reasons, and thereby a practical conflict which is not an illusion but a real aspect of how things are.

There is a question whether we are simply to abandon the less specific versions of our principles, as Scanlon seems to suggest, or whether they can remain in play in some way. Richard Holton (2002) offers a picture which is broadly similar to Scanlon's but which allows the superseded principles to remain on the scene.[15] Holton is pursuing the idea that there is no one set of

---

[15] As does Richardson in his (1990).

principles that entails, and hence justifies, each true moral claim. But he takes this to be compatible with holding that each true moral claim is entailed by some true principle (together with appropriate non-moral truths). The thought is that we can find a way of adding new principles to the old ones, principles that are in some way built on the old ones, but do not amend or replace them. We have, as it were, a nested set of principles of different layers. There is the principle 'do not kill', and there is the principle 'do not kill except in self-defence'. Where Scanlon would say that the latter principle replaces the former, Holton says that both remain sound, but that the question which one we are to use depends on the circumstances, in the following way. We can perfectly well apply the simple principle 'do not kill', in cases where there is no further relevant feature to be borne in mind (such as that one needs to defend oneself). So a moral argument could run like this:

1. It is wrong to kill.
2. This would be a killing.
3. There are no further relevant features.
4. So: it would be wrong to do this.

If, however, self-defence is at issue, the third premise is false, and we need a different argument, thus:

1. It is permitted to kill in self-defence.
2. This would be a self-defending killing.
3. There are no further relevant features.
4. So: it is permissible to do this.

Holton is suggesting a possible 'principled particularism' under which every wrong action is made wrong by its relation to some principle, but that the principle only 'applies' in cases where there are no features relevant to how to act other than those already specified in the principle. This enables him to sidestep the particularist's complaint that in other circumstances application of the principle will give the wrong answer. In those other circumstances it will not be the case that there are no further relevant features (the 'That's it' clause, as Holton calls it, will fail), and so we really need to find a more specific superseding principle, as shown above. But the superseding principle is not somehow a replacement of the superseded one; both remain in play, and we allow circumstances to determine which to use on which occasion.[16]

Despite these subtleties, Holton's picture shares one weakness with Scanlon's. This is that he can give no account of a contributory moral reason. If moral reasons are given in principles, and if we understand the behaviour of such principles in the way that Holton suggests, there is only ever one

---

[16] It is interesting to compare the structure of Holton's picture with the structure of Brandom's example, quoted in Ch. 1.

principle applicable to each case; for if there were more than one, the 'that's it' clause would fail and the whole approach be subverted. The idea then has to be that only one principle applies at a time, and the consequence of this is that there are no opposing moral reasons, and we never have more than one on the same side either. This renders Holton vulnerable to the complaints made against Scanlon, that certain predicaments can only be understood if we retain the idea of contributory reasons, and that the conception of a defeated reason is required if we are to make sense of regret and residual duties.

These attempts to write a theory that does without contributory reasons altogether seem therefore to have failed. This leaves us with the other option, of retaining contributory reasons but of trying to understand them in their own terms, rather than in terms of some relation to the overall ought. The only way that I know of doing this is to say that to be a reason for action is to stand in a certain relation to action, and the relation at issue is that of favouring. This is where Scanlon starts his book (1998: 17), and it seems to be the right way to start. The only weakness in it is that it seems terribly uninformative. Talking about the favouring relation, or that of counting in favour of, offers us no analysis of the reasons-relation, nor in any other way does it seem to do more than tell us what we knew already. So what is the great excitement here?

I think that the answer is that there is no great excitement, but that it is better that what we say should be true than that it should be exciting. Further, the appeal to the favouring relation does have at least the advantage of causing us to look in the right place. We will, that is, be trying to understand the nature of a certain relation, not the nature of a certain monadic property such as goodness, which has been the focus of so much attention. And this will have its effects when we come to ask in what sense the notion of a reason is normative, and whether it is *the* basic normative notion. If it is the basic normative notion, the fact that the basic normative notion is that of a relation will make a difference to the ways in which the debate between naturalists and non-naturalists will proceed. And it seems to me that the reasons-relation is going to be a lot harder to naturalize, and will raise rather fewer hackles, than were such supposed monadic normative properties as goodness and rightness.

4. TWO BASIC NOTIONS?

We have decided that we can neither understand the contributory in terms of some one relation to the overall, nor do without the contributory altogether. This leaves us with a further strategic choice. One option is to take it that there are two basic notions, that of a contributory reason and that of an overall ought, neither of these being definable in terms of the other. We might have a local holism, with the contributory being impossible without the overall, and vice versa, but no reduction of either to the other. For an analogy (which I owe to Daniel Stoljar) consider the local holism of belief and desire. It might be that only a creature capable of desire (an agent, that is) is also capable of belief, and vice versa. Suppose that to be true: it is an entirely independent question which, if either, of these notions is primary. It may turn out that belief is primary; perhaps desire will eventually be shown, as many suggest, to be some form of belief. But it may equally turn out that neither is primary. Still, we may say, we learn much about the nature of belief by laying out the elements of the local belief/desire holism; and similarly about desire. So, by analogy, we learn about the nature of a reason by learning about the relations between reasons and overall oughts (and perhaps between reasons and beliefs, and between reasons and desires). What we get in this way is a sort of functional characterization of reasons, and at the same time a functional characterization of the other elements in the now more complex local holism. There cannot be reasons unless there are oughts for them to contribute to; there cannot be overall oughts unless there are features that contribute to them; there cannot be beliefs without reasons, nor desires without reasons—and so on. Lay all this out, and much becomes clearer in a way that does not require us to identify any one concept as primary.

Someone pursuing this general line would be likely to say that what was wrong with the various accounts of the contributory that have been considered and rejected in this chapter was really that each was taken separately. True enough, none of them is sufficient on its own. But if you take them all together in an appropriately flexible way, the combination might achieve what no part can achieve. This approach, then, allows that the notion of favouring is a distinct notion that cannot be *analysed* in terms of the overall, but suggests that it can still be *understood* or *explicated* in terms of the various relations in which favourers stand to other things (which may include desires, beliefs, actions, overall oughts, motivation, and anything else that seems appropriate.) The general idea is that once we have given this sort of functional characterization, claims that the notion of favouring is unanalysable lose their force.

My view of this programme is that it is fine in principle: I have no general objection to functional analyses. The difficulties that I see in the present case are that we are trying to put together an understanding of the ways in which reasons function by piling on top of one another a set of thoughts each of which is strictly speaking false. At least, I argued of each attempt to characterize reasons in overall terms that it was false; if I was right each time, it is not as if the refuted claim is still capable of contributing to a better characterization of a different sort. Functional characterizations are supposed to contain truths which together make up the relevant explication; it would not be enough for it to consist of things that are by and large true, or normally true. But that seems to be all that is available. And matters do not much improve if we enlarge the local holism to include remarks about the relation between reasons and belief, and between reasons and desire. What we will end up with, I suggest, will never be anything more than a partial characterization of how reasons behave. There is just not enough there to persuade us that eventually we will have a complete explication of the notion of a reason. *Some* reasons are such that they behave in this way: alone, they decide the issue. *Some* reasons are such that in their absence things are worse rather than better. *Some* reasons are such that they should affect how one deliberates. And these last three claims differ; the first two specify a sufficient condition for being a reason, and the last specifies a necessary but not sufficient condition. But when we have said everything of this sort that occurs to us, we have something like this: all reasons are the right sort of thing to behave in some of these ways, though some of them don't actually do so. I think this is not enough to count as a functional explanation. It is not that one would not understand the various clauses of the functional specification unless one was already a competent user of the concept of a reason. This is probably true, but true or not, it is irrelevant; it is true of all functionalist characterizations, and no objection, for such characterizations are trying to get it right about which things are the reasons, not to train people up in the use of a concept when they don't have it already. The problem as I see it is that the relevant characterization can never be made complete.

5. OUGHT AND MOST OUGHT

If it cannot be completed, we will have to abandon the functionalist programme that promised to explain the nature of reasons in a way that simply avoided the question whether the concept of a reason is the primary normative concept. Our other main option is to reverse our original direction, and to try to explicate the overall ought in terms of some relation to reasons. This general programme is extremely attractive, for reasons that I now turn to investigate.

The matter can be brought out by considering the difficulties that Ross gets into when he tries to relate what he calls prima facie duty to what he calls duty proper. First, he says that 'the phrase "prima facie duty" must be apologised for, since it suggests that what we are speaking of is a certain kind of duty, whereas it is in fact not a duty, but something related in a special way to duty. Strictly speaking, we want not a phrase in which duty is qualified by an adjective, but a separate noun' (1930: 20). Second, he says that prima facie duty 'may be called a parti-resultant attribute, i.e. one which belongs to an act in virtue of some one component in its nature. *Being* one's duty is a toti-resultant attribute, one which belongs to an act in virtue of its whole nature and of nothing less than this' (1930: 28). Each of these claims causes problems.

The first one is awkward because by denying that prima facie duty is duty in any sense, Ross makes it impossible for himself to make sense of the idea that duty proper is in some sense the product of various normative pushes or forces coming up from below—from the various features that stand as reasons. Ross effectively maintains that there is nothing like duty at the contributory level, and so leaves nothing there that we can think of as contributing to duty. But this is to sever what he has to say about duty from its proper ground. To put the matter another way: we have to find some way of understanding right-making features so that the 'right' in 'right-making' is the rightness of duty proper, and Ross has prevented himself from doing that.

The second one is awkward because it reinforces the divide between duty proper and the things that contribute to it. If the ground for duty proper is really every feature of the relevant action, and the ground for prima facie duty is some particular feature or other, we have deprived the relevant right-making features (which occur at the contributory level) of the ability to be what in some preferential sense make the action right. It is impossible to conceive how they can be what make the action right because we have been explicitly told that they play no special role in the construction of duty proper—no role, that is, that is not played by every feature of the action whatever, including even the reasons on the other side.

It is interesting that these points seem to have been the ones that persuaded H. A. Prichard to write to Ross in 1932 criticizing Ross's theory of prima facie duties (Prichard 2002: 286–7). Prichard's letter ends:

> The truth is that the more I consider it the less I can make sense out of 'the act which I am bound to do'—as distinct from 'an act which I ought to do'—and the more I get to think that the only fact corresponding to the phrase is 'the act which I ought to do more than I ought to do any other', and that your 'prima facie' duty is really a duty, your 'my duty sans phrase' is really that of a man's duties which he most ought to do, i.e. that so far as these phrases can be made to stand for facts these must be the facts.

What Prichard is doing here is opting explicitly for an account of duty proper in terms of the contributory. One's duty proper is the act which one most ought to do, and the 'ought' we are dealing with now is a contributory 'ought'—something we have not seen before. There is no separate overall 'ought'; and the reason why not is that to introduce such a thing severs the vital link between that which contributes and that to which it contributes. And, as Prichard says elsewhere, nothing is gained by trying to reintroduce a notion of overall duty in addition to that which we ought and that which we most ought to do. According to him (2002: 79), this would imply that 'while the one act is a duty the other is not, and that the latter is a duty though to a lesser degree than the former. Putting this otherwise, if we think that of two acts there is a greater obligation to do one of them, we cannot go on to think that we ought to do that action without implying that there is no obligation to do the other in any degree whatever. Consequently we gain nothing by maintaining the existence of degrees of obligation in addition to absolute obligation.'[17] Another way of putting this might be as follows: the act we ought not to do is still one which we ought to some extent to do, even though we ought not to do it at all. The greater obligation to do A implies that this is what we ought to do, and that we have no duty to do B at all, indeed a duty not to do it, even though we ought to some extent to do it. This sort of incoherence seems to be the result of combining talk of what one most ought to do (the strongest or most stringent prima facie duty) with talk of what one ought to do (full stop).

It may be that there is some other resolution of these difficulties, but by far the easiest is to take Prichard's route and work with a contributory ought, which is a matter of degree. I think of this contributory ought as a monadic feature of an action that is consequent on, or resultant from, some other feature—the 'ought-making' feature, whatever it is. So oughts of this sort are not relations. But for them to be present there must be a certain relation between the ought-making feature and the action. If I have some duty to do this action, there must be some feature of the situation that makes it so. If in some more general way I ought to do it, still there must be some feature of the situation that makes it so. But the ought, and the duty, are what is made; the making is a relation, but what is made is not.

One might suppose that this duty-making relation must be the favouring relation, but that would be wrong. Things are a little delicate here, but I am still inclined to say that there are two normative relations in the offing, not just one. The monadic ought is reached by detaching from the ought-making relation. The train of thought here is 'Feature F ought-makes action A; Feature F is in place; so one ought (so far as that goes) to do action A'. This expresses the idea that the relevant relation is not favouring, but ought-making (or right-making, if you like—so long as 'right' does not mean only morally right). So we can stick to our intuition that favouring is a relation between a feature and an action, and ought-making is a making-the-case relation that holds between a feature and the (contributory) rightness/oughtness of an action.

The programme of understanding the concepts with which we operate at the overall level in terms of those whose real home is at the contributory level would be much helped if we were willing to adopt what have come to be called 'buck-passing' accounts of all thin evaluative or deontic concepts. Such concepts are, or include, the concepts of the right, wrong, good, bad, ought, duty, obligation, evil—and so on. A buck-passing account of the good, for example, would understand a good action as one that has features that give us

---

[17] This passage is supposedly from a student's notes on one of Prichard's lectures, on conflicts of duties. One might think that, if so, the student has done a truly miraculous job of capturing Prichard's tone and style, but it appeared that Prichard lectured at dictation speed.

reasons to do the action, to help someone else do it, to admire the person who does it, and so on. A buck-passing account of rightness would be almost exactly the same, except that rightness is an overall concept and goodness is not (bestness is the nearest we get to an overall concept on the evaluative side).[18] Now if all the thin properties could be understood in this sort of way, it would be clear that the concept of a (contributory) reason plays a foundational role. Unfortunately the buck-passers cannot agree among themselves. Some (Scanlon and Parfit) want to pass the evaluative buck but not the deontic one; they want, that is, to understand goodness as suggested above, but they think of rightness as a property distinct from any suggested *analysans* in terms of having reason-giving properties of some sort or other. Others (myself included) are happy to pass the deontic buck, for reasons to do with the idea that the overall ought and right are verdictive concepts, but are less convinced that goodness (which is not verdictive) can be understood in similar ways. Then there are some brave souls who want to pass every buck. This is an internecine debate, but it is relevant to our present concerns. The minimal form of buck-passing required by the attempt to understand the overall in terms of the contributory is that which applies to any overall concept. Such concepts are right and ought; best is not itself an overall concept, but the top degree of a contributory concept. So we do not need to pass the evaluative buck, so far as the main issue about the relation between the overall and the contributory is concerned. Being good could, for all we care, turn out to be having a property whose presence makes it the case that there are reasons of certain sorts, but which is not identical with the existence of such reasons. The presence of the reasons could be a consequence of the goodness, not identical with it.[19]

6. OUGHTS WITHOUT REASONS?

I have been gently moving towards the conclusion that the overall ought should be understood as some function of a contributory ought. To go this way is to insist that we can make good sense of such remarks as:

So far as this goes, you ought to ϕ.
You ought to do this more than you ought to do that.
In this respect, you ought to ϕ.
What you most ought to do is not what you are most likely to want to do.

***

[18] This is one difficulty for the general buck-passing programme; there ought to be more difference between the right and the best than the programme seems capable of allowing.

[19] There is, however, another purpose for which it would be important to understand (contributory) goodness as the presence of reasons of certain sorts, namely that of supposing that the basic normative concept is that of a relation, not that of a monadic normative property.

I now want to mention two potential difficulties for this position.[20] One I have already referred to; it is the existence, or at least the possible existence, of enticing rather than peremptory reasons. The other is the possible existence of overall oughts that are not grounded in contributory reasons. These two possibilities are relevant because I did not only suggest that we understand overall oughts in terms of contributory oughts. I also suggested that the presence of a contributory ought is much the same as the presence of a reason. Now if that last suggestion were true, two things seem to follow, both of which should give us pause. First, there could be no enticing reasons, because (at least so the suggestion goes) such reasons have nothing to do with oughts, contributory or otherwise. Second, there could be no overall oughts without reasons, because there could be no overall oughts without contributory oughts, which, as I was in danger of presenting the matter, merely consisted in the presence of a reason.

Let me take the first issue first. There is some confusion here, which needs to be sorted out. The crucial question is whether, if we understand the overall in terms of the contributory, we therefore understand it in terms of reasons, and so end up identifying reasons in terms of contributory oughts. And part of the point of the distinction between the two normative relations, favouring and ought-making, is that reasons for action are not to be directly understood in terms of any relation to oughts, but directly in terms of favouring. Some forms of favouring are essentially related to ought-making; but others (enticing) are not. So that disposes of the worry about enticers.

The possibility of overall oughts without contributory oughts is, however, a genuine problem for the general attempt to treat the contributory as basic. How can there be something that one most ought to do if the 'most' here does not express some degree of the contributory? Now since the examples that are offered here are not to do with enticing reasons but with peremptory ones, we can without error think of ourselves as dealing with the suggestion that there are overall oughts in cases where there are no favourers. We owe these examples to John Broome (2004). First, he defines a 'weighing explanation' of why you ought to ϕ as an explanation that mentions at least one 'pro tanto' reason for you to ϕ, and associates that reason with something that we can call its 'weight'. Then he offers two examples of oughts whose explanation is not a weighing explanation in this sense—one theoretical and one practical. The theoretical one is this. Suppose that you ought not to believe both that it is Sunday and that it is Wednesday. A plausible explanation of this is that these propositions are contraries and one ought not to believe two contrary propositions. This, Broome says, is not a weighing explanation, because no weight is associated with either of the facts to which it appeals.

---

[20] There is a third difficulty, raised by Carla Bagnoli: how can the position make sense of tragic dilemmas?

The practical example is rather different. Suppose you ought to pay £12,345 income tax for 2000–1, and that the explanation of this is that £12,345 is what the tax laws say you owe, and that you ought to pay what the tax laws say you owe. Again, neither of these considerations is a *pro tanto* reason for your paying £12,345. So, Broome says, the explanation here is not a weighing explanation. (One can run the account through again using 'contributory reason' for Broome's *pro tanto* reason.)

These examples are interesting but they do not persuade me. In the second case, there are two things one can say. The first is that it is perfectly possible for a contributory reason to be a complex of considerations none of which is a separate contributory reason. So it is possible to see the two elements in Broome's explanation as combining to make a contributory reason even if neither separately favours paying £12,345. Second, that this is the right way to view the case is shown, I think, by the fact that we can conceive that there might be something else which one ought to do with the money, and Broome has not yet mentioned any such reasons for doing something other than paying £12,345 to the taxman. One does not establish that an explanation is not a weighing explanation simply by not mentioning opposing explanations of the same kind. And one does not establish it by pointing out that its parts are not weighing explanations, either.

Broome has something of a reply to this. He points out that, like the previous example, this one appeals to a principle, that one ought to pay what the tax laws say that one owes. The question is whether this principle is absolute. In objecting to the example, I implicitly claimed that the principle is contributory; we end up with some reason to pay £12,345, and some reason not to, perhaps. But Broome says that though the principle is defeasible, this does not show that it is not absolute. A principle can contain a condition, such that if the condition fails, the principle generates no ought (because it does not apply any more). He meant his principle to be conditioned, but absolute. Now if this were right, it is true that we would have an overall ought and an explanation of that ought which is not a weighing explanation (because nothing is here serving as 'weight'). But in fact it does not seem to be right. A conditioned but absolute principle would generate no reason at all in any case where the condition fails. But the principle that one ought to pay what the tax laws say one owes does generate some reason to do this even if the supposed condition should fail. So the principle is not a conditioned absolute, but something like a principle of contributory reason, which specifies an ought which can be weighed (in whatever sense we give to that notion) against the oughts specified by other principles that also apply to the case (such as the principle that one ought not to give any money to any government that will use that money to give weapons to oppressive regimes).

Now consider Broome's other example. He says, in this connection: 'Suppose the only way a nuclear war can be averted is by your believing both that it is Sunday and that it is Wednesday. You might doubt that, in those circumstances, you ought not to have both beliefs.' So, again, he concludes that the principle that one ought not to believe two contrary propositions is, though absolute, still a conditioned absolute; there is a condition under which it fails to apply, or ground, any ought. Properly understood, the principle says something like: 'One ought not to believe two contrary propositions unless enormous harm could be avoided by doing so.'

But this seems vulnerable to the same complaint; if the principle is a conditioned absolute, it will ground no ought of any sort in any case where the condition fails. Broome suggests that the condition (whatever exactly it is) fails in the case where I can save the world by believing these two contraries. But I suggest that in such a case there would still be a good reason for me not to believe both of them, which is that no pair of contraries can be true.

This is the final point I want to make in favour of my general programme of understanding the overall ought in terms of a contributory ought.[21]

The situation now is that an enormous amount of weight has been thrown onto the notion of a contributory reason, since we have understood overall oughts in terms of contributory oughts, and those in terms of contributory peremptory reasons. But the only account of a contributory reason that I have offered is the not very helpful one that just tells us to think about favouring. I hope to show in the next chapter that the situation is not as bleak as this makes out.

---

[21] Note that if this programme is sound, it makes trouble for Broome's distinction between slack and strict 'oughts' (Broome 2000). His suggestion is that there is a strict sort of 'ought' such that, if you do not do what you ought (in that sense) you are not entirely as you ought to be, and another slacker sort for which this is not the case (the latter is the contributory sort of 'ought'). My programme involves doing without this distinction, or perhaps rather reworking it so as to say that if you fail to do what you most ought, you are not as you most ought to be. We can say this without appealing to a strict sort of 'ought' at all.

3

Beyond Favouring

---

1. FAVOURING AND ENABLING

If one cannot explicate a philosophically significant concept, there may be other ways of giving people a sense that the concept is itself in good order and that they have a reasonably clear grasp on it. One way of doing this is to work through a range of examples, showing how the concept applies to them and showing that there is a graspable distinction between cases in which it applies and cases in which it does not apply. In this way one can hope to train people up in the use of a concept on which (we are supposing) they already have an implicit grip. My experience is that, in the case of favouring, not too many examples are needed. Consider the following piece of practical 'reasoning':

1. I promised to do it.
2. My promise was not given under duress.
3. I am able to do it.
4. There is no greater reason not to do it.
5. So: I do it.

Note here that there is a similar train of thought that ends not with (5) as presented, but with:

5*. So I ought to do it.

If we end with (5) we are dealing with the favouring relation, and if we end with (5*) we are dealing with the right-making relation. Think of (5) and (5*) as 'conclusions' of the reasoning presented in (1)–(4). This is a bit odd, because I intend (5) to be, or to represent, an action undertaken in the light of the reasoning that leads to it, and it is perhaps awkward to think of an action as the conclusion of anything (except a series of other actions, I suppose). If (5) is an action done in the light of (1)–(4), somewhere in (1)–(4) we should be able to find something that favours that action. And indeed there is; the only question will be how many favourers there are there. For ease of reference, I will call (1)–(4) the 'premises' of the reasoning, for the while at least. Later I will suggest that they are not premises at all, whether the conclusion is an action, as in (5), or an ought, as in (5*).

Premise (1) presents a clear favourer. That I promised to do it is (in this context at least) a reason in favour of doing it. I am not going to argue for this; it is an assumption of the example. What I am going to argue for is that none of the other premises is a favourer. They play other roles; they are relevant, but not in the favouring way. Take (2). I want to say that the fact that my promise was not given under duress is not a second reason for doing the action, to be set alongside the first one. What is true here is that if my promise had been given under duress, I would have had no reason to keep it. What this means is that in the absence of (2), (1) would not have favoured the action. In this sense, the presence of (2) *enables* (1) to favour (5). In my preferred terminology, (1) is a favourer, and (2) is an enabling condition or enabler.

Various people have suggested to me a rather different picture: that the favourer here is not that I promised but rather that I freely promised—a combination of (1) and (2). I have no objection to this idea in principle; there will be many cases where a favourer is a complex no part of which is itself a favourer. The suggestion requires, then, that promising does not of itself favour acting, since we must be dealing now with a complex favourer which does not contain simpler favourers. (If promising itself favours, it is hard to think that freely promising also favours.) I would only object to all of this if it were premised on the idea that one can always put a favourer and an enabler together to make a more complex favourer. This 'agglomerative principle' does seem to me to be false. One does not construct a larger favouring consideration merely by putting together a favourer and an enabler. The enabler no more becomes now (part of) a favourer than the favourer becomes (part of) a larger enabler. The distinction in role should not be elided by agglomeration.

The reason why I don't need to insist that (1) is an independent favourer is that nothing really hangs on the fortunes of this one example, the official purpose of which was anyway only to train people up in distinguishing favouring from other forms of relevance. Those who want to argue that the real favourer is really (1 + 2) are thereby showing that they don't need a lot of training. Still, it may be that their grasp on the notion of favouring could be improved. For I don't myself accept the idea that the real favourer is that I freely promised rather than that I promised, so that it is a mistake to think that promises only give a reason if they are freely made. I stick to the view that what favours my doing the action is that I engaged myself to do so. But it is hard to know how to tell whether this is correct or not. One clue is that those who recognize that their promise was deceitfully extracted from them often feel some compunction in not doing what they promised, even though they themselves recognize that in such circumstances their promise does not play its normal reason-giving role. I think their attitude would be different if what plays the reason-giving role were not that one promised but that one 'freely' promised (where to be free a promise must not be extracted by deceit). For on that hypothesis there would be no sign of a favourer in the case at all. Another example: that someone is asking you the time is a reason to tell them, a reason that would not exist if their purpose were to distract you so that their accomplice can steal your bag. I would not be very tempted to say that the reason is really that they are asking you the time for a genuine rather than a surreptitious purpose.

Now consider (3). That I am able to do an action is not often a reason in favour of doing it. There are unusual occasions, such as when I have been paralysed for a while and the mere ability to flex my arm is a reason for me to do so.[1] But this is not one of those, I am supposing. What then is the importance of (3)? Suppose we agree that in some suitable sense 'ought' implies 'can'. This tells us that (5*) cannot be true unless (3) is true. But officially we are thinking about the relation between (3) and (5), not (5*). Well, in the sort of sense that 'ought' implies 'can', we might also suppose that 'has a reason' implies 'can'—that one cannot have a reason to do an action that one is (in the relevant sense) incapable of doing. I have, perhaps, a reason to run as fast as I can but no reason to run faster than that. If so, then in the absence of (3), again (1) would give me no reason to act. What (3) does is to enable (1) to favour (5). It is another enabler, perhaps not quite of the same type as (2).

Are we sure that (3) is not a favourer? I think there is a conclusive reason for saying that it is not, which is that if it were, all favoured actions would share one and the same favourer: that they are actions of which the agent is capable. But it is not the case that if an action is favoured, we already know at least one of the reasons for doing it, namely that the agent is capable of doing it. The agent's capacity to act must therefore be playing some other role, and I suggest that the role that it is playing is that of a general enabler. We could think of (2), by contrast, as a specific enabler, one specific to the particular case, or at least to a limited class of cases.

Now consider (4). The presence of (4) does not enable (1) to favour (5). (1) would have favoured (5), we may suppose, even if something else had more strongly favoured not doing (5); that one promised can be some reason to act even if there is greater reason not to. What (4) does enable is the move from (1) to (5). In the absence of (4), that move should not be made. This is a different sort of enabling from what is done by either (2) or (3).

Are we sure that (4) is not a favourer? Again, there is a conclusive reason for saying that it is not. Judgements like (4) are verdictive; to assert (4) is to pass judgement on the balance of the reasons present in the case. If (4) was itself a further reason over and above those on which it passes judgement, we would be forced to reconsider the balance of reasons once we had asserted (4), in a way that would continue ad infinitum. Which is ridiculous. So (4) is not itself a favourer. We can add to this the sort of point I made about

---

[1] Walter Sinnott-Armstrong suggested to me that, in a case where the mere ability to act is a reason, it is also an enabler for itself. I see no reason to deny this amusing possibility.

(3): that if (4) was a favourer, all actions that we have overall reason to do would have at least one common favourer, which I take to be intrinsically implausible. In saying this I don't mean to be appealing to any first-order theory, idiosyncratic or otherwise. What is implausible is that the structure of reasons alone should guarantee that all right actions share a common favourer, which it would if (4) were taken to be favouring rather then enabling. It might be that, as Christians presumably think, all right actions please God, and so have a common favourer; but that this is so, if it is, is not guaranteed merely by the structure of reasons.

So what we have in the present example is one favourer and three enablers, none of which is doing exactly what any of the others is doing. The crucial point for further reference is just that there is a difference between favouring and enabling, even though there are different sorts of enabler.

For a simpler example of a similar sort, consider Plato's suggestion in his *Crito* that agreements should be respected so long as they are just. The ordinary reason for respecting one's agreements is, I suppose, that one agreed to them. Plato's idea seems to be that this would be no reason if the agreement itself were unjust. But that the agreement is not unjust does not seem to be another reason for respecting it; that something is not unjust is not ordinarily a reason for doing it, and it does not seem to be one in this case either.

So far, then, I have distinguished between favourers and enablers. There are favourers and there are disfavourers, and if there are enablers, there must be such things as disablers; trivially, the absence of an enabler will disable what would otherwise be a reason. So favouring comes along with disfavouring, and enabling comes along with disabling.

My discussion has focused on the relation between (1)–(4) and (5). But exactly similar points could be made about the relation between (1)–(4) and (5*). Just as the favouring relation can be enabled and disabled, so can the right-making or ought-making relation. So there are enablers and disablers for right-making as well as for favouring. For the remainder of this chapter I will move back and forward between these two relations, making my points in terms now of one and now of the other, in a way which I hope will not be too confusing.

In addition to favouring or disfavouring and enabling or disabling as two different sorts of things that relevant considerations can do, there is a third role that a relevant consideration can play. To see what this might be, consider a rather different example:

1. She is in trouble and needs help.
2. I am the only other person around.
3. So: I help her.

That she is in trouble and needs help is a consideration that favours my helping her. That I am the only other person around does not seem to be another reason, on top of the first one. It is not as if, even if she were not in

trouble, that I am the only other person around would still favour my helping
her. The reverse, however, is true; even if there were others around, I would
still have a reason to help her, a reason given by the trouble she is in. But my
being the only other person around does make a rational difference, all the
same. I suggest that what it does is to intensify the reason given me by her
need for help. Instead of two reasons, what we have here is one reason and
an intensifier. Presumably there is the opposite of an intensifier, an attenuator. An example might be this:

1. She is in trouble and needs help.
2. It is all her own fault, and she got in this situation through trying to spite
    someone else.
3. But still: I help her.

One might think that there is reason to help her even though it is all her own
fault, etc., but less reason than there would otherwise be.

The notion of an intensifier (and that of an attenuator) is in some ways
more stable than that of an enabler. The tendency to agglomerate favourer
and intensifier is much less strong than the tendency to agglomerate favourer
and enabler. After all, the reason I have to help her surely exists whether I am
the only one around or not; it is just stronger in the one case than in the
other. And there is, or should be, no pressure to suppose that the intensifier is
part of a larger reason which includes her need for help. This is because her
need for help is already a reason, and is unlikely to figure *in addition* as part of
a larger reason. If her need for help is not part of a larger reason, we can take
it that the relevant intensifier is not either.

But this itself can be used to support the notions of enabling and disabling,
should support still seem to be needed. If we are happy with the idea that a
reason can be attenuated by a consideration which is not itself a reason, why
should we fight shy of supposing that it can be reduced to nothing? And if we
accept this last possibility, why should we not suppose that the reduction can
be achieved all at once rather than by degrees?—which is after all exactly what
a disabler does. And if we allow the idea of a disabler, we will have to allow
that of an enabler as well.

So far, then, we have identified three sorts of role that a relevant consideration can play: a relevant consideration can be a favourer/disfavourer, it
can be an enabler/disabler for another favourer/disfavourer, and it can
intensify/attenuate the favouring/disfavouring done by something else. All
such considerations are relevant, which just shows that there is more than one
way of being relevant—more than one *form of relevance*, as one might say. Are
there more ways than these three? Note that I have not counted six ways,
but three. And I have not supposed that to favour an alternative to an action
is the same thing as to disfavour that action, though I have supposed that
disfavouring is effectively the same sort of thing as favouring, even if it has the
opposite normative polarity.

The main further suggestion is that as well as favourers and disfavourers, there are decisive reasons. These operate in a different manner, and so there must be a further way of being relevant, beyond the ones already mentioned. In ordinary cases we have an action that we have overall most reason to do, but none of the reasons for doing it is in the relevant sense decisive; they each count in favour but none of them is decisive on its own. Nor should we think of the winning collection of reasons as decisive, either. Or rather, if we do, we will merely need a new term to express the possibility that there are reasons that are decisive on their own, even when there are further reasons on the same side. So the idea is that what is done by a decisive reason is not the same as what is done by a collection of reasons when together they manage to defeat the opposition. I am sympathetic to the general thrust of this suggestion (because it warns against the sort of narrowness of focus that often bedevils analytic philosophy), even though if it were true it would unsettle one of my basic themes, that all reasons are contributory reasons. True, we may say, there are no overall reasons; but a decisive reason is not the same thing as a very strong (or at least strong enough in the circumstances) contributory reason.

Why not, though? It seems to me that there are two possibilities here. One is that there are reasons that are decisive in context. I don't think this is a very interesting possibility. It seems to collapse into the more mundane idea that in a given context, a certain reason is enough to tip the scale, or that it alone would have defeated such opposition as there was. For this we don't require a different sort of reason over and above the contributory. The more interesting idea is that there is a sort of reason that is in its own nature decisive. The obvious example is a moral reason. Many people suppose that in a battle between reasons, where there are moral reasons on one side and none on the other, the moral reasons will be decisive. Morality always wins. Of course if we have moral reasons on both sides, as sadly we often do, those reasons cannot now be all treated as of their nature decisive. But still, moral reasons are of their nature decisive vis-à-vis reasons of other sorts.

My own view about this is that the matter is exaggerated. First, it seems to me that weak moral reasons are on occasions defeated by strong practical reasons. Maybe I ought to grade this last essay this evening, having promised the class that their essays will be returned at the meeting tomorrow; but I have stronger reasons to go to bed. Second, the supposed intrinsic decisiveness of moral reasons may be a product rather of an independent commitment to the paramount nature of the moral. Many people are committed to morality in this sense, and treat moral reasons as decisive. But one could be committed to doing the right thing case by case without supposing that moral reasons have an intrinsic decisiveness. Until further notice, then, I will go on supposing that all reasons are intrinsically contributory and none intrinsically decisive.

2. NON-MORAL CASES

In attempting to establish the soundness of a general distinction between two distinct roles, those of favouring and of enabling, I started from examples that involved moral reasons. But when we move away from moral reasons to ordinary practical ones, we find similar phenomena. The reason why I am going to Edinburgh this weekend is to see my daughter Kate, who is a student there. If she were a student at York, I would not have any reason to go to Edinburgh. But that Kate is not at York is no reason to go to Edinburgh. This is at the contributory level. At the overall, suppose again that I have reason to go to Edinburgh to see Kate, but that if there were a bomb hidden somewhere in that part of town I would have an even stronger reason not to go. That there is no bomb lurking up there is, I would claim, not itself a reason in favour of going there, though it is a feature in the absence of which my perfectly good reason for going there would be by no means good enough to make it the case that I ought to go.

We went out for the evening last week, and sadly Mary could not join us. As things turned out, however, the smaller group that her absence made possible made a great party; the very smallness of the group was the key feature in how well the party went. That Mary was not there was not one of the good things about the party. Indeed, if she had been there, things would probably have gone equally well (she is a lot of fun)—but differently. Her absence, then, enabled the party to go well in the way that it did, but was not among the things that were good about the party. It was an enabler, and not a contributor.

Now for an example that is not really in the realm of good reasons at all, whether practical or moral, but which nonetheless has the same structure. What makes this ice-cream taste nice is not that it is not salty, even though if it were salty it would not taste nice. What makes it taste nice are the ingredients it has actually got and the ways in which their tastes combine, not the absence of things that would subvert what is there already. That absence plays a role, but it is a different role.

A very different example comes from the film *Bedazzled*. Here someone is given seven wishes, and he wishes to be alone with his girlfriend, who is to be besotted with him. He gets this, indeed, but in circumstances that he did not think to exclude, and in such a way that the fulfilment of his wishes is entirely subverted. For instance, in one scenario they are both nuns; he hadn't thought to specify his own sex or an absence of religious constraints. And so on. What he had failed to specify was an absence of specific disablers.[2]

I now take myself to have established a distinction between favourers and enablers (of which there are various sorts). And I take that distinction to be of considerable importance in the general theory of reasons. This is not only

---

[2] Thanks to Don Garrett for this nice example.

because it is the first move in the attempt to distinguish different styles of relevance. The distinction has many other salutary effects, as we will see. One is that it reveals yet another thing that is wrong with Ross's general metaphysical picture of the difference between the contributory and the overall, which in his terms is the difference between prima facie duty and duty proper. Ross's claim that duty proper is toti-resultant and prima facie duty parti-resultant is driven by a sense that certain factors are relevant to the wrongness of the action, even though they do not figure in prima facie principles. In this he is quite right, but he is wrong to think that there is only one style of relevance, which comes in two varieties, the 'parti-' variety and the 'toti-' variety. Thinking this, he is condemned to say that an action is made right by (among others) features that count against doing it, as well as by features that, though they are required if it is to be right, are clearly playing a different role from that played by features that appear in prima facie principles. For instance, it is required that there be no stronger reason on the other side, but there is no prima facie principle that says 'if there is no stronger reason on the other side, this is some reason to do the action'. Ross lumps all relevant features together, as part of the right-making base (the ground, as one might call it), and this metaphysical picture of the situation is far too indiscriminate.[3]

In fact, I suggest that the distinction between favourers and enablers can be generalized: there is a general distinction between a feature that plays a certain role and a feature whose presence or absence is required for the first feature to play its role, but which does not play that role itself. The distinction between favouring and enabling is a special case of this general distinction, whose earliest explicit instance, so far as I know, is in Plato's Phaedo 99b: 'Fancy not being able to distinguish between the cause of a thing and that without which the cause would not be a cause!'[4] I now give two further applications of the more general distinction, one in the theory of explanation and one in epistemology. These are both rather more contentious.

3. ENABLING AN EXPLANATION

To explain, or to contribute to an explanation, is to play a certain role. There should therefore be a distinction between the features that play that role and the features whose presence or absence enables the explainers to play that role but which do not play it themselves. Now it is common in the theory of

---

[3] Other salutary effects of the distinction between favourers and enablers crop up throughout this book. A signal instance is at the end of Chapter 6.2.

[4] This is from the Hackforth translation, p. 127; 'cause' here is αἴτιον. I owe this reference to Constantine Sandis.

explanation for people to reject this distinction. They do this in the service of a doctrine that could be called 'the completeness of a full explanation'. They hold that every condition necessary for an explanation genuinely to explain must itself be part of that explanation. By contrast, if one applies to this case the distinction between contributors and enablers, it should be possible to find a case where E1 only explains E2 in cases where it is the case that p, but where it is no part of the explanation of E2 that p. There are two possibilities of this sort. The first is where, if it were not the case that p, E1 would not have occurred. The second is where, if it were not the case that p, E1 would still have occurred, but would have been unable to explain E2. To suppose that these apparent possibilities cannot occur is to suppose that explanations are guarantees of a certain sort.

There is a potential example of the second type in the theory of causation. A full causal explanation of an event might be thought of as one that specifies a sufficient set of events as causes. Now what about the laws governing the whole transaction? It looks as if they are not a proper part of this explanation at all, because it is a specification of a sufficient set of events, and no law is an event. The role of the laws lies elsewhere. They are the conditions required for those events to necessitate this one, and thereby they stand as enabling conditions for the explanation rather than as a proper part of it.

Another such instance, in my own highly contentious view (2000b, chs. 5–6), is found in the explanation of action. The standard way to explain an action is to specify the features that induced the agent to do it. Having specified those features, we do not need to add to them that the agent believed them to obtain. This consideration is no part of a *rational* explanation at all. If we insert it, we in fact spoil the rational explanation by inserting something that bears the wrong sort of relation to the action (see Schueler 2003). For the fact that the agent believes the relevant features to obtain is not itself a reason in favour of doing the action, and inserting it among those reasons turns what would otherwise have been a good explanation, one that reveals the light in which the agent chose the action, into one that is unstable because it contains irrelevancies. That the agent has those beliefs is no part of the light in which he saw the action, no part of the perspective from which he chose to do it— and as such it can play no part in what is, in its own terms, a perfectly sound explanation. The agent's having those beliefs is, however, something without which the features mentioned in the explanation would have been unable to do the explaining.

We should also consider examples of explanations of the first sort, ones where if it were not the case that p, the *explanans* would not have occurred or been the case, but where that p is not a proper part of the explanation. Here is an instance from the theory of motivation: another ice-cream example. What motivates me to buy this ice-cream is that it will taste nice. That it would taste nice would not motivate me (in the sense of 'get me to do it') if I thought that ice-cream was bad for one's teeth. We should not for that reason conclude that I am partially motivated by not believing that ice-cream is bad for the teeth, nor that purely motivational explanations of action are somehow incomplete. I have seen it suggested, for example by Roger Crisp (2000: 44) that a 'full explanation' of my action will have to include that I don't believe that ice-cream is bad for teeth, because if I had believed this I would not have acted, even though the original *explanans* is still in place (that is, the ice-cream would still be very nice). He concludes that 'one of the reasons for my buying the ice-cream is that I do not believe that it will damage my teeth'. So according to Crisp, the motivational explanation is never a full explanation; the full explanation of an action will need to make reference to every belief which I don't have but such that, had I had it, I would not have been motivated. But here I want to say that, quite apart from the question whether we will ever finish listing all these beliefs that I don't have, Crisp's 'full' explanation is answering a different question, and so is a different explanation, from the original motivational one. If we want to know what motivated me, the answer is that it was that the ice-cream would be nice. If we want to know how that could have motivated me, that is, if we want to know how that explanation could be the correct one, the answer (if we need this thought at all) is that I do not believe that ice-cream is bad for teeth.

The point at issue here is significant because Crisp makes it the basis of a general attack on particularism. What he suggests is that particularist conceptions of rationality are at odds with basic features of explanation. He does not respect the distinction between right-making features and enabling conditions. We must mention both, he thinks, if we are to provide a 'complete explanation' of why this action is right. To explain the action's rightness, we can start by listing the features that make it right (in my sense). But the features that make this action right might be present in another case without making that action right. So Crisp thinks we need to do more if we are to explain why the first one is right. What drives us is mainly the comparative question why this action is right when other similar ones are not. In response to this question, we attempt to complicate our explanation, and we only reach an end of that process if we manage to produce something capable of acting as a guarantee. Our original explanation must be expanded so that it becomes such that whenever an action satisfies the *explanans*, it is right.[5]

The central point here is not whether this process is possible or desirable. What is at issue, I think, is the relation between the eventual product and the explanation with which we started. Crisp seems to think that the eventual explanation is effectively the correct, fuller version of the initial one. I, by contrast, think that these two explanations are doing quite different jobs, and that the possibility of a final version of the second, larger explanation is not really required for the initial, smaller one to do its job. In my view we are dealing not with incomplete and complete explanations, but with two nested

---

[5] Raz makes similar complaints (2000c: 225/55–6).

explanations, each of which is complete as it stands. There are, after all, two questions:

1. Which are the features that make this action right?
2. Would those features make right any action that had them ?

Suppose that we have an answer to the first question, and that our answer to the second question is no. We need an explanation why, in another case, the features that here make their bearer right are not doing the same there. Suppose that we find one; some enabling condition fails. What does this tell us about our original explanation, which told us what made the first action right? Does it tell us that it was incomplete or enthymematic? No. Does it tell us that the presence of the enabling condition was among the features that made the action right? No. The comparative question—why was that action made right by these features when this one is not?—is interesting and important, but the answer to it is not really part of the answer to the question what made this right. So the supposed larger explanation is not a larger version of the original smaller one. Or, to put it another way, our account of the reasons why the action is right, the grounding reasons, is not shown to be incomplete by the fact that those reasons obtain in other cases where the action is not right.

My general conclusion is that the supposed expanded explanation is not a fuller version of the original one. It is answering a different question and doing a different job. In fact, it seems to me that the features mentioned in the original explanation do not properly appear in the 'expanded' explanation at all. Consider the ice-cream example again. I suggested that though I would not eat this ice-cream if I thought that ice-cream was bad for one's teeth, what motivates me is that it will taste nice, not that I do not think it bad for teeth. Crisp suggests (2000: 44) that my not thinking ice-cream bad for teeth will be part of the complete explanation of what he calls 'the reasons for my buying the ice-cream'. He supposes, however, that my expecting it to taste nice will also be part of that complete explanation. And this seems to me to be a mistake. It is a mistake because one can be motivated by considerations that are *not* the case, but such considerations can play no role in the supposedly broader account of why one acted.[6] The situation here is, according to me, analogous to the relation between direct and comparative explanation. If we ask what made this action right, we are told the grounding reasons. If we ask why this action was right when that other one, so similar, was wrong, presumably we cannot mention the grounding reasons, since they are, as it were, part of the question, not part of the answer. It is as if the comparative question concerns the answer to the direct question; but if so, it just has a distinct subject matter. This means that the 'complete' explanation that answers all comparative questions, supposing such a thing to be possible,

---

[6] This thought depends on my view that what motivates us is what we believe, not our believing it; where what we believe is false, we are motivated by something that is not the case. This admittedly contentious view is defended in my *Practical Reality*, ch. 6.

does not subsume the original direct explanation at all. It is, in this sense, not more 'complete'. It is an explanation of the success of an explanation.

4. EPISTEMIC ENABLERS

I now turn to the epistemological example. The general idea here is that what is required for one to know on the basis of evidence need not itself count as more evidence. For instance, I am only capable of diagnosing the problems with my central heating system because I have reasonable experience of similar systems. But that experience does not function as a premise, or a reason, in my diagnosis. It is not part of my evidence, nor part of the evidence that my diagnosis is correct. Again, I am a competent speaker of the language only because I underwent serious training at an early age. What is required for me to have the skill I do never functions as something that I appeal to in the exercise of that skill. Perhaps these two points are about skills. (I am not convinced that the first is, but even if they do both concern skills, they are none the worse for that.) So let us look for one that lies clearly in the area of propositional knowledge—knowledge-that.

I know that q, and I know that it would not be the case that q if it were not the case that p—but I do not know whether it is the case that p or not. This is the structure of various examples offered by Dretske (1970). I know that this is a zebra, but I also know that if the zoo had taken to disguising its mules by painting them with black and white stripes, this would probably not be a zebra; and I also know that even if it were a zebra, in those circumstances I would not know that it was. Crucially, I do not know that the zoo has not taken to disguising its mules as zebras in this way, but, as Dretske claims, I do know that this is a zebra. That the zoo has not started painting stripes on its mules is a necessary and so enabling condition for me to stand in the 'knowing' relation to this being a zebra, but we need not for that reason suppose that I know whether the zoo has done so or not.

Wilfrid Sellars writes: 'It might be thought that knowledge (not belief or conviction, but knowledge) which logically presupposes knowledge of other facts *must* be inferential. This, however, as I hope to show, is itself an episode in the Myth [of the Given]' (1956: §32). The idea he is attacking is that if I only know that q because I know that p, I must be inferring that q from my knowledge that p. And lying behind that is the suggestion that he is really after here, which is that since I only know that there is a book in my hands because of my knowledge of how things look and feel, my knowledge that there is a book in my hands must be inferred from that more basic sensory knowledge (the standard inferentialist version of what I call classical foundationalism). What is wrong with this? It cannot be that the supposedly more basic sensory knowledge is not propositional and so cannot stand as a premise, because that is at odds with Sellars's talk of 'knowledge of other facts'. Luckily we need not pursue Sellars's own reasons for his claim. For our purposes, the point is just the idea that subjunctive conditionals (the instance in point here being that if I had not known how things are looking and feeling, I would not have known that there is a book in my hands) are very indiscriminate. Subjunctive conditionals are held in place, or made-true, in all sorts of ways. The insistence that where we come across one it must be functioning in this or that particular way is always something to be wary of.

This is exactly the point we started with, reformulated to suit Sellars' example. Consider the following two propositions:

(1) If it had not been the case that *p*, that action would not have been so wrong.
(2) That *p* is part of what makes that action so wrong.

One might suppose that even if (1) does not entail (2), at least (2) certainly entails (1). But in fact neither of these propositions entails the other. There are many conditions necessary for the wrongness of an action which do not play the special role of a wrong-maker; so (1) does not entail (2). Conversely, that *p* may be part of what in fact makes the action wrong, in a case where, were it not the case that *p*, the action would be made equally wrong or even worse by some other feature which is either already the case but lying dormant, as it were, or which would become the case if it were not the case that *p*. We have seen this point before, and we will see it again.

We might think that (2) here could be reformulated in a variety of ways, which are certainly entailed by (1):

(2′) That *p* is among the reasons why the action is so wrong.
(2″) The action is so wrong partly because *p*.
(2‴) The action's being so wrong depends on its being the case that *p*.

I want to allow that there are ways of hearing (2′)–(2‴) that make them true wherever (1) is true. But we should not suppose that in such cases they are also equivalents of (2). They are only equivalent to (1) if we hear them in senses that differ from the sense of (2). In the case of (2′), for instance, we have to hear the relevant sense of 'reason why'.

A further epistemological application of the general distinction is given by Marcus Giaquinto (1998). He suggests that a belief that is caused by certain experiences may still be able to count as a priori or conceptual knowledge, so long as the experiences that cause it do not act as grounds for it. There is of course the classic Quinean objection to any such claim that a priori or conceptual knowledge is possible, which is that any sentence might come to be rationally rejected as false in the light of experience. Giaquinto admits this, but claims that it is irrelevant. The truth of the relevant sentence is indeed dependent on experience, in the way that Quine claims, but this is *negative dependence*; a belief is negatively dependent on experience if its retention is dependent on the absence of awkward experience. A belief is *positively dependent* on experience if experience acts as its ground, that is, if the acceptability of getting the belief depends on the presence of supporting experience. Giaquinto's point is that a belief can be negatively dependent on experience without being positively dependent on it. And to constitute a priori, or conceptual, knowledge, the belief only needs positive independence. Quine's point that it is negatively dependent on experience is irrelevant.

The purpose of all this has been to reinforce the soundness of a distinction between the favouring role and the much less specific role of being an enabling condition. This is an instance of the more general distinction between what plays a certain role and what is required for it to play that role; the latter features may not play that role themselves. Suppose that we all agree on these points. This does not mean that we are all going to agree on any suggested instance. In fact, it is easy to find examples of cases where it is not clear which side of the favouring/enabling distinction a given feature is to fall. Suppose that the way he is driving is perfectly safe, even if the road is icy, so long as it has been salted. Is the fact that the road has not been salted one that makes his driving dangerous, or is it merely a condition under which various features of his driving (the speed, the violence of his braking) make it dangerous? It is hard to be sure. Is the fact that I did not intend this outcome a condition under which the disastrousness of the outcome does not make my action wrong, or is it rather a mitigating or attenuating factor in some way? Is this action partly made right by the fact that it has better consequences than any other, or is that only a condition necessary for other features (the goodness of its own consequences, in this case) to make it right? In all these cases one's grip on the distinction between favourers and enablers seems unable to generate a clear answer.

One response to this situation is to insist that until a clear criterion has been found for this distinction, it is useless as a theoretical tool (cf. Shafer-Landau 1997). Given the number, or perhaps the practical importance, of cases in which we are rightly uncertain how to apply it, the distinction does not apply itself, and stands in need of a criterion if we are to work with it at all. It seems to me, however, first that there are clear cases—cases in which the applicability of the distinction is not controversial at all. That there are unclear cases does not destabilize the distinction, but should rather lead one to be cautious in applying it. I don't take it to be a general rule that every distinction needs an independent criterion. If one does suppose this, one collapses immediately into Pyrrhonist scepticism, for the criterion itself will require a distinction, and so on indefinitely, as Pyrrho so joyfully pointed out. So distinctions do not *as such* require criteria for their application, and I maintain that the many cases where it is not clear how to apply this one do not constitute a reason why it should need a supporting criterion when others don't. One thing I do want to insist on is that the many unclear instances do not constitute a reason for thinking that there is no real distinction at issue here at all.

The general message of this chapter has been that there is more than one conception of moral relevance, or more than one way of being relevant to the answer to moral questions. A feature that favours one action or another, at least if it does so in a certain way,[7] is certainly relevant. So are the enabling conditions, those which do not favour but whose presence or absence is required for others to do the favouring job. There may be forms of relevance beyond these, but these will be the ones we need for what is to follow. The crucial point, perhaps, is that terms like 'dependent on', 'because', 'are affected by', and so on, like subjunctive conditionals, are not discriminate enough for our purposes. Moral properties are as much dependent on the enablers as on the favourers, but nonetheless the favourers play the central role.

Subjunctive conditionals are crude tools in the theory of reasons because they fail to distinguish enabling conditions from favourers. And this fact is the real reason (promised in the previous chapter) why we cannot characterize a reason to ϕ as a consideration in the absence of which we would have had less of a duty to ϕ, or maybe no duty at all. The second part of this (maybe no duty at all) is as true of enabling conditions as of reasons; the first part (less of a duty) is as true of intensifiers as of reasons.

---

[7] This caveat alludes to the problem of distinguishing moral reasons from (some) practical reasons, especially those of prudence.

4

Dropping the Catch

This chapter is concerned with the question which metaethical positions are well placed to capture the notion of a contributory reason, given the points made so far. Unfortunately, many significant figures in recent debates in ethical theory have said little or nothing on the topic. One has to work out for oneself what they might say (or, perhaps better, ask them).

1. HUMEAN REALISM

Michael Smith sometimes characterizes rightness as the property an action has of being such that one's fully rational self would advise one to do it (1994: 151ff.). If we converted this directly to yield an account of reasons, we would get something like this: for there to be a reason for me to ϕ is for my fully rational self to advise me to do it, so far as that goes. But this is clearly wrong, for reasons which should now be familiar. The notion of advice is an overall notion. There is no such thing as partial or contributory advice. One cannot say, 'To some extent (or in some respect) I advise you to do this, but overall I advise you not to do it.' So if the appeal to advice were central to Smith's position, he would be stuck at the outset. But in fact the official way of expressing Smith's position is this: for an action to have the property of rightness is for it to be such that one's fully rational self would desire that one do it. And now things are looking more promising, for there does seem to be some prospect of finding a suitable notion of desiring something in a certain respect, but not overall.

If there is such a notion, we can use it in the following analysis of a reason: for there to be a reason for me to ϕ is for my fully rational self to desire in a certain respect that I ϕ. So far, then, things are going well for Smith. But what exactly is this notion of desiring in a respect? I know two ways of understanding this notion and I do not think that either will work. The first is to construe desiring in a respect in terms of desiring that respect. For Smith, to judge that one has a reason to ϕ is to judge that ϕ-ing is valuable. Suppose that I value, or judge valuable, honesty, integrity, kindness, and thoughtfulness. The action I propose to do will be dishonest, and to that extent lacking in integrity, but it will be kind and thoughtful. I judge that I have reasons to do it and reasons not to do it. We are to understand all this in the following way. What I am judging is that my fully rational self would desire honesty and integrity and kindness and thoughtfulness, and those independent desires for features are construed as partial desires for any action that has those features in virtue of their presence. We then work backwards and understand valuing an object for a feature that it has in terms of one of these partial desires in one's fully rational self. And this, finally, gives us our understanding of what it is to have a reason to ϕ.

The crucial move in this is the understanding of what it is to value an object for one of its features in terms of what it is for one's fully rational self partially to desire complexes in which that feature occurs. I don't think that this move will work, for reasons to do with organicity. It is generally agreed that the value of a complex whole is not to be identified with the sum of the independent values of its parts. If that is so, we cannot move automatically from an independent evaluation of the parts to any judgement of how valuable they are in the whole. But our first way of making sense, on Smith's behalf, of a notion of desiring in one respect and not in another involved exactly that move. It involved the identification of desiring a part wholly and desiring a whole partly, and this is flatly at odds with the organicity of value (if value is understood in terms of desire in this sort of way).

But perhaps a contextualized version of this strategy is still possible. The idea would be that instead of trying to work to a desire for the whole from independent desires for the parts, we should be trying to work from desires for the various features of the whole as they appear in that context. If we do things this way, we avoid the problem of organicity altogether. We are identifying desiring the whole for the presence of a feature with desiring the feature in that context, and using this in Smith's way to understand what it is to have some reason to ϕ. For me to have a reason to ϕ is for my fully rational self to desire some feature that my ϕ-ing would have in the relevant context. This does *not* amount to the thought that my ϕ-ing would have that feature in the context and not elsewhere, and that my fully rational self only desires my ϕ-ing when it has that feature. Nor does it mean that my fully rational self would desire this feature if that self were in one context (a men's club) but not if it were in another (a tea party). The idea is rather that my rational self desires the feature in that context and not necessarily in others where the feature occurs. Now this is certainly better. But what does it mean to desire a feature in one context and not in another in this sort of way? I value my double bass for its rich sonority—something that I would not much value in a friend. I treat its rich sonority as a reason; perhaps I am more careful about the instrument for that reason. On Smith's account, that means that I judge that my fully rational self would desire rich sonority in the context of my double bass but not necessarily elsewhere. But it is hard to be sure what this would amount to. My fully rational self would certainly want this object to be richly sonorous and not that one. But wanting that this object be richly sonorous is not the same thing as wanting this object for its rich sonority;

wanting that a person be absent is not the same as wanting them for their absence. Nor is wanting that a person be absent the same as wanting the absence they would have. So wanting that an object be richly sonorous is not the same as wanting rich sonority in that context. We have to make sense of the idea of wanting a feature in some way that does not amount to wanting the feature-bearer for the presence of the feature, nor to wanting that the object have that feature. At the moment I don't see how to do this.

There is, however, another way of working. To desire a whole partly might be to desire the whole more with the part than without it. There is a sub-junctive conditional operating here: I desire O partially for being F iff I desire it as it is more than I would if it were not F. This subjunctive conditional should remind us of one of the failed definitions of what a contributory reason does. And I suggest that the problems we had with that definition are repeated here. The crucial point is that the following things are compatible:

1. Part of the value of the whole is contributed by the presence of F-ness, i.e. derives from its being F.
2. If it had not been F, the whole would be even more valuable than it currently is.

There are two ways to show that these two are compatible. The first is simple; any attenuator will satisfy (2) above, but not satisfy (1). But I suspect that this point will seem unpersuasive to many, and that it is better to tackle the issue at a more intuitive, less structural level. We need an example. The simplest sort of example is one where being not-F is even more valuable than being F. I have already suggested an example of this sort of win-win situation. I might praise you for doing something nice for a friend, and praise you even more fervently were you to do it for someone who is not a friend. But perhaps this suggestion appears fanciful. A different sort of example would be a case where, if the whole had not been F, it would have had a different feature, G-ness—and its G-ness would have contributed even more value than its F-ness would have done. In such a case, we can say that the whole is the better for the presence of F-ness, but we had better not mean by this that it would be worse without it. Let us suppose that had Mary been at the party, her presence would have been one of the respects in which the party was enjoyable; it would have contributed largely to the value of the evening. But as things stood, her absence enabled a more intimate gathering which was even better than the party would have been had she been there. Now is this a relevant example? If it is, it is easily repeatable, and will defeat any attempt to understand partial valuing in terms of an overall ranking of alternatives (whether desire-based or not).

There seems to be only one effective objection to such examples, which is that they involve appeal to the wrong subjunctive conditional. Instead of appealing to how things would have been if they had not been F, it may be said, we should start from how they are, with feature F present, and create a contrast with *that very same situation minus F*. So in the case of the party with

Mary, we should extract Mary from that party and then ask about the value of the resulting object, the ebullient party minus Mary. The greater value of the other party, the one we actually had, is irrelevant.

I do not think that this manoeuvre can possibly be got to work across the board; and it has to work across the board if it is to be the basis of a sound general understanding of 'desiring in a certain respect'. The idea had been that we are to rank alternatives, and alternatives have to be ways in which things might have gone. Now there are certainly two ways things might have gone, to pursue the party and Mary a little further. There was the larger party with Mary, and the smaller, more intimate one without her. What is not a way things might have gone is the ebullient party without Mary. Look at another example. Suppose that my wife and I hire a car and drive across the country to the west coast, spend a day there, and then drive back. (I wrote this on the east coast of New Zealand.) Now I want to assess the value of having a car to make the trip in. Do I compare the value of the trip with a car and without a car, leaving it somehow unspecified how we are to get from east to west coast and back again? No, I compare doing it by car with doing it by bus, let us say—or by bicycle, perhaps. Do I compare doing it by car with the weighted average of doing it in the various alternative ways, or with doing it in no particular way, but in some way or other (shades of Berkeley on abstraction here)? No, again. There really only seems to be one coherent comparison. And the same applies to Mary and the party; we need whole alternatives to compare for value, and the Mary party without Mary is no such thing. Or rather, if it is anything at all, it is the intimate party, not a less well attended ebullient one.

Perhaps we could cope with this by supposing that context, rather than logic, should determine the appropriate subjunctive conditional. This is of course a wise sort of thing to say in general; the problem is how to apply it to the Mary case so as to get the right answer. The right answer is that Mary would have contributed to the value of the ebullient party, but that 'it' would have been even better without her. So: what might the 'it' be here? To fill out the context a little: the three of us who made up the intimate party would, with Mary, have had an ebullient rather than an intimate evening. We want to find something in between the incomplete ebullient party—that party but Maryless, as it were— which seems to be incapable of existing, and the intimate party, which could exist but gives us the wrong answer (that Mary did not contribute to the ebullient party). And I don't think that there is anything intermediate to be found here. So the tactic of allowing the subjunctive conditional to vary according to context does not seem to be even applicable to the present case.

All this seems to me to show that as things stand Smith is devoid of any suitable notion of 'desiring in a respect'. And if this is true, it is at best moot whether his general approach is capable of capturing the notion of a con- tributory reason. If it is not, the probable diagnosis is that it was constructed with only the overall in mind, in a way that turns out not to be as flexible as it needs to be if it is to cover all the normative ground.

Since this conclusion is of general importance, I want to confirm it by a short excursus into what one might call the logic of *pro tanto* preference. Let us try to think of this as *ceteris paribus* preference. The most prominent approach to this concept tries to understand preferring A to B as some function of preferring A without B to B without A, all within some context that is contextually determined (cf. Hansson 1996). An immediate objection to such an approach is that it cannot capture every notion of *ceteris paribus* preference. Suppose that I am offered three choices for a meal:

1. The entrée without the dessert.
2. The dessert without the entrée.
3. Entrée and dessert.

Now if I am only to have one course, I would prefer the entrée. But suppose that I choose to have both. I could then be asked, of the two courses that I ate, which I preferred. To this question no official answer can be provided, on the approach we are considering. Or if there is an answer, it looks as if it might be the wrong one; for it might be that of the two courses I preferred the dessert, even though if I could only have had one course I would have preferred the entrée.

This should merely serve to remind us that preferring in the sense of choosing is a different matter from preferring in the sense of liking more, or wanting more. But which of these things is the one that matters for our purposes? If we are trying to understand the idea of 'desiring in a certain respect' we are likely to be looking at liking or wanting more, rather than at choosing. But the comparative analyses of preference don't seem to apply well to this sort of preferring; it seems to be about choice rather than desire and liking. To prefer A to B when one has both is not the same as to prefer A without B to B without A. Indeed, it doesn't seem to be comparative in this sort of way at all. (It is of course comparative in another way.) The point is even more obvious when we try to understand preferring A with feature F to A without feature F, which would be what desiring in a certain respect should come down to. The official analysis apparently tells me that this is to prefer [A with feature F and not-A without feature F] to [A without feature F and not-A with feature F]. I suppose that one can hardly fault such an 'analysis', but it could hardly be said to share any merits enjoyed by the analogous approach to choice. It certainly does not offer an account of 'desiring in a certain respect' that avoids the objections already made.

2. EXPRESSIVISM

For an expressivist attempt to capture what it is to be a reason or (perhaps better) what it is to take something to be a reason, we need to look at Allan

Gibbard's *Wise Choices, Apt Feelings* (1990: 160–6).[1] To see the problem from Gibbard's point of view, we need to ask what we might expect an expressivist to say about the notion of a reason. An initial suggestion might go something like this:

> To say that R is a reason for S to ϕ in circumstances C is to express acceptance of a system of norms that direct S to ϕ in C.

The trouble with an account of this sort is that it does not address the notion of a contributory reason. We want to know what it is to say that R is some reason for S to ϕ in C, and what we are told is surely directed more at the notion of overall reason. After all, I might say that R is a reason for S to ϕ in C while actually adhering to a system of norms which forbids S to ϕ in C. What is required, then, is to find some other term than 'directs'. What then does Gibbard in fact offer? He writes:

> To say that R is some reason for S to ϕ in C is to express acceptance of a system of norms that direct us to award some weight to R in deciding whether to ϕ in C. (1990: 163)

Note that our initial suggestion supposed that the norms I sign up to in saying that there is a reason for S to ϕ in C are norms that require (or recommend) that S should be doing the ϕ-ing in C (or the deciding whether to ϕ in C). On Gibbard's account, by contrast, they require *everyone* to be doing something, not particularly S. But that is by the by. The real weakness is that the account makes explicit use of some appropriate conception of weight—of normative weight, as one might put it—and that was pretty well exactly the thing we were trying to understand. Further, we should note the way in which the account is entirely in terms of how one should go about *deciding* whether to ϕ in C. But to award weight to R in one's decision is not the same as taking R to favour ϕ-ing in C. I might think, for instance, that I should always consider the question whether R if I am deciding whether to ϕ in C, but suppose nonetheless that on many occasions the question whether R or not will be in fact irrelevant to how I ought to act. This would happen if R was very commonly relevant, so that it is a consideration one ought always to bear in mind, even though sometimes its relevance is defused by other considerations. If, by contrast, awarding weight to R is another way of saying 'take R to count in favour or against' we are left groping for an expressivist account of *these* notions, which were surely the ones the analysis was supposed to be addressing in the first place.

---

[1] Simon Blackburn's *Ruling Passions* (1998: 257) offers the suggestion that a reason is 'a feature that prompts concern'. But I don't think he meant this to be taken very seriously, and anyway the notion of prompting is not normative enough to do the work required here. Something might very well prompt concern without deserving to do so. If we were to read 'prompt' as 'ought to prompt', things look better. But the 'ought' in this phrase is either itself a contributory ought, in which case we are no further forward, or it is an overall ought, in which case the analysis (if such it is) would be plain wrong.

We might therefore try the following slightly different version:

To say that R is a reason for S to ϕ in C is to express acceptance of a system of norms that would lead one to approve of S's ϕ-ing, at least to some extent, in respect of R.[2]

The problem now is that, though one thinks there is indeed some reason for S to ϕ in C, it might well be that one also thinks that there is conclusive or overall reason for S not to ϕ in C at all. The difficulty is to make sense of the idea that one might approve of S's ϕ-ing to some extent while being overall firmly against it. But isn't there such a phenomenon as approving of an action in one respect and not in another? Let us say that the action is that of my son's buying a car (a 1971 Citroen DS). The elegance of the car is some reason to buy it, I think, and its liability to rust is some reason not to buy it; the liability to rust wins, and there is overall reason not to buy it. One way to understand what is going on here is to say that I approve overall of the elegance (my approval of the elegance is unmixed, as it were) and disapprove overall of the liability to rust. These will be two overall approvings or disapprovings, and we are going to try to construct a notion of contributory or partial approving of buying the car out of them. This should remind us of the previous discussion of Smith. The difficulty for Smith in this connection arose because of the organicity of value, and I suggest that the same problem arises now. Wholesale approvals of parts considered apart cannot be converted directly into focused approval of those same parts when they are parts of wholes, or of wholes in virtue of the presence of those parts, because a feature need not have the same value in every whole in which it appears.[3]

One can say, 'I partly like him and partly dislike him; I like his wit and charm but I dislike his manipulativeness.' This is overall liking and overall disliking, directed at a part. Whether overall one likes him or not will be determined by the balance between these partial likings (likings of parts) in an organic way. What the expressivist needs here is a notion of overall liking whose object is the whole but which is somehow also focused on the part. I like *him* for his wit and charm; I dislike *him* for his manipulations. But so far we have not seen how to do this.

The second approach we might try on behalf of the expressivist tries to piggy-back on an expressivist conception of an overall 'ought'-judgement.

---

[2] Note that this suggestion could be turned into a non-Gibbardian one by dropping the explicit reference to the system of norms. I would prefer this because I think it wrong for an *analysis* of the notion of a reason to include the stipulation that reasons must be part of some *system*. This would give us:

To say that R is a reason for S to ϕ in C is to express approval of S's ϕ-ing, at least to some extent, in respect of R.

This version is more amenable to the general thrust of expressivism; it is something that Simon Blackburn, for instance, might espouse. But the criticism offered in the text applies to this simpler suggestion as well (or badly) as it does to the Gibbardian one in the text.

[3] This is a tendentious version of organicity. Those who dispute it are asked to wait until the direct discussion of Moore's version (which is indeed different from the one given here) in Chapter 10.

We are, for present purposes, allowing that there is nothing wrong with the standard expressivist approach on *this* topic:

> To say that S ought overall to ϕ in C is to express acceptance of a system of norms that would require S to ϕ in C.

So we might try something like the following, for the contributory:

> To say that R is some reason for S to ϕ in C is to say that, if it had not been the case that R, S's ϕ-ing in C would have been less right than it is.

But this can hardly succeed, for reasons most of which we have seen too often before. First, our expressivist has not yet established a good sense for the notion of more and less right. We just have the notion of requiring that appears in the account of overall oughts, and we have not been shown any expressivist way of taking requiring to come in degrees of stringency. (Note that there is a difference between degrees of acceptance of a norm and degrees of stringency of the norm accepted.) Second, the subjunctive conditional we are now considering is anyway incorrect as an analysis of the contributory. First, again, it is true of intensifiers, which are not favourers—not reasons, that is. Second, we saw in our discussion of Smith that this sort of appeal to subjunctive conditionals does not work, because it can be the case both that this feature counts in favour of the action and that the action would have been better (more right) without it.

Some will feel that this is all mere skirmishing. Suppose, then, that we try to capitalize on the approach to *pro tanto* or *ceteris paribus* preference considered earlier. What we are looking for, again, is a notion of approval of an act in virtue of the presence of some feature F, to take this as a model for taking the presence of F as a reason for doing the action. We could try to do this in terms of approving of the act with that feature more than one approves of 'the same' act without it. But we have already seen all sorts of difficulties with this approach. And what if the presence of a certain reason against doing the action was required for the presence or force of other stronger reasons in favour of it? For a formal example of this, what if I promise that I will ϕ, but only if there is some significant reason against ϕ-ing?

My conclusion is that the expressivists have failed to offer any effective account of a contributory reason, and that they do not seem to have the resources to do better.

3. NEO-PRAGMATISM

I now turn to the neo-pragmatists, in the person of Robert Brandom and the views expressed in his *Making it Explicit* (1994). For Brandom, an inference (practical or theoretical) is valid or sound if entitlement to the premises generates entitlement to the conclusion. Entitlement is a matter of permission. So a valid argument is one such that, if you are permitted (entitled) to believe the premises, you are also permitted (entitled) to endorse the conclusion. You can be entitled to incompatible conclusions, in the sense that you have the right to endorse any one of them—though once you have endorsed one of them, you are committed to that one and lose entitlement to the others. You can, therefore, be committed to the premises of various entitlement-preserving inferences without yet being committed to any particular conclusion. This should remind us of the familiar thought that one can have and recognize good reasons for and against various alternative views or actions, but not yet be committed to any one of them. So Brandom writes at this point that 'the notion of entitlement-preserving inferences accordingly provides a pragmatic analysis . . . of the notion of *prima facie reasons* (whether doxastic or practical)' (1994: 249). I want to dispute this claim. It seems to amount to saying that one may be in a position in which one has sufficient reason for any of a number of conclusions. But the notion of a sufficient reason is not the same as the notion of a prima facie reason.[4]

What features of prima facie reasons might Brandom be thinking he can capture with his notion of an entitlement-preserving inference? His thought must be that where there is such an 'inference' from reason to action, one is entitled to the reason, and thus to the action, but not committed to the action even if one is committed to the reason. Now of course when we are dealing with practical reasons, reasons for action, this is indeed the situation. You can have and recognize good reasons for each of several alternatives, say ways of spending your holiday, without being 'committed' to spending your holiday in one way rather than another. But so long as the reasons are equally good in each case, you are 'entitled' to draw any one of the conclusions, that is, to take whichever holiday you choose.

One thing to be borne in mind here, however, is that there is a difference between theoretical and practical reason in this respect (though Brandom says 'whether doxastic or practical'). Suppose that I want to stay dry, and that it is raining. There may be various ways of staying dry. I might just not go out; I might take my umbrella; or I might put on my rainproof cape. This gives me three possible 'inferences':

1. It is raining: so I'll stay in.
2. It is raining: so I'll take my umbrella.
3. It is raining: so I'll put on my cape.

I could 'draw' any one of the three 'conclusions' specified in these 'inferences', and the 'could' here is normative; I am entitled to draw any one of them. Suppose, now, that the inference is not, as we have so far been supposing,

---

[4] The context of the quotation given above establishes beyond doubt that Brandom is thinking of prima facie reasons in a Ross-like sense; so it is fair to take him as claiming to capture the nature of the contributory.

practical, but theoretical. We can make it explicitly theoretical by making it third-person rather than first-person. He wants to stay dry and has three ways of doing so. That gives us three inferences:

1. It is raining: so he'll stay in.
2. It is raining: so he'll take his umbrella.
3. It is raining: so he'll put on his cape.

Now *none* of these inferences is sound; we are not entitled to *any* of the conclusions even though we are entitled to the common premise.[5] The matter turns on the notion of good enough reason—sufficient reason. What is sufficient reason in a practical sense is not sufficient reason in a theoretical sense. In theoretical reason there is no analogue of the kind of plural entitlement that we find in practical reason. What we do get, in theoretical reason, is a different notion of a sufficient reason, which is that of a good enough, though not conclusive reason. (This sense of 'sufficient reason' of course is applicable in practical contexts as well.) What we don't get in the theoretical context is the right to draw one conclusion when there are others available to us that are equally good.

This matter, however, is nothing whatever to do with the notion of a prima facie reason. A prima facie reason is a consideration that favours a certain action, even though it may be defeated by considerations that favour the other side more strongly. Even when defeated in this sort of way, it remains as a reason, and it continues to favour the action that overall one has more reason not to do. But can Brandom capture this? He writes that, 'the premises of these inferences entitle one to their conclusions (in the absence of countervailing evidence) but do not compel such commitment. For the possibility of entitlement to commitments incompatible with the conclusion is left open' (1994: 169). This remark appears to use a notion of entitlement that is rather like that of having separate good reasons. But this is a mere appearance. The sort of entitlement Brandom is talking about vanishes in the presence of countervailing reasons. Good reasons on the defeated side, by contrast, do not vanish just because there are better reasons on the winning side. But in Brandom's terms, entitlement cannot exist where there is another conclusion better supported. The idea of an entitlement that is defeated but still holds good (that is, retains some normative force) is not available to him.

The only way out of this apparent impasse, so far as I can see, is to be found in the words, 'the premises of these inferences entitle one to their conclusions (in the absence of countervailing evidence)'. We might take this to imply that, though the entitlement vanishes if there is countervailing evidence, still the role of a reason has been captured by saying that a reason is a consideration

[5] Bill Lycan suggested that this claim is an instance of Cliffordian prissiness; it only holds if we suppose there to be an overarching duty only to apportion belief according to the strength of the evidence. If this is right, yet another potential distinction between theoretical and practical rationality falls to the ground.

that does entitle one to the relevant conclusion (an action, perhaps) in any case where there is no reason on the other side. (Actually it might do more than entitle, in that situation; it might commit one to the action.) But we have already seen, and rejected, attempts to capture the normative role of a contributory reason by appeal to how things would be if there were no opposing reason.

Brandom, we can now see, is in a familiar situation. He is trying to work with just two concepts, entitlement and commitment, whose home is really the overall level. Entitlement, though it does come in degrees, is still (for Brandom) a success term. A defeated entitlement is one that has lost its normative status. One can have a defeated but still operating contributory reason, but such a reason does not ground any entitlement—not even a little one or a *pro tanto* one—to do the thing favoured by that reason. So the question is whether it is possible, in terms of entitlements, to construct any conception of what is better called the *pro tanto*—the separate contribution made by each distinct reason. Almost the only move available to Brandom at this stage is to try to understand a *pro tanto* entitlement as an overall enti-tlement that one would have in some counterfactual situation, and this is what he does, suggesting that a contributory reason generates an entitlement in cases where there is no countervailing reason. But this characterization of what a reason does is effectively the same as Ross's account of a prima facie reason (perhaps not surprisingly), which we have already seen to be unsus-tainable on several counts. The tempting conclusion is that there is an aspect of normativity (of the way in which reasons behave) that cannot be captured in terms of commitments and entitlements—the terms to which Brandom wants to restrict himself.[6] He cannot make room for contributory reasons.

4. AUSTRALIAN NATURALISM

Frank Jackson is a doughty representative of a vigorous tradition in philo-sophy, and his *From Metaphysics to Ethics* (1998) contains substantial dis-cussion of the normative, leading to the conclusion that all normative properties and concepts are descriptive. He reaches this conclusion by arguing that for every evaluative property, there is a descriptive property that is necessarily co-extensive with it, and then arguing that in fact these necessarily co-extensive properties are identical. The tools of this argument are the notions of entailment (especially mutual entailment) and super-venience; there is a sense in which Jackson uses a limited weaponry in a self-denying way, just as Brandom does. So the same question arises, namely whether this weaponry can be got to cover the normative ground. The natural

---

[6] Many thanks to Mark Lance for help with Brandom.

way to try to capture the notion of a contributory reason, if one is wanting to work with Jackson's basic tools, is to try to provide an analysis in terms of subjunctive conditionals—the same resource as is used to construct the notion of supervenience. I have no complaint against this manoeuvre in itself. It is just that there are manifest obstacles in its way, as we have already seen. Subjunctive conditionals cannot capture the favouring relation, because they cannot distinguish between favourers and enabling conditions. They are too indiscriminate for our purpose, then. We cannot say that a reason for doing an action is a feature in the absence of which the action would not have been right. For enabling conditions are of this sort, but they are not favourers. We might try saying rather that a contributory reason will be a feature in the absence of which the action will be less right than it would otherwise have been. But this is also subject to counter-examples. First, it is as true of intensifiers as it is of reasons. Second, it might be, as we have seen, that we have here a feature which favours the action, but such that if that feature were absent the action would have been even better.

Might we hope to do better by using the notion of entailment? No, for we have already seen that the features that favour an action, even if they succeed in making it right, do not entail that it is right. It is perfectly possible for those features to be present in another case without making the relevant action right—this is just what would happen if an enabling condition were to fail. So this avenue is blocked too.

These considerations are rather abstract; I have merely looked at the tools of Jackson's trade and suggested that they are of the wrong type to do the job. It might then be suggested that one could do to the concept of a reason something rather similar to what Jackson does to the concept of rightness in his book. What he does is to argue that the predicate 'is right' is necessarily co-extensive with some natural predicate, argue that necessarily co-extensive predicates pick out the same property (whether one-place or many-place), and then use Ramseyfication as the method of determining which natural property that is. The question for us is whether this method, always assuming that it can be got to work for the one-place predicate 'is right', can also be got to work for the (at least) two-place predicate 'is a reason for', which we are reading as 'favours'. I will suggest that it cannot, and so that the second phase, that of Ramseyfication, is not applicable here.

The first phase goes as follows. Start from a representative evaluative predicate E, perhaps 'is a right action'. Wherever E is satisfied, we can give a larger description of the action in its context, and as we cast the context wider and wider we will eventually end up with a complete description of the world in which the action is done (let that world be World 1) which is given by the enormous descriptive predicate 'D^1'. Call this a 'world-description', though really it is a description of an action-in-its-world. Now D^1 entails E, by supervenience, for any world descriptively similar to the first one must also be one in which things are evaluatively similar, and so it is impossible for D^1 to be satisfied in any other world without E being satisfied there as well. But E does not entail D^1, for there may be other different worlds (Worlds 2, 3, 4, 5, . . .) in which E is satisfied but in which D^1 is not. In those worlds different descriptions will be satisfied: D^2, D^3, D^4, D^5, and so on. There may even be an infinite number of descriptive ways a world can be, compatible with the satisfaction of E. Let us form, however, the disjunction of all such world-descriptions, Δ. What we find is that E entails Δ, since if E is satisfied in a world, that world must be one of the worlds in which E is satisfied and so be one in which the disjunctive description Δ is also satisfied. But Δ also entails E, for if the enormous disjunctive description is satisfied, one of its disjuncts must be satisfied, and all such disjuncts entail E. So E both entails and is entailed by Δ. And since E was merely a representative evaluative predicate, we can conclude that for each such predicate, there is at least one descriptive predicate that both entails and is entailed by it, i.e. that is necessarily equivalent to it.

Now how are we to run this argument when we are dealing with a two-place predicate? No problem, it seems. We start with our two-place predicate, and move out to a world description whose satisfaction entails that of the two-place predicate with which we started. We then construct a potentially infinite series of such world-descriptions and announce that the disjunction of them entails and is entailed by the original two-place predicate. We then argue, as before, that necessarily co-extensive predicates pick out the same property, be it a one-place property or a two-place property (otherwise known as a relation).

The difficulty that I have with this does not derive from the fact that the favouring relation is a relation. It is a two-place relation, and no doubt the infinite disjunctive world-description can be seen as an enormous two-place predicate as well. The problem that I have in mind derives from the fact that the favouring relation is necessarily asymmetrical. It does not seem to me that Jackson's procedure guarantees that there will be a matching asymmetry in the complex disjunctive predicate which he offers as necessarily extensionally equivalent to the predicate 'favours'. One might dispute this on the general ground that two necessarily equivalent relational predicates must be either both asymmetric or both symmetric. But that does not seem to be true if the necessary equivalence is extensional rather than intensional. My conclusion therefore is that even if we allow that the relevant two predicates are necessarily extensionally equivalent, there is no chance of supposing that they pick out the same relation. One of them picks out a relation that is necessarily asymmetrical, and the other does not—or at least there is nothing in Jackson's process to guarantee that it will do so, which is enough for my purposes.[7]

Jackson does, however, make a further suggestion, which is in fact the only explicit characterization of a reason in his book. He writes:

Again, the principle that acts that cause suffering are typically wrong is not the principle that the suffering causes the wrongness of the act. An act may be wrong because

---

[7] Thanks to Paul Studtmann here.

it causes suffering, but the 'because' is not a causal one. (The act does not become wrong a moment after it causes the suffering.) The principles of folk morality tell us which properties typically go together, but not by virtue of causing each other. (p. 131)

About this, I want to say that even if one can make some sense of the notion of an epistemic reason in terms of which properties typically go together, since such generalities can perhaps underlie the credence quotients (or the changes in such) required of us by epistemic rationality, this approach is not likely to work for contributory moral reasons. It is not that causing suffering commonly goes together with being wrong—though it does, no doubt; the causing of suffering is rather the ground of the wrongness or generates it—it makes the action wrong. This is a different relation from that which holds, say, between the pronouncements of a recognized moral authority and the moral facts of the matter. In the latter case, we really are dealing with things that 'typically go together', and not with contributory reasons that go to make the action right. That this moral authority pronounces our action right cannot be among the things that make it right (except in very unusual circumstances), even if it favours our believing that the act is right.

A final suggestion about how we should treat the notion of a reason is to be found in a paper by Jackson, Pettit, and Smith (2000: 97). They are here suggesting that the particularist doctrine of the holism of reasons can be captured even within the terms of expected-value utilitarianism—as un-particularist a context as one might hope to find. They write:

According to expected-value utilitarianism, the moral value of A is a weighted sum of the value of each possible world at which A obtains: $V(A) = \Sigma_w Pr(w/A).V(w)$, where $V(w)$ is a measure of the total happiness at w. And R is a reason for A if and only if the value of A given R is greater than the value of A... which obtains if and only if $V(A.R) > V(A)$.

As it stands, this seems to tell us that one thing is a reason for another if the value of both together is greater than the value of the second alone. Of any two things that are of independent value, then, each is apparently a reason for the other. A possible way of avoiding this result would be to distinguish $V(A.R)$ from the value of A given R, and think of this last in terms of the idea that if the presence of R raises the value of A, R is a reason for A. My question at this point would be: what account has been given of this notion of 'raising the value of A'? It looks to me as if the only way to make sense of this, within the constraints of the approach, is to run things in terms of subjunctive conditionals, in a way that should by now be familiar. The presence of R raises the value of A iff A has greater value when R is present than it would have in the absence of R. But we have seen over and over again that a feature R can favour A, can contribute to its value, even though in its absence A would be more favoured, not less.

It is worth pointing out that the analysis is probably wrong anyway. There are counter-examples. I promised to lend my friend David my Christmas tree stand, knowing that he was in need of one. But I could have just turned up with it and surprised him by my friendly thoughtfulness. We would normally think that my having promised to turn up gave me some reason to do so. But it is quite probable that the expected welfare generated by my turning up unexpectedly would be greater than that generated by my promising and then turning up. But even if this were true, we would still think that my having promised to do it gave me some reason to turn up that I did not have before—contrary to the position we are considering.

The real point, of course, is that the value of my promising and not turning up is much less than that of my just not turning up. But this is the claim that R is a reason for A in case the value of R without A is much less than the value of $R.A$, or perhaps rather that (in this case) once R is in place, the value of not-A becomes much less than that of A—and that was not the theory's point. Raising the value of A is a different thing from reducing the value of not doing A (most obviously if value is understood in terms of expected utility).

The theory might retort that if I promise, this means that my action now has the value-adding property of being a promise-keeping, so that it is true that the action, given that I promised, has more value than it would have had if I had not promised. But this has more than one defect. The first defect concerns the relevant comparison class. The action of turning up unexpected is the action of turning up without having promised to do so. So if we want to stick to the idea that being a promise-keeping is a value-increasing quality (which we do, because promise-keeping is a reason and we are trying to understand reasons in terms of increases in value), we have to do so in a way that is compatible with the idea that if I had not promised, my action would have had more (expected) value than if I had promised. It is not clear to me how to do this.

5. KANTIANISM

The writers who have been discussed so far in this chapter would all, I think, accept that an inability to capture the nature of a contributory reason is a significant failure from the point of view of their overall enterprise. Kantian approaches, which I discuss in this section, are quite different in this respect. It would be characteristic of a Kantian approach to be suspicious of the very notion of a contributory reason, and to try to capture the relevant phenomena in other ways. Complaining that they are not trying to do what I think they ought to be doing would not cut much ice in this context. More to the point would be to show that there are some aspects of our ordinary moral thought that they have not captured quite as well as they suppose, or that they have failed so far to address at all. If one could show that there is little prospect of any improvement on these fronts, that would be even better; but I renounce this further aim for the present.

In discussing Kantian conceptions of reasons, one needs to remember that Kant has a bifurcated conception of practical rationality. As far as ordinary practical rationality goes, his conception is broadly Humean, and this means that for that domain he can take over more or less completely any acceptable Humean account of the contributory. Rather than try to show (beyond anything shown by my discussion of Smith's views earlier in this chapter) that Humeans can offer no satisfactory conception of the contributory, I am just going to leave that issue aside and concentrate on Kant's views about moral reasons. Morality is special, for Kant, in ways that render his ability to capture the nature of a contributory *moral* reason very dubious.

The worry, of course, is that the Categorical Imperative appears to function entirely at the overall level. It tells us that it is overall wrong to act on a maxim that cannot be appropriately universalized. But it seems impossible to convert this so that it acts as a test of whether a consideration is morally relevant, in the sense of being a moral reason for or against doing the action proposed. Nor can it tell us that we have some reason to do the action but more reason not to. Nor can it tell us that there is more than one reason to do this action, and that the separate reasons for doing it are together, but not separately, enough to make it our duty.

In pursuing these issues I am going to take as my focus the excellent discussion by Barbara Herman (1993, chs. 7 and 8). Herman's general procedure is to argue that everything of real significance here can be captured in Kantian terms (that is, by Kant as she interprets him), and that the rest is probably a misconception in one way or another. Her main discussion concerns the notion of moral conflict. A crucial reason for thinking in terms of the contributory is that moral reasons can conflict, and that the conflict between different reasons must be taking place at the contributory level. Herman offers a Kantian account under which the nature of conflict generates no reason to think in contributory terms at all. 'It is not a matter of weighing independent reasons', she claims (p. 168). I will outline her account and say why I think it cannot be right, and then try to suggest that there are further aspects of the behaviour of contributory reasons that Herman has left unaddressed.

Herman takes it that the maxims that are tested by the Categorical Imperative procedure are of a special sort. They provide a joint specification of an action to be done and a type of reason for doing it. Such maxims Herman calls 'general maxims'; an example might be, 'I will deceive others to serve my own purposes'. This maxim fails the Categorical Imperative test. But that fact does not establish that one ought never to deceive others intentionally (which is the sort of thing that Kant is normally taken to be saying). Suppose that in order to help my friend A, I must make a deceitful promise to B. How am I to proceed, that is, deliberate? As Herman sees things, the rejection of the general maxim mentioned above officially establishes only a 'deliberative presumption' against doing actions of that sort. This presumption 'can be rebutted by reasons (justifications) of a different sort' (p. 148). What she means by this is that if there is some moral justification for deceiving B, I may still do so despite the presumption against doing actions of that sort that is generated by the rejection of the general maxim. But this is, for Herman, quite a different matter from the presumption's being overridden by more stringent moral considerations; the presumption is not overridden but rebutted. What is it, however, for a presumption to be rebutted? The language of rebuttal makes it appear that the thing rebutted is somehow shown false. But on Herman's account a rebutted presumption is not shown false so much as shown not to be reason-giving (or conclusive?) in this context. She considers the suggestion that helping A is part of the obligations between friends, and I might make the deceitful promise on that ground. One might take it, then, that there is some moral reason to help and some moral reason not to help (since helping involves deceit); but that would be the wrong way of looking at things, apparently. There is no reason not to help in this case, and hence no sense in which a duty not to deceive is overridden by some stronger duty of friendship. Why is there no duty not to deceive? Because the presumption against deceit has been rebutted in this case.

One worry here is how the general presumption against deceit is supposed to emerge from the rejection of the 'general maxim' of deceiving for one's own purposes. What I think this means is that if you are going to deceive someone, you have to be doing it for some other reason than because it will achieve something that you want, some end in which you have an interest, or something that is of no value independent of its value to you (pp. 148–9). The 'presumption' amounts to the thought that deceit is wrong unless it is done for some other type of reason. (So it is not what I mean by a default, a notion that will be introduced in Chapter 6.6.)

Now all this is in the service of the view that one never has moral reasons both for and against a certain action. It is not that I have some moral reason not to deceive B but more moral reason to go ahead. Properly understood, there is, in the present case, no reason not to deceive B at all. The only reason there might have been is carried by a presumption that has here been rebutted. I don't think that this description of things is adequate to the situation. What has been established is that there would have been a (conclusive) reason not to deceive B if I had been going to do it for my own purposes. As things stand, however, my motive is more respectable. Since I am not doing it for my own purposes, the fact that it would be wrong so to act is irrelevant. What has got lost in this is the possibility that my deception might be done for a reason which in its own way is respectable enough, but which is not good enough to make the deceit acceptable. Perhaps I am going to deceive B, a stranger, in quite a gross way for the sake of some fairly trivial advantage to someone else C in whom I have no interest either. It seems to me that Herman's structures don't capture this sort of situation. The fact that my action would be deceitful has not become irrelevant or ceased to be a reason, even though the presumption against deceit has been rebutted by the fact that my motivation is not one of those excluded by the rejection of the general maxim.

I think that Herman's response to this would be to say that all this is left up to judgement, in a way that is controlled by deliberative principles. She writes, for instance, that, 'resolution of conflict ... requires a principle of deliberation. It is not a matter of weighing independent reasons' (p. 168). But, though it is true that the question whether one has an adequate justification for acting in ways that the deliberative presumption would prohibit is a matter of judgement, which in Kantian terms would require a principle, it seems to me that the subject matter of that judgement is whether one has enough moral reason to justify engaging in deceit, which is not the same question as whether there is no reason not to—which is how things look on Herman's account.

This, then, is my first reason for thinking that Herman's Kant cannot capture the behaviour of reasons. There is conflict between moral reasons, and there are aspects of that conflict that have got swept under the carpet by the structures that Herman offers us.

My second reason is that conflict is not the only thing to think about. A second phenomenon to be captured, according to my way of thinking, is that one reason can strengthen the case for doing an action that has already been made by a first. Suppose that I am torn between two courses of action, both admirable in their way, but incompatible. I might, say, spend my holiday taking underprivileged kids on adventures in Wales, or I might spend it helping villagers in India dig a well. I am trying to work out which way my time would be best spent, and I am not sure which need is the more pressing. There is something to be said, a lot to be said, for either choice. Then I learn that the need in India is urgent in a way that the kids' need for adventures is not. (There has been a sudden and unexpected drought.) I now take it that I have more reason to go digging than to go adventuring. I don't see how to describe this situation in Herman's terms.[8]

---

[8] The main worry with this example is that the urgency might not be a second reason. It might merely intensify the first reason, and intensifiers are perhaps less of a problem in the present context. But I think that the need for water is a reason to go and help dig (now, or if not now then later), and the urgency is a reason to do it now rather than later. If you don't agree, other examples are not far to seek.

PART II

From Holism to Particularism

5

Holism and its Consequences

In previous chapters we have been pursuing general themes in what one might call the theory of reasons. After trying to locate particularism among a range of options, some more and some less extreme, I have been concerned to stress the importance of the notion of a contributory reason, and of the normative relation of favouring. I tried to suggest that we cannot explicate what it is for a reason to make the sort of contribution it does in terms of any relation to the overall; we are forced to understand it in its own terms or not at all. And I tried to stress the fact that there are many different ways in which the presence or absence of a consideration can make a difference to how one should respond, the main distinction in this connection being between favouring and enabling something else to favour.

It may not have been obvious why a book that is officially on particularism in ethics should have started with so much material that is apparently only tangential. But the favouring/enabling distinction is in fact central to the particularist's approach to these issues, and the more general enquiry into the nature of the contributory was intended as a pre-emptive strike against a form of generalism that grounds itself on one of the (now refuted) attempts to understand the contributory in terms of the overall. This last matter will return (in Chapter 6.3).

1. HOLISM IN THE THEORY OF REASONS

So I now plunge into the main theme. In the present chapter I lay out what I see as the main argument for particularism in ethics, which is based on holism in the theory of reasons. I start by repeating two distinctions introduced in Chapter 1, particularism vs. generalism and holism vs. atomism:

Particularism: the possibility of moral thought and judgement does not depend on the provision of a suitable supply of moral principles.
Generalism: the very possibility of moral thought and judgement depends on the provision of a suitable supply of moral principles.
Holism in the theory of reasons: a feature that is a reason in one case may be no reason at all, or an opposite reason, in another.

Atomism in the theory of reasons: a feature that is a reason in one case must remain a reason, and retain the same polarity, in any other.

I am going to work with a distinction between theoretical reasons and practical reasons, reasons for belief and reasons for action.[1] It doesn't matter for my purposes whether this distinction is exhaustive or not. The holism that I am talking about is intended to hold on both sides of it, and in the middle too, if there is anything in between. I start by trying to establish that theoretical reasons are holistic. We will quickly find that theoretical reasons are perfectly capable of changing their polarity according to context, without anyone making the slightest fuss about the matter. For instance, suppose that it currently seems to me that something before me is red. Normally, one might say, that is a reason (*some* reason, that is, not necessarily sufficient reason) for me to believe that there is something red before me. But in a case where I also believe that I have recently taken a drug that makes blue things look red and red things look blue, the appearance of a red-looking thing before me is reason for me to believe that there is a blue, not a red, thing before me. It is not as if it is some reason for me to believe that there is something red before me, though that reason is overwhelmed by contrary reasons. It is no longer *any reason at all* to believe that there is something red before me; indeed, it is a reason for believing the opposite.

As I say, it seems to me that nobody ever thought of denying what I am claiming here. I know of nobody who has nailed themselves to an atomistic conception of how theoretical reasons function. If generalism is taken to be the view that all reasons are general reasons, i.e. that if a feature is a reason in one case, it is the same reason in any other case, generalism is uncontentiously false of theoretical reasons.

Let us now turn to ordinary practical reasons. We will find just the same thing there. There are plenty of examples to persuade us that such reasons are holistic. For instance, that there will be nobody much else around is sometimes a good reason for going there, and sometimes a very good reason for staying away. That one of the candidates wants the job very much indeed is sometimes a reason for giving it to her and sometimes a reason for doing the opposite. And so on. Now examples of this sort would be of little use if there were some theoretical obstacle to taking them at face value. But again we should remind ourselves that nobody has ever really debated the question whether ordinary practical reasons are holistic or not. There should be no *parti pris* on this issue; so the examples, which are legion, should be allowed to carry the day without resistance.

Perhaps this is too quick. There is a theory-based reason for doubting my claim that practical reasons are holistic, a reason that derives from the common thought that practical reasons are grounded in desires of the agent

---

[1] Nothing hangs on my identification here of reasons for belief as theoretical reasons and reasons for action as practical ones. All that I am doing is introducing a little convenient terminology.

in a way that theoretical reasons are not. What one wants should not affect what one judges to be the case, on pain of charges of bias or prejudice. But what one wants can perfectly well affect what one has reason to do. Indeed, many find it hard to conceive of our having any practical reasons at all if we had no desires. My own view on this matter, however, is that even if a desire-less creature could not have any reasons at all, it is not our desires that give us or ground our reasons. Reasons stem from the prospect of some good. If we have no other reason to do a certain action, wanting to do it will give us no reason at all; nor can wanting to do a silly action make it marginally less silly. (These are only the first moves in a long debate.[2] I mention them here only to show the sort of way in which I find myself denying the possibility of grounding practical reasons in desires of the agent.) This view of mine is, of course, an independent input in the present debate. I mention it only to show that a certain motive for doubting the analogy I have been drawing between theoretical and practical reason is itself contentious.

It may be that here we come across the real motivation for atomism in the theory of practical reason—an adherence to the view that reasons for action are partly grounded in desires. For if we accept that view, and if we then think of desires as giving the desirer the same reason wherever the desire occurs, the result looks atomistic. The right response to this, however, is to claim that even if all practical reasons are grounded in desires, the same desire need not always function as the same reason. Consider first the third-person case. That she wants power and he does not may be a reason to give the power to him rather than to her, as I have already said. But it may at the same time be a reason to give it to her, since according to me one feature can be a reason on both sides at once. Now consider the first-person case. Suppose that I am trying to train myself into indifference towards a woman. I want very much to spend time with her. But I also want not to have this want, since she is permanently indifferent to me. It is better for me not to think of her at all. If I spend time with her, this will make things worse for me rather than better—so long as I have not yet suc-ceeded in training myself into indifference towards her. Once I am indifferent towards her, I can spend time with her without loss. In this situation, it seems, my desire to spend time with her may be a reason for me not to do so.[3]

So far we have it that theoretical reasons are holistic, and so are ordinary practical ones. Beyond the ordinary practical ones, what remain? There are two categories of reasons that have often been thought special: the aesthetic and the moral. Aesthetic reasons are difficult to categorize. They may not even be practical, but theoretical; that is, they may be reasons for judge-ment rather than for action. Luckily, I don't have to decide about that here.

---

[2] For the remainder of the debate, see my *Practical Reality*, ch. 2; or, perhaps better, Quinn (1993a), Raz (1986, 1998), and Scanlon (1998).

[3] In this connection I cannot resist reporting an advertisement I saw in a bus in Washington, DC, which said 'Do you always want to look at pornography? If so, ring this number'. The number was that of a clinic which was offering to help one get rid of this intrusive and socially awkward desire.

Whatever they are, they are largely holistic. It is undisputed that a feature that in one place adds something of aesthetic value may in another make things worse; a given metaphor may be telling in one context and trite in another. Converted into talk about reasons, there are reasons to introduce that metaphor in the one case and reasons not to do so in the other. We might think that *some* features behave atomistically, that is, always provide the same reason wherever they occur. Most of these will be picked out using thick concepts. Perhaps imaginativeness is always for the better; I don't know. Painterliness seems to me a quality that can sometimes be out of place; symmetry too. And the same goes for most of the concepts with which aesthetic appreciation deals. Perhaps then there are some invariant aesthetic reasons, but I know of nobody who has ever suggested that one could erect a principle-based structure for aesthetic judgement in the sort of way that almost everybody thinks one can do for moral judgement. This, despite the many respects in which judgments of the two sorts are similar.

Now could it be the case that moral reasons are quite different from all the others in this respect, being the only atomistic ones? This is what many have supposed, in taking it that moral rationality is necessarily based on the existence of a suitable supply of moral principles. Moral reasons, they have held, necessarily behave in regular (or rule-bound) ways, though other reasons see no need to behave in that way at all. About this, I want to say that straight off it just seems incredible that the very logic of moral reasons should be so different from that of others in this sort of way. Consider here the sad fact that nobody knows how to distinguish moral from other reasons; every attempt has failed. How does that fit the suggestion that there is this deep difference between them? Not very well at all. Then of course there are examples to be considered, examples of apparently moral reasons functioning in a holistic way. I forbear to bore you with these. It just seems inevitable that moral reasons should function holistically in the way that other reasons do.

This certainly makes it hard to hold, as many do, that the very possibility of moral distinctions, of moral thought and judgement, is predicated on the existence of a range of moral principles. Moral principles, however we conceive of them, seem all to be in the business of specifying features as *general* reasons. The principle that it is wrong to lie, for instance, presumably claims that mendacity is always a wrong-making feature wherever it occurs (that is, it always makes the same negative contribution, though it often does not succeed in making the action wrong overall). The principle that it is wrong to lie cannot be merely a generalization, a claim that lies are mostly the worse for being lies, for if all moral principles were of this sort, the argument that moral thought and judgement depend on the possibility of moral principles would simply be the argument that such thought is impossible unless there is a considerable preponderance of normal cases over abnormal ones. I have never seen this argument made, and I doubt, what is more, whether it would be persuasive if restricted to ethics.

If moral reasons, like others, function holistically, it cannot be the case that the possibility of such reasons rests on the existence of principles that specify morally relevant features as functioning atomistically. A principle-based approach to ethics is inconsistent with the holism of reasons.

All the same, it might be argued, we have to admit that there are some invariant reasons—some features whose practical relevance is invariant. And surely I should allow this, because holism, as I expressed it, concerns only what may happen, not what must. It could be true that every reason may alter or lose its polarity from case to case, even though there are some reasons that do not do this. If they don't do it, this will be because of the particular reasons they are. Invariant reasons, should there be any, will be invariant not because they are reasons but because of their specific content. And this is something that the particularist, it seems, should admit. It is like the claims that a man can run a mile in four minutes, that Sam Smith is a man, and that Sam Smith cannot run a mile in four minutes. These claims are compatible, and so are the claims that reasons are variable *qua reasons* though some reasons are (necessarily, given their content) invariant. The invariance, where it occurs, derives not from the fact that we are dealing here with a reason, but from the particular content of that reason.

So can the particularist admit the existence of *some* invariant reasons? The obvious examples are things like the causing of gratuitous pain on unwilling victims. Surely, it is commonly urged, this is always for the worse, even if overall we might in some case be morally forced to do it. Well, the first thing to say is that admitting the possibility of some invariant reasons is a far cry from admitting that the very possibility of moral thought and judgement is dependent on our being able to find some such reasons. To support any such suggestion, we would somehow need to be able to locate a sufficient range of invariant reasons, ones that together somehow cover the moral ground entirely and themselves explain the nature and role of the variant reasons. This is quite a different matter from simply trying to refute particularism by producing one counter-example of an invariant reason, which is normally what happens.

Further, we should remember that the question whether reasons are atomistic or holistic is a very basic question about the nature of rationality, of how reasons function from case to case. It is, I suppose, conceivable that though the vast bulk of reasons function according to a holistic logic, there are a few whose logic is atomistic. But if this were true we would have a hybrid conception of rationality. There would just be two sorts of reasons, each with their own logic, and moral thought would be the uncomfortable attempt to rub such reasons together. It is *much* more attractive, if at all possible, to think of our reasons as sharing a basic logic, so that all are atomistic, or all holistic.

Let us consider, then, how the supposed invariant reasons function as reasons in the particular case. Take the well-known example of the fat man stuck in the only outlet from a cave that is rapidly filling with water from below. We and our families are caught in between the fat man and the rising water. But we have some dynamite. We could blow the fat man up and get out to safety. But the fat man is unwilling to be blown up (he, at least, is safe from drowning, being head up); and, let us immediately admit, he is blameless in being where he is, and in being fatter than the rest of us. So what we propose to do involves the destruction of an unwilling and blameless victim. As such, we might say, this is *some* reason against lighting the fuse and standing back. The question I want to raise is whether the fact that this feature (that we are causing the death of an unwilling and blameless victim) is functioning as the reason it here is, is in any way to be explained by appeal to the (supposed) fact that it functions in the same way in every case in which it occurs. It seems to me that this feature is the reason it is here quite independently of how it functions elsewhere.

Of course, if the feature is genuinely an invariant reason, this fact, should we discern it, will be of use to us in any case where we might be in doubt as to the contribution it is making. We can say, 'This is an invariant reason, it makes such-and-such a difference there, and so it must be making that difference here.' But suppose that we were to treat one of these supposedly invariant reasons as potentially variant, so as to deny ourselves the use of that inference. What sort of mistake would we have made? Would it be a failure of *rationality* to treat an invariant reason as potentially variant, or just a mistake of fact? I suggest that the invariance of the reason is an epistemic matter rather than what one might call a constitutive one. If we know or even merely suspect that the reason functions invariantly, this tells us, or at least gives us some idea, how it is functioning here, but in no way constitutes the sort of contribution it makes to the store of reasons here present. In that sense, the invariance of its contributions is not a matter of the logic of such a reason.

I conclude, then, that we should accept the possibility of invariant reasons, so long as the invariance is not a matter of the logic of such reasons, but more the rather peculiar fact that some reasons happen to contribute in ways that are not affected by other features. We can admit this without adopting a hybrid theory of rationality, so long as we treat the invariance of any invariant reason as an epistemic matter rather than as a constitutive one.

2. FROM HOLISM TO PARTICULARISM

This concludes the argument. So I now turn to ask what exactly it establishes. There are two reasons for thinking that any such simple attempt to present particularism as a direct consequence of holism will not work. The first reason is that particularism is about the ways in which actions are made right or wrong, and the argument in the previous section doesn't even address that topic. It is simply silent on the question whether the ways in which features can combine to make actions right or wrong are holistic or not. To think otherwise is to forget the distinction between two normative relations. The first is the favouring relation, the relation in which features of the situation stand to action or to belief when they are reasons for doing one thing rather than another or for believing one thing rather than another. The second is the right-making relation, the relation in which features of the situation stand to an action when they make it right or wrong. I seem to be suggesting that a feature can make an action right, or stand in the right-making relation to it, in one case, but not in another. But the argument for this, if it is contained in the previous section, seems to establish only the holism of the favouring relation. The holism of the right-making relation is something else, and it is not at all obvious, one might say, how this second holism is supposed to follow from the first. Of course it is not nothing to have established that the favouring relation is holistic. But particularists surely want both holisms, not just one. How are they going to get the second holism out of the first?[4]

There are various ineffective responses to this difficulty. The first is to appeal to the notion of a reason. There are reasons for belief and for action; these are favourers. Then there are the reasons why the action is right or wrong. These are reasons like the others. So if the argument of the previous section has established the holism of reasons in general, it has already established the holism of right-making reasons, and there is nothing left to be done. But this is all rather specious. We cannot really hope to establish one holism on the back of the other by this sort of appeal to the notion of a reason. The very notion of a reason why an action is right or wrong needs to be shown to be suitably similar to that of a reason to do the action, and that is exactly what we have not yet done. This sort of appeal to a supposedly single notion of a reason begs the question.

Nor can we hope to make progress by pointing out that most features that stand in the favouring relation to an action are also right-makers. This is true enough; the left-hand sides of the two relations largely coincide case by case. But this does nothing to show that if one relation is holistic, so must the other be. The holisms we are after are holisms of the relations, not of the relata.

It looks as if it is conceivable that the metaphysics of the situation (the nature of rightness and the way it is made) might have a different logic from that of the favouring relation. And if this is so, no appeal to the holism of one will be enough on its own to establish the holism of the other. This being so, two avenues are open to me. The first is to argue directly, in much the same way as that in which I argued for the holism of the favouring relation, that the right-making relation is variable, holistic too. To do this, I would bring examples, or adapt earlier examples, to show that if there is good reason to

[4] Thanks to Nick Zangwill and Margaret Little for helping me see the force of this question, though not in these terms.

think that the first relation is holistic, there must be similarly good reason to take the second one to be holistic. This would not, I think, be very hard. All that would be necessary is to convert every suggested case in which a feature is a reason for doing the action, or for believing it right, into a case in which that feature is a reason why the action would be right. I don't think this would be very difficult. By this, I don't mean, of course, that every reason for believing an action to be right is a reason why the action is right, in the constitutive sense of being part of what makes the action right. I only mean that the examples offered should be ones that lend themselves to character-ization in either way.

But this avenue, though it seems perfectly effective to me, fails to address the interesting question whether it is technically possible for the favouring relation to be holistic while the right-making one is not. Is it possible for the epistemology of a domain to come apart in this sort of way from its metaphysics? It is natural to think that were this to be the case, a peculiar sort of dislocation would have emerged. The canons of rationality for a given domain would not be directly related to, or be held in place by, the way that domain is itself structured. Perhaps this is indeed possible. It might be, for instance, that the rules for chess are capturable in a set of finite rules expressing the powers of each sort of piece, and that this set is effectively atomistic, while the reasons to which we are responsive in actually playing the game operate holistically. For this to be the case, there would have to be an explanation of how the move from the domain of the rules of play to the domain of actually playing can take us from an atomistic to a holistic context. Perhaps the point is that when we are dealing with living agents rather than the abstract structure of a game, or a rational practice, or something like that, a far wider range of considerations enters the scene, which function in ways that can only be conceived holistically. But no such explanation is available in the case that we are officially concerned with here, namely the move from the domain of moral metaphysics (supposedly atomistic) to the domain of reasons for action and belief (supposedly holistic). I conclude that it is safe to think that if either of these two domains is holistic, so must the other be. Whether we are thinking about reasons for doing an action or about reasons why it would be right to do it, any feature that is a reason in one case may be no reason at all, or an opposite reason, in another.

This result already establishes more than that reasoning is not always monotonic (not that this needed establishing, of course). Holism takes us beyond the claim that some reasoning is non-monotonic, as we saw in Chapter 1. It does this because non-monotonicity tells us only that a feature that alone is a reason in favour may be part of a larger reason that is a reason against. Holism looks within that larger reason, and notices that sometimes the sup-posed 'larger reason' is in fact a combination of two distinct reasons against.

But going beyond non-monotonicity is not very exciting. The real question is what our general holism establishes about moral principles. On occasions

I have been rash enough to claim that, given holism, moral principles are impossible. I still think something of the sort, as we will see, but the passage of years brings caution. Already the argument, as I advanced it, admitted the possibility of invariant reasons; and if there can be such things, and some of them are moral reasons, there can certainly be true general statements whose role is to articulate that fact. If we can think of such general statements as principles, holism will turn out to be compatible with the existence of at least some principles. The issue then becomes how many such invariant reasons we can find, with principles to go with them, and that does not seem to be the right sort of point to get stuck on. The question whether morality is principle-based will not really be being addressed, if we approach the matter this way. For one might think that nothing can count as a principle, as a source of moral distinctions, unless all morality stems from principles; it couldn't be that some of our moral distinctions are principle-based and others are not, though it could be that some of our reasons are invariant and others are not. All one would be left with, on the present showing, is the occasional appearance of invariant reasons, and the recognition that this is so will not take us straight to the claim that we are here dealing with a principle.

I now turn to my second reason for suspecting that the move from holism to particularism cannot be as simple as I have so far suggested. This is the fact that a principled ethic can accept and indeed stress the truth of holism. The simplest way to see this is by looking at a candidate principled ethic that is explicitly holistic. Consider the following 'principle':

P1. If you have promised, that is some reason to do the promised act, unless your promise was given under duress.

This principle specifies a contributory moral reason, but explicitly says that the feature that gives the reason does not always do so. (One can even imagine a principle of this sort which ends up, 'in which case it is a reason not to do the act', if one wanted a principle which allowed for reversed polarity.) Now suppose that we have a set of such principles, all of them explicitly allowing for cases in which the normally reason-giving feature would fail to perform that role. And suppose that our set is wide or large enough to cover the ground, in the sense that it specifies all the moral reasons that there are. (There is nothing in the holism argument to show that such a thing is impossible.) The result is a principled but holistic ethic.[5]

To be sure, this result only emerges if we were lucky enough to be dealing with a set of morally relevant features whose defeasibility conditions, if we can use that phrase, are finitely specifiable. Nothing can guarantee that this

[5] I am very much in Michael Ridge's debt at this point. It is worth saying that the same point is made at the end of Jackson et al. (2000), but in that instance the point is associated with such a contentious example (as I tried to show in Chapter 4) that it is impossible to know what, if anything, it can hope to establish. The Ridge approach, which is the one I have laid out in the text, is far more direct and forceful.

will be so; nor does the suggestion at issue suppose otherwise. The point is only that one cannot argue from holism directly to the conclusion that moral principles are impossible.

What this shows is that the argument (if there is one at all) from holism to particularism is at best indirect. I suspect, indeed, that particularists will not agree among themselves about how best to proceed at this stage. I know some who will not be swayed by the point at all. I have in mind those who don't much care about what sort of moral outlook is officially possible or impossible, since their main interest is in showing that the morality we actually have is not grounded in any principles. I certainly accept that our actual morality is unprincipled, but I was hoping to cast the net rather wider than that.

I think the best way to put the particularist conclusion is that, given the holism of reasons, it would be a sort of cosmic accident if it were to turn out that a morality could be captured in a set of holistic contributory principles of the sort that is here suggested. Most importantly, of course, it would be a cosmic accident if *our* morality could be expressed in this way, but the same would apply to any workable moral scheme. It would be an accident because, given the holism of reasons, there is no discernible need for a complete set of reasons to be like this. If our (or any other) morality turned out to be that way, there could be no possible explanation of that fact. It would be pure serendipidity. There is no need for things to be so, and therefore there is nothing for the moral principles to do.

It was because of this issue that I characterized particularism as I did above, as the claim that the possibility of moral thought and judgement (and in general, one might say, of moral distinctions) in no way depends on the provision of a suitable set of moral principles. So characterized, it seems to me that particularism does follow from holism. What does not follow is a straight denial of the possibility of a moral principle, or at least of an invariant moral reason. But the loss of those conclusions is no real damage to the particularists' assault on the standard principle-based conception of morality. Their picture of what is required for there to be moral reasons, duties, obligations, and so on remains in place.

The thought that the existence of a suitable provision of principles would be a cosmic accident depends on the claim that there is no discernible need for such a provision. In a sense, this claim is a challenge to the opposition to come up with a picture of moral thought and judgement which, though it respects the truth of reasons-holism, still *requires* (rather than merely makes possible) a provision of principles that cover the ground. Some subject matters are such that we can expect such principles. In arithmetic, for instance, dividing one number by another will not always yield a smaller number; sometimes it will, and sometimes it won't. So the situation is holistic, in a sense. But nonetheless we can expect to find specifiable laws or principles that govern these operations. If morality were relevantly similar to arithmetic, a similar expectation would be appropriate.

Richard Holton's 'principled particularism', which I outlined in Chapter 2, is a response to the challenge here. He starts from the thought that, if an action is right, there must be certain features of the world that make it so. Those features would perhaps not have the same effect in other cases, but this doesn't matter. For if we specify those features and then announce that there are no further morally relevant features in the case (this announcement being the so-called 'That's it' clause), we know that such a combination will always have the same effect. For the interfering effects of changes elsewhere will not be capable of making any difference.

The important aspect of this picture is that it offers just the sort of motivation that the unprincipled particularist is saying cannot be found. But does it respect the truth of reasons-holism? I would say not. In fact, Holton's picture doesn't really admit the existence of the sort of reasons that I have been talking about at all. I argued in Chapter 2 that there is no room in his story for the sort of reasons-talk that drives holism, in which we pick out individual features of the situation and say that some are reasons and others are not. There are no doubt awkward aspects of this sort of talk, such as the imprecise nature of the distinction between one larger reason and two smaller ones combined. But Holton is really producing a sort of agglomerative picture in which the different contributions of different features are not distinguished at all, those features being lumped together as the features of the world that combine to make the action right. This is not really a holistic picture at all.

What we are looking for is some positive suggestion as to why the behaviour of moral reasons might *need* to be capturable in some principled way, even though we continue to respect the truth of holism. Holton offered one such—but there are others to be found. One is that morality is essentially a system of social constraints, and as such it must meet certain conditions. It must be reasonably simple, so as to be operable by the populace at large. It must be explicit, so as to give clear guidance so far as possible. And it must be regular, so that we can tell in advance what effects this or that feature will have on how we and others should behave. My own view about this is that it is a description of something like a set of traffic regulations. But morality was not invented by a group of experts sitting in council to serve the purposes of social control. It may be that it does serve those purposes, but even if so, it does not follow that one can derive from that fact a set of requirements on the nature of any effective moral system. The particularist claim would be that people are quite capable of judging how to behave case by case, in a way that would enable us to predict what they will in fact do, and which shows no need of the sort of explicit guidance that a set of principles (of a certain sort) would provide. (I return to this issue in Chapter 7.5.)

An alternative move is to abandon the idea that the behaviour of moral reasons can generally be captured by some collection of contributory principles, but to insist that any possible moral scheme must contain *some* substantial invariant moral reasons, despite the general truth of holism; the behaviour of these reasons, at least, will be capturable in principles. The best form of this suggestion takes its start from the distinction between thick and thin ethical concepts. The thin concepts are those of right, wrong, evil, good, bad, duty, obligation, ought, and so on. The thick concepts are those of the thoughtless, the tactful, the kind, the brave, the obscene, the patronizing, and so on. This distinction is not fully defined (e.g. it is not clear whether justice is a thick concept or a thin one), but it is still operable. The general idea seems to be that the thin concepts are used in overall judgement, and the thick ones are used on the way to that judgement. Below the thick ones, as one might put it, will be other concepts that are not moral concepts at all. So one might judge someone's action wrong because he turned up late (thick concept), and judge that he turned up late because the time printed on the invitation was 8 p.m. (Maybe the concept of an invitation is a thick concept, but I hope that the point is clear.) Overall, then, there are three layers: the non-ethical at the bottom, the thick ethical in the middle, and the thin ethical at the top.

With this picture we are in a position to make two claims. The first is that morality needs the thick intermediate layer. The second is that the thick layer is the one where interesting invariability is to be found. Thick concepts, that is, have an invariant relevance; if an action is thoughtless, that is always for the worse, and if it is brave, that is good so far as it goes. But one can say this while still supposing that there is no regularity about the relations between the non-ethical base and the thick layer above it, nor between the non-ethical base and the thin layer at the top.[6] The conclusion will be that there will be no moral principles expressing invariant relations between (sets of) non-ethical concepts and thin ethical concepts, but that there will be moral principles expressing invariant relations between thick and thin ethical concepts. So, for instance, a particularist who takes this line will maintain that relations between non-ethical and thin ethical concepts are always variant; the same non-ethical concept may be instantiated in different cases and make quite different differences to how one ought to act. So there are no principles telling us how we ought to act (or how we have reason to act) in situations described entirely in non-ethical terms. But there are intra-ethical principles that capture the regular relations between thick and thin ethical terms.

Both of the two claims at the beginning of the last paragraph are interesting. I have never seen a decent argument for the first one, though I am very tempted to believe it true. The idea must be that thick concepts put the non-ethical material below them into a sort of practical shape, in a way that enables overall judgement to see how it fits in and thereby see what effect it has on how one ought to act (the thin). But I don't know of anyone who has managed to tell this story in convincing detail. So that part of things is unfinished business.

[6] For this suggestion, see Little (2000) and McNaughton and Rawling (2000).

As for the second claim, I will return to this in greater detail in Chapter 7.1. But my main point will be that I see no reason to allow that *all* thick ethical concepts have an invariant polarity. Plenty don't, I will be wanting to say. This might still leave a good many that do. But that would only be significant if the invariant ones can be shown to constitute some sort of a centre or core. The aim here is to reach a picture which has an invariant core of thick ethical concepts, surrounded by a variable periphery. With this picture in hand, one could say that invariance of this sort is required for ethical thought, even though many thick concepts are not invariant in their relevance. The promise will be to show that the variable ones depend in some way on the invariant ones; there is to be an ethical core, and it is to be invariant, and variability only makes sense against a context of invariability.[7]

3. SUPERVENIENCE AND RESULTANCE

I now turn to a quite different way of showing that holism and principles are compatible. Remember that our question at the moment is whether, despite the truth of holism, the enterprise of morality necessarily brings with it a suitable array of principles. The new answer to the question is that holism is not incompatible with the supervenience of the moral on the non-moral, and supervenience alone generates a vast array of general principles linking natural descriptions of the world to moral evaluations, in the sort of way that moral principles purport to do.

To see what is going on here we have to start by distinguishing two relations, supervenience and resultance. These two relations are often confused, but it is absolutely vital for present purposes to keep them apart. Resultance is a relation between a property of an object and the features that 'give' it that property. Not all properties are resultant; that is, not all properties depend on others in the appropriate way. But everyone agrees that moral properties are resultant.[8] A resultant property is one which 'depends' on other properties in a certain way. As we might say, nothing is just wrong; a wrong action is wrong because of other features that it has. The obscure 'because of' in this claim is sometimes expressed using the equally obscure phrase 'in virtue of'; a wrong action is wrong in virtue of other features than its wrongness. None of the phrases that are used to express the relation I am calling resultance is at all helpful, really, in trying to get a good intuitive grasp on the nature of that relation. But it is still of the utmost importance to get such a grasp, and in particular to distinguish it from other relations with which it is very easily

---

[7] In McNaughton and Rawling's terms, there can only be secondary reasons if there are primary ones.

[8] Moore (1942), p. 588; Ross (1930: 121–3). Ross sometimes talks in terms of the 'resultant' (1939: 168) and sometimes in terms of the 'consequential' (1939: 280).

confused. The 'resultance base' for the wrongness of a particular action consists in those features that make it wrong, the wrong-making features. There is, however, no such thing as the resultance base for a property (wrongness, say) *in general*. This is because a property that is resultant may be one that there are very many different ways of acquiring, and there need be no way of capturing all those ways at once. I would say this is how it is with wrongness: there are many different ways in which an action can get to be wrong.

So the resultance base for the wrongness of an act will consist in the properties that make that act wrong, which are sometimes called the 'ground' for its wrongness. At this point a crucial question arises: should we say that the properties in the resultance base for this act's wrongness are the same as those which disfavour the act (in the sense of 'disfavour' that I developed in Chapter 3, which is roughly equivalent to 'count against'), or should we take the resultance base to range rather more widely? For the moment, and for the sake of a clear initial contrast between resultance and supervenience, I am going to take it that we should say they are the same. So the resultance base for this act's wrongness consists in those features that make the act wrong in the sense of being the ones that count against doing it, that disfavour it.

There is a vast difference between resultance, so conceived, and super-venience. Moral properties supervene on others in the sense that if an action has a moral property, then any other action exactly similar to the first in non-moral respects will have that moral property too. Here the base we are talking about—the supervenience base—consists in *all the non-moral features of the action*, not just those that make it wrong. The supervenience base is far larger than the resultance base, then, and it includes crucially all the features that count in favour of the wrong action (defeated reasons for doing it) as well as those that count against, all enablers and the absence of all disablers, quite apart from all the other non-moral features as well. So the relation between the wrongness and the resultance base is going to be quite different from that between the wrongness and the supervenience base. Most obviously, if the action is made wrong by the features in the resultance base it cannot also be made wrong by the features in the supervenience base (unless we are dealing with a quite different sense of 'made wrong'—the sort of sense that people must have in mind when they talk of 'fixing the wrongness', a horrible expression).

There is an issue here about whether it even makes sense to talk of the supervenience base of this action's wrongness. Wrongness, like other moral properties, supervenes on non-moral properties. As I expressed things above, those properties are still properties of the action concerned. But I will suggest later that we should cast the supervenience net wider, so as to include features other than those of the relevant action. (We can do this by thinking of features of other things as 'Cambridge features' of this thing.) If so, there is no obvious point in thinking of supervenience as a relation between this action's moral properties and a supervenience base that consists in all the non-moral properties of anything whatever. It is better just to think of supervenience as a syncategorematic relation between moral and non-moral properties in general, expressed in the fully general claim that if we start from a wrong action and move out to the entire non-moral nature of the world in which it is situated, and then replicate that in a new world, we are certain to have a wrong action in the replicating world. There is nothing more to supervenience than this.

The point of the distinction between resultance and supervenience, for present purposes, is as follows. It is extremely plausible to suggest that if an action is wrong, every other action that is exactly similar in non-moral respects must be wrong also.[9] (Though the immediate attractiveness of this maxim is somewhat vitiated by the way in which we broadened our conception of supervenience in the previous paragraph.) It is nothing like so plausible to suggest that if an action is wrong, every other action that shares the features that make the first one wrong must also be wrong. Two actions may be similar to each other in a limited way, that is, in the respects that disfavour the first one wrong and thereby make it wrong, but differ in other respects so that the second is not wrong; the features that manage to make the first wrong are prevented from doing so in the second case because of variations that lie beyond the common resultance base. I take this point to be established by appeal to the distinction between favourers and enablers.

Suppose that a moral principle says things of the following form: where things are in non-moral way N, there will be an action with moral property M. Supervenience generates things of that form, whose distinguishing feature is that they have an enormous left-hand side. Can we announce that this at least (*pace* the renegades who reject the supervenience of the moral on the non-moral) guarantees that there is a complete set of principles, even though they are much longer than the ones we are used to? Not really, I fear. First, these principles specify complexes of such a size and in such detail that there is effectively no chance that they should be capable of recurring. A principle that has only one instance is worse than useless, for no such principle could ever be a guide for judgement. Second, these things do not really have the form of a principle either. For they contain all sorts of irrelevancies. Principles are in the business of telling us which actions are wrong and why they are wrong. But the vast propositions generated by supervenience fail utterly to do this; they don't select in the right sort of way. They do no doubt contain the relevant information, but they do not reveal it; as far as supervenience is concerned, all features of the present case, including those that count in favour of the actually wrong act, are equally relevant. Supervenience, as

---

[9] I don't mean to suggest that the claim that moral properties supervene on others is not in any way controversial. Joseph Raz, for instance, denies it (2000c), and I at least have seen some reason to dispute it (1995: 278–9). But I will assume that it is true here, so as not to make life more difficult than it is already.

a relation, is incapable of picking out the features that make the action wrong; it is too indiscriminate to be able to achieve such an interesting and important task. Finally, it is surely not irrelevant to point out that nobody could ever come to know the sort of supposed 'principle' generated by supervenience. So even if such 'principles' could have more than one instance, nobody could ever be guided by them.

Matters are quite different with the principles supposed to be generated by resultance. These principles are short, usable, and restrict themselves to specification of right-making and wrong-making features. It is sad that, despite these advantages, they rest on sand, since resultance, as we are currently characterizing it, is not a generalizable relation. The resultance base, in a given case, is too narrowly delimited to ensure that where it recurs it will have the same effect.

This means that while supervenience has the advantage of generating truths, what it generates cannot serve as a moral principle, while resultance, though what it generates could serve as a moral principle, only manages to 'generate' such things by appeal to a fallacy. If one were somehow to amalgamate these two relations, one might suppose that one had established a way of extracting principles from particular cases. Here is Jonathan Bennett, to that effect:

Moral judgements supervene on non-moral facts; so if some particular act is wrong, it is made so by some of its non-moral properties and relations, ones that would suffice to make wrong any act that had them. (1995: 19; cf. 1–2)

There are two fallacies in this. The first is the inference from supervenience to resultance. This cannot be defended. (I will suggest below that the inference goes in the other direction.) Its indefensibility is clear when we consider other suggested instances of supervenience. If in other cases we get supervenience without resultance, we must suppose the same to be possible in the moral case. Consider the supposed supervenience of the psychological on the physical. This means that if I believe that London is in the UK, then any other creature that is physically indistinguishable from me, and whose surroundings are physically indistinguishable from mine, will also have that belief. Suppose that this is true. Would it *follow* that there is some restricted group of physical properties (of mine or of my surroundings) that bear the same sort of relation to my having that belief as the harmfulness of an action can bear to its wrongness? I cannot see that it would.

The second fallacy is the supposition that if an action is made wrong by certain non-moral properties and relations, those properties and relations would together suffice to make wrong any action that has them. This fallacy we have already exposed. It looks less bad because of the close association with supervenience; for the non-moral facts on which the wrongness of this act supervenes (if we can make sense of such talk at all: see above) do indeed suffice to ensure that any action that is similar in those respects will also be wrong. They will not, though, necessarily be those that make the action wrong, in the sense we are beginning to give to that expression. They will include the facts that play this role, but also include many others that do not.

My final question about supervenience is how to explain it. We saw Bennett attempting to derive resultance from supervenience—that is, to derive the resultance of moral properties from their supervenience on the non-moral. I complained that this cannot be done and that in fact it reverses the true order. What then explains the fact that moral properties supervene on the non-moral? My own view is that this is a consequence of the fact that they result from the non-moral. The properties from which the wrongness of this action results are the reasons why it is wrong, the ground for its wrongness. Now we know already that if we move to another case holding just these properties fixed, we may yet get an action that is not wrong; differences elsewhere may conspire to prevent the original wrong-making properties from doing that job in the new case. But if we move to another case holding fixed all the non-moral properties of the case whatever, we know in advance that no conspiracy of that sort can happen. Whatever was a reason in the first case must remain a reason in the second, and nothing that was not a reason in the first can become a reason in the second. So necessarily the reasons must remain the same, and if so, their rational result must remain the same. So if the first action is wrong, the second one must be wrong too.

4. EXPANDING THE RESULTANCE BASE

This is all that I have to say about supervenience. My general view is that it is certainly no threat to particularism. But in constructing the contrast between resultance and supervenience I assumed that the resultance base was very restricted in scope: it amounted to no more than the favourers—or the disfavourers, if we are dealing with wrongness rather than rightness. And this was certainly a challengeable assumption. What tells us, for instance, that the enabling conditions should not be included in the resultance base? This is a question which can be discussed in its own right, without our being in danger of unsettling our conclusion that supervenience—the relation we are contrasting with whatever resultance will turn out to be—generates nothing worth thinking of as a moral principle.

Given the unsatisfactory way in which I introduced the concept of a resultant property (by appeal to mere locutions such as 'in virtue of', 'because of', and so on rather than by appeal to any professional-sounding metaphysics), we already know that there is nothing in our starting point that will prevent the resultance base from being expanded in the sort of way we are now considering. What is the core intuition here? I think it is just this: that if an action is wrong, there must be something that makes it wrong, and not all its features play that role. But it should be obvious that this leaves things wide open for more than one conception of resultance.

Now this is an important point, because the way in which I tried to show that resultance generates no moral principles relied on the very restricted conception of a resultance base. Principles that specify favouring features are very vulnerable to changing situations; I took this point to be already established, by means of the distinction between favourers and enablers. But the point will be by no means so obvious once we start expanding the resultance base by putting the enablers inside it.

The core intuition itself is capable of multiple interpretations. One might express it thus: if an action is wrong, something must fix its wrongness. This sounds congenial to the friends of supervenience, who often talk about what fixes what; so let us think of it in that way, and thereby put it at one end of the scale. At the other end we interpret the core intuition as saying that if an action is wrong, something must count against doing it. This is the way we understood resultance originally, in terms of favourers and disfavourers. The question then is whether there is a sense of 'make wrong' which is to be located between these two extremes.

What is driving the idea of an intermediate sense is the hope that we will be able to find something which makes the action wrong in a sense such that whatever is a wrong-maker will also be a guarantee of wrongness. (It must be a guarantee of overall wrongness rather than of prima facie or *pro tanto* wrongness, because the core intuition is about the overall, not the contributory.) Then moral principles could be thought of as specifying such guaranteeing wrong-makers. Such principles would be decisive, since, whatever is on the left-hand side, on the right-hand side we find overall wrongness. Without this hope for a guarantee—a set of conditions that when satisfied are guaranteed to give us a wrong action—matters would not be so interesting. If, say, we expanded our resultance base to include all specific enablers, without any suggestion that when we have done this we have reached a guarantee of wrongness, not much would have changed. The resultance base could exist without the action being wrong, and we are returned to the point that resultance does not yield principles.

The thought might be that if we expand the resultance base, we will eventually reach a stable stopping point, one beyond which nothing could overturn the wrongness that is established by the presence of the expanded base. This is technically true, since it is guaranteed by supervenience. But it is, as we have seen, an uninteresting truth. The question is whether there either is or needs to be any stable point on the way, any point, that is, short of the entire supervenience base, that would have the same result. As far as I can see, there is no need for such a point and no reason to expect that we can find one; if one were to be found, this would be more serendipidity.

None of this does anything to show that we might not find such a point in some cases. Some cases will be more amenable than others. The less amenable ones will be those where there are enablers for enablers, and so on; since there are plenty of such cases, merely mentioning all the enablers will not end up with a guarantee. But this is by the by. The main target here is what follows from holism (and the distinction between favourers and enablers). Again, the issue turns on the fact that until we are given some reason to suppose that moral thought *needs* a sufficient provision of such stable stopping points along the way to supervenience, I think that particularists can rest content.[10]

At this point I want to return for a moment to W. D. Ross's distinction between the parti-resultant and the toti-resultant. In drawing this distinction, Ross writes:

An act that is right is right in virtue of its whole intrinsic nature and not of any part of it. In respect of certain elements in its nature it may be *prima facie* right and in respect of others of them *prima facie* wrong; whether it is actually right or wrong, and if it is wrong the degree of its wrongness, are determined only by its whole nature. (1930: 123)

A property that is 'determined by the whole nature' of the object that bears is toti-resultant; one that is 'determined' by certain elements in its nature is parti-resultant. Ross here claims that rightness, that is to say duty proper, is toti-resultant, not parti-resultant; prima facie duty is parti-resultant, not toti-resultant. Now we can use Ross's official account of the prima facie (given in Chapter 2) to make this combination of views sound pretty silly. For the whole thing amounts to saying that an action is a prima facie duty in virtue of being a promise-keeping if, were it to have no other morally relevant characteristics, it would be a duty proper in virtue of *all* its characteristics. This is noticeably worse than what we would wish to read Ross as saying, namely that if an action is a prima facie duty in virtue of being a promise-keeping, then, were it to have no other morally relevant characteristics, it would be a duty proper in virtue of *that* characteristic alone. One reason why it is noticeably worse is that in a case of conflict of reasons the overall right act will have some features in virtue of which it is prima facie wrong but which count among those in virtue of which it is *a duty proper*.

But there is some defence for Ross here. He does not fail to point out that he has somewhat exaggerated matters 'to avoid complicating unduly the view I am putting forward' (1930: 33n). Further, he allows that many features of an action are ones 'which make no difference to its rightness or wrongness' (ibid.). What is driving him is the thought that 'no element in its nature can be dismissed without consideration as indifferent' (ibid.). This epistemological point is of course not enough to ground such a large metaphysical distinction between the grounds for prima facie duty and the grounds for duty proper. We could perhaps add on his behalf the point that, at least as we

---

[10] Of course, some think that expressivism is committed to generalism, and that since expressivism is true, there is a need for these intermediary stopping points. But that was not the sort of need that I had in mind.

ordinarily think, some features that crop up in the ground for duty proper are never present in the ground for prima facie duty. Here I am thinking of such comparative features as that there is no alternative action that produces more good, or that involves breaking a less stringent promise. Ross would, I think, maintain that such features are part of the ground for duty proper. Suppose that this action is a duty proper despite being a promise-breaking; there is some reason why I have to break my promise here. That no admissible alternative involves breaking a less stringent promise is part of what makes it the case that this action is right *despite* the fact that it requires promise-breaking. For otherwise I ought to take the alternative course (so long as it is not worse in other ways). So, Ross concludes, the ground for duty proper is always more extensive than the ground for prima facie duty, since it always includes this sort of comparative fact (or the absence of such a comparative fact). Generalizing now, if an action is a duty proper there can be no greater reason for doing something else. So the absence of such a greater reason is, Ross would say, part of the ground for *any* duty proper, in a way that serves to distinguish duty proper from prima facie duty.

For present purposes I introduce this distinction between parti-resultance and toti-resultance (perhaps better called mini-resultance and maxi-resultance), not because it is something that Ross is wrong about, but because it returns me to the idea of expanding our conception of resultance to include more than the favourers or disfavourers. What is driving Ross here is the sense that the ground for duty proper is more expansive than the ground for prima facie duty.

It is important, on the way as it were, to distinguish the relation of supervenience from that of toti-resultance. First, toti-resultance is not really what its name suggests, since Ross admits that many of an action's properties are irrelevant to its rightness or wrongness. Supervenience is not like this. An action's moral properties supervene on *all* its non-moral features without exception. Second, I cannot believe that Ross really wanted to suggest that an action's rightness results in any way from the features that count against doing it. It is *despite* those features that certain other features are capable of actually making it wrong. We need to keep any sound notion of toti-resultance distinct from any notion of supervenience.

It is also worth distinguishing between two different expansions. The first is the one discussed earlier, where we add enablers to favourers. The second is the one that Ross had in mind, I think, where we add to the favourers some thought such as that no competing action is a more pressing duty. In some sense this thought can stand as an enabler—but remember that it is an enabler of a rather different style from the others discussed at the beginning of Chapter 3. There is a difference between features that enable another to stand as a reason, and features that enable some of those that stand as reasons to ground an actual duty. That no competing action is a more pressing duty is an enabler of the second sort, not of the first.

Remember the core intuition that if an action is right there is something that makes it right. Should we suppose that among the features that make this act right is that there is no more pressing duty? If we say no, this will probably be because the relation between the rightness of this act and the absence of a more pressing duty seems too close. First, if the action is right, it *follows* that there is no more pressing duty. Second, if rightness is conceived in a ver-dictive way, so that to judge an act right is (among other things, perhaps) to claim that the reasons come down on the side of doing this rather than any competing action, the fact that there is no more pressing duty is part of what one is judging when one judges that *this* is one's duty, and so cannot stand as part of the ground for that judgement.

But even if we allow this point to persuade us that the absence of a more pressing duty is not part of the resultance base for rightness, we still have to consider what role is played in the whole story by the reasons for doing competing actions. Those reasons cannot be thought of directly as enabling conditions for this action to be a duty. So where are we to place them? It would be convenient if one could announce that to favour one action is *ipso facto* to disfavour any alternative; but this does not seem to be quite right. We might say, however, that the reasons for doing other things generate a sort of secondary reason not to do this action. This manoeuvre is intended to capture the force of reasons for doing something else, while enabling them to be treated *as if* they were defeated reasons against doing this action (which they are not, exactly), and so as no part of what makes the action right. This suggestion is the best I can devise to deal with this very awkward conundrum.

6

Can Holism be True?

In this chapter I consider various reasons that have been given for supposing that holism must be false. There will be a certain amount of recapitulation of results already achieved, but I am trying to pull together into one chapter all considerations whose effect is supposed to be that holism is impossible. I end by looking at a couple of suggestions to the effect that though there is truth in holism, that truth is much less dramatic than I have so far been suggesting, both in itself and in its consequences.

1. VARIOUS FORMS OF ATOMISM

The opposite of holism is atomism. Atomism comes in two or three varieties. Full atomism is the claim that if a feature is a reason in one case, it must be a reason (and on the same side) wherever it occurs. I call this full atomism because it takes features one by one; one could also call it single-feature atomism. Full atomism is false because of the distinction between favouring and enabling.

But there is another form of atomism, to be called cluster atomism, which takes features in clusters rather than one by one. This claims that if everything relevant to this case were reduplicated in another, what is a reason here must be a reason there. This needs a more subtle refutation. The problem is that in allowing that full atomism is false, as cluster atomism does, we have to allow that the polarity of each separate feature in the cluster could be affected by changes elsewhere. All that we claim, as cluster atomists, is that the polarity of the set as a whole cannot be affected in the same way. But this seems an inexplicable combination. If it is really true that each single feature can change its polarity, there could be no explanation of the supposed fact that if all the others are retained, the polarity of the last one cannot change. If full atomism is false, the polarity of the last fact should be able to change. If cluster atomism says that it cannot, it should be able to say why not, and no possible answer seems available. So cluster atomism seems to be an unstable halfway house between full atomism and holism. Further, it seems that even if we do take everything relevant (in however broad a sense) in this case and transport it *en bloc* to another case, there is still no guarantee that what was relevant here will be what is relevant there. Essentially, the point is that there might be some disablers present in the new case.

The only way in which this result might be disturbed would be if there were principles of relevant similarity—principles that tell us when one case is relevantly similar to another. Such a principle would tell us that two cases related to each other in a certain limited way must be such that what is a reason in one of them must be a reason in the other. But all such 'principles' seem false.

Of course, there is an even weaker claim, that if two cases are relevantly similar, what is a reason in one must be a reason in the other. This claim is true, but toothless. It has no ability to harm anyone. In the absence of principles of relevant similarity, if I want to establish that two cases are relevantly similar, all I can do is to show that what is a reason in the first is a reason in the second, and vice versa. But that is what was supposed to be established by our showing that the cases are relevantly similar. We have not made any progress this way.

A rather different tack is taken by those who suggest that what is sufficient reason in one case must be sufficient in all. But this claim fails to distinguish between what is sufficient in the circumstances and what is sufficient in any circumstances. It seems obvious that what is sufficient in these circumstances need not be sufficient in different circumstances, and this is all the holist needs to say.

2. COMPLETE REASONS AND FULL EXPLANATIONS

I now consider arguments to the effect that once we distinguish more carefully than the holist does between parts of reasons and whole or complete reasons, we will be able easily to accommodate everything the holist has to say without anything like the results that the holist supposes to emerge. Roger Crisp introduces a conception of an 'ultimate reason', defined as 'a reason that we can rest satisfied with as grounding [the rightness of] the actions in question' (2000: 37). This notion of an ultimate reason seems innocuous, until one sees what Crisp requires before one can rest satisfied. For he suggests that what we would ordinarily offer as an account of a reason present in the case is one with which we cannot rest satisfied. We cannot rest satisfied with any account which offers as a reason why an act is right something that might not play the same role on other occasions; for Crisp, if a feature or set of features is offered as a reason for rightness in one case and not in another, we already know that feature is not an ultimate reason, not one with which we can rest satisfied. Our question what the reasons were in the first case, then, can only be fully answered if we produce a guarantee, in the sense of something that guarantees that there is a reason to do the relevant action in all cases in which it appears. So for Crisp, we cannot rest satisfied with anything short of a guarantee. Every ultimate reason is a feature whose presence guarantees that there is a reason (i.e. that there is something to be said for doing the action), and any reason we can rest satisfied with is an ultimate reason.

One problem with this demand is that a guarantee that there is a reason to do the action need not itself be a reason in favour of doing it, so that in moving from our original account of the reason to the guaranteeing, ultimate reason, we may move from something that is a reason to something that is not, something that only guarantees that there is a reason. I would suppose that I get nearer a guarantee by adding as many enablers as I can think of and also the absence of as many disablers as I can think of to my account of the favourers in the case. But by doing this I establish, I think, that Crisp's complete reasons are not even reasons; anything that could be a reason for doing the action has got submerged in a host of considerations that are doing other jobs. The crucial point here is that a combination of a favourer and an enabler need not itself be a favourer at all; Crisp needs to suppose otherwise if his complete reasons are to be reasons.

But the real point for me is that I myself see no need to be dissatisfied with a *correct* account of the reasons in the case, even though one admits that those reasons are present in other cases without making the action right. When properly specified, the reasons, in my sense of the favouring features, will constitute an ultimate reason in Crisp's sense—or at least so I would claim— even though they do not function as guarantees of anything.

Of course what underlies Crisp's claims here, and in general his conception of an ultimate reason, is his idea of a full explanation, discussed in Chapter 3. A 'full' explanation is a guarantee, just as is an 'ultimate' reason. Crisp thinks of giving the reasons why the action is right as giving an explanation of why it is right, and he thinks that a full explanation is incompatible with the non-occurrence of the *explanandum*. So if we have a full explanation why the action is right, we have something that guarantees that there will be a right action in any case in which it obtains.

What drives Crisp in this direction—what makes him, as I put it, an 'expander'—is a sense that if an explanation is not a guarantee, it cannot answer the question why the *explanandum* occurs in some cases and not in others. But if it could answer that question, we would just add that answer into our explanation until we eventually reached a 'complete' explanation for which that expanding question does not arise. So an explanation that is not complete, for Crisp, is necessarily incomplete, and thus inadequate.

The same applies to the reasons for doing the action. If the reasons we give for doing it would not always be reasons, we know that we have not yet specified them completely. Our reasons-explanation must still be partial or incomplete. And Crisp writes accordingly that 'particularism about reasons focuses on non-ultimate reasons' (2000: 39). The idea is that holism about reasons is a true claim about partial reasons, but a false one about the ultimate reasons which must exist if there are any partial ones.

I reject this suggestion that reasons that do not carry a guarantee are necessarily only partial. And I reject the idea that we cannot 'rest content' with anything short of a guarantee. I gave my reasons for this in Chapter 3. Essentially, the point is that what we have here is not a relation between partial and complete explanations, but between nested explanations, the second of which is concerned in some way with the success of the first. Crisp's notion of an ultimate reason shares the defects of his notion of a complete explanation.

But there are others who want to expand our reasons until we reach something of which holism will no longer be true. Jonathan Bennett seems to think that one can see particularism off in short order by simple appeal to some notion of a 'whole reason' (1995: 80), but since he does not develop this idea it is hard to respond to it. Joseph Raz has similar, though no doubt more cautious, ambitions for the notion of a complete reason (sometimes he speaks of 'his reason in its entirety' (2000c: 228/59)). In a long footnote to his paper on particularism (ibid.: 228–9n/59n) he defines a stipulative notion of a complete reason as consisting of 'all the facts stated by the non-redundant premises of a sound, deductive argument entailing as its conclusion a proposition of the form "There is a reason for P to ϕ" '. He claims, in support of this definition, that 'An examination of the use of expressions such as "this is a different reason", "this is the same reason", and similar expressions, will show that this notion of complete reason captures an important aspect of our understanding of reasons', though he does allow that those expressions are ordinarily used in ways that invoke differing, context-dependent, standards of completeness.

Of course, on Raz's account of a complete reason, whose parts (which he thinks of as premises, and which I would think of as reasons, some of them) are not reasons, it will be true that whatever is a reason is always a reason, and always on the same side. The premises of a valid deductive argument suffice for the conclusion in any circumstances whatever. So what is going on here is that Raz is so defining a 'complete reason' that atomism is established by fiat— though only for complete reasons, of course, not for the parts of them that most of us originally thought of as reasons, but which Raz announces are not.[1]

But it is easy to show that Raz's account is inadequate. Here is a sound deductive argument whose conclusion is in accordance with Raz's definition above:

1. Someone in the room has a reason to ϕ.
2. There are only three people in the room, P, Q, and S.

---

[1] So Raz's position is quite like that of R. M. Hare. Both are cluster atomists, thinking of reasons as groups of features rather than those features one by one; and both suppose that a cluster that plays a certain role in one case must play that role wherever it appears. I say cagily 'plays a certain role' here because for Raz that role is the role of being a reason, but Hare has no conception of a reason. Raz is a cluster atomist about the contributory, Hare about the overall.

3. Neither Q nor S has a reason to ϕ.
4. So P has a reason to ϕ.

It seems to me that none of the premises of this argument is a reason for P to ϕ, and the combination of them is not a reason either, complete or otherwise. All we have here is a guarantee that there is a reason, which is not at all the same thing as a specification of the reason that there is guaranteed to be. Note also that the reason referred to in the conclusion is not the reason referred to in the first premise, on Raz's way of looking at these things; the reason referred to in the conclusion consists of the three premises together, but the reason referred to in the first premise can hardly be supposed to consist of a whole of which a proposition referring to it is a part.

Leaving these criticisms aside, my own view about Raz's stipulative definition of a 'complete reason' is that it obliterates the distinction between favourers and enablers, and that it makes it appear that a contributory reason is somehow of its own nature incomplete. These further criticisms, if correct, will apply equally to versions of the view that escape the objections in the previous paragraph. I think that what Raz has in mind is really the idea that we start from a premise specifying a contributory reason, and then add further premises which will specify the presence of enabling conditions and the absence of disabling conditions, until we reach a valid deductive argument to the effect that there is a reason here; and that once we get this far, we are to say that all the premises together count as a complete reason. So a now familiar example might be:

1. He promised to do this.
2. He is capable of doing it.
3. His promise was not extracted by duress or subterfuge.
4. What he promised to do is not immoral.
5. So: he has some reason to do this.

The complete reason consists in the conjunction of the four premises, always supposing that the argument is indeed deductively valid.[2] Now, first, I have already suggested—insisted, indeed—that the last three premises are doing quite different jobs from that done by the first. The first specifies a consideration that, in my sense, favours doing the action; the other three do not. I would want to say that the reason why he should do it is that he promised to do it, while the fact that what he promised to do is not immoral is not a reason to do it. So unless we retain a sense that the first premise specifies a reason in a way that the others do not, we lose something important. However, once we have this, a question arises about the relation between the reason specified by the first premise and the supposedly 'complete' reason specified by all the premises together. If the latter reason is complete, presumably the former one—the one that specified what one would ordinarily want to think of

---

[2] It is only informally valid, of course; no more could be expected.

as a contributory reason—is incomplete. But there is nothing incomplete about an ordinary contributory reason. Whatever it is that such reasons do, they do it perfectly well, and completely. They are not hopelessly trying to do something else, something that can only be done by several considerations acting together (as Raz would have it, acting as the several premises of an argument to the conclusion that there is a reason for P to ϕ). Furthermore, in defining 'complete reason' as he does, he is in danger of making it impossible to understand the relation between what is contributed by an ordinary, incomplete reason and what is achieved by a 'complete' one. Finally, whatever it is that a contributory moral reason does, it must, just in virtue of that contribution, be capable of standing as the ground for overall duty. If it were the only relevant feature, the only one actually making a difference here, our duty overall would be to do the action which it favours. But it is not at all clear, on Raz's picture, that an incomplete reason is capable of playing this sort of role; only complete reasons can do that, for him.

I have been trying to destabilize Raz's picture, supposing that this will leave mine at an advantage. But Raz has an argument against my picture, which is that particularism is committed to the view that some things relevant for the evaluation of an action are not reasons for or against the action. As he puts it, on my account the things that determine the rightness of an action extend beyond the reasons for doing it. Raz makes this the basis of a criticism, since he supposes that there must be a broad coincidence between what makes the action right (sc. the reasons for doing it) and what determines that it is right (2000c: 219–20/49–50; also 229/60). But once we have distinguished between favourers and enablers, we can see that the supposed need for this coincidence is fictitious. It is bound to be the case that there are features (enablers) that are relevant to whether the action is right but which are not reasons for doing it. We should distinguish between the two questions which Raz runs together: what makes the action right and what determines whether it is right. To answer the latter question we have to mention everything that is in any way relevant; Raz supposes that when we have done this, we have the premises of a valid deductive argument to a normative conclusion. To answer the former question we have no need to go into such enormous detail. Reasons are not trying hopelessly to play the role of premises in a valid argument.[3]

3. ATOMISTIC CONCEPTIONS OF RELEVANCE

So much for attempts to maintain that particularism (or the holism on which it rests) is true of partial reasons but false of complete ones. I now turn to

[3] As well as Crisp's notion of an ultimate reason, and Raz's of a complete reason, and Bennett's of a whole reason, there is also John Broome's notion of a perfect reason; see his (2004). Broome's notion is built on views about explanation that are similar to those of Crisp.

a rather different sort of reason for denying holism, a reason that led me into the intricacies of Chapter 2. This is that relevance is itself to be understood in ways that defeat holism; that is, the correct account of relevance will show directly that holism is false. We have already seen that this is what Raz is trying to achieve. Ross is after the same thing in a different way. He wants an account of what we notice when we notice that a feature is morally relevant to how to act in a particular case, and he wants an account of how, noticing this, we can know immediately that the same feature would be relevant in the same way on every occasion. He achieves both of these ends by his account of what it is to be morally relevant. On this account, for an act to be a prima facie duty in virtue of having a certain feature is for that feature to be such that, if it were the only relevant feature, the act would be a duty proper. The point here is not so much that this account of relevance is just plain wrong, as I argued perhaps over-forcibly in Chapter 2. It is rather that it gives Ross exactly what he needs. For if a feature is relevant here, in Ross's sense of relevance, we know in advance that it will be relevant on any occasion on which it crops up. For what we notice when we discern a reason is that if that feature were the only relevant feature, the act would be a duty proper. So what we notice is essentially general, and immediately gives us a principle of a rather peculiar sort, namely that all actions that have this feature and no other relevant feature are duties proper. But that will be true of this feature wherever it occurs; wherever it occurs it will be true of it that if it were the only relevant feature, it would determine the issue. So it is established that every moral reason is a general reason, and one for which there is a (rather peculiar) principle.

This is all technically correct, I think. The sub-text of Chapter 2 was that it could not be substantially right; this notion of relevance cannot be accepted, for quite independent reasons. I further argued there that all attempts to characterize the nature of a contributory reason in terms of some relation to the overall were going to fail. One might be pardoned the suspicion that at best all I managed to establish was that all the attempts I had come across or dreamt up for myself were failures; there might be others that are more robust. I had something of a reply to this, which was that all attempts to explicate the nature of a contributory reason by appeal to some relation to an overall ought conflated two distinct normative relations, the favouring relation and the ought-making relation. But however that may be, for me the interest of the matter lay largely in the threat that, if relevance could be understood in one or other of these ways, it might turn out to be *essentially* general in the sort of way that it seems to turn out in Ross's hands. To that end, I argued against each suggestion; and to that end I wanted to put in their place a conception of relevance as favouring (among other forms of relevance, as enabling, intensifying, and so on) which showed absolutely no signs of needing to function in a regular way. The notion of favouring is putty in the hands of particularists.

4. PRACTICAL REASONING AND INFERENCE

The next reason for supposing that holism must be wrong stems from the idea that practical reasoning is a form of inference. If it is a form of inference, we are told, then there must be principles. On the deductive side, we cannot have a distinction between valid and invalid inferences unless there are principles of inference. Instances of *modus ponens*, for example, are valid only because *modus ponens* is a valid principle. And the same applies to non-deductive inference, *mutatis mutandis*. Non-deductive inferences cannot be valid, officially, but they can be cogent. And their cogency depends in each case on the existence of a cogent principle such as the principles of probabilistic reasoning or of evidence.

There are two ways of responding to this. The first allows that there cannot be sound practical reasoning without a principle of inference to back it up. The second denies that we need principles of any sort in order to distinguish between sound and unsound reasoning. Strangely, however, these two tacks amount to the same thing in the end.

Taking the first, we might allow that wherever there is sound reasoning there is a principle, but think of that principle as particular rather than general in its application. Suppose that I reason as follows:

1. The train is about to leave.
2. If I don't run, I will miss it.
3. There won't be another train for over an hour.
4. I have had a hard day at the office.
5. Hanging around the station for another hour is very unenticing.
6. So: I run.

What does the supposed principle according to which I am reasoning actually say? It is common ground to think that a principle is a sort of inference ticket; the principle says 'it is OK to move from (1–5) to (6)'. (Others might say, more strongly, that one *must* move from premises to conclusion, or perhaps more cautiously that one must either accept the conclusion or reject one of the premises.) Inference tickets are permissions, just like railway tickets; they permit one to travel, in the mind as on the railway. But we could see this sort of permission as focused on the particular case, saying something like 'in the circumstances it is OK to move from these premises to that conclusion'. Such a particularized principle is one that the holist should have no trouble with.

On this tack, then, we allow that practical reasoning is inference, and that if there is inference there must be (permissive) principles of inference, but deny that those principles need to be general principles. But there is another tack, on which we deny that practical reasoning is inference at all.

Practical reasoning is often thought of as a movement of thought which ends with some decision about what to do. What is the nature of that movement of thought? In particular, is it inferential? People often speak of the premises of a piece of practical reasoning, just as they speak of the premises in theoretical reasoning. But there is some reason to suppose that this is a mistaken conception of what is going on when people try to decide, or work out, what to do (or what they should do). Now admittedly someone may say to herself, 'this action would involve harsh treatment (say), and so I won't do it'. There is a 'so' in this, which could even be expressed as a 'therefore'; and it is very natural, especially for a philosopher, to suppose that where there is a 'therefore' we must be dealing with an inference. We may be given pause, however, by recognizing that the following three sentences are practically equivalent:

> This action would involve harsh treatment, and so I won't do it.
> This action would involve harsh treatment, and therefore I won't do it.
> This action would involve harsh treatment, and for this reason I won't do it.

The same is true if we change the 'won't' to 'shouldn't':

> This action would involve harsh treatment, and so I shouldn't do it.
> This action would involve harsh treatment, and therefore I shouldn't do it.
> This action would involve harsh treatment, and for this reason I shouldn't do it.

The question, then, is whether we should take the 'therefore' as a signal that there is inference going on. In my view the fact that it can be replaced by 'for this reason' is a clue that the answer is no. Only a clue, one might say. But there is more to come. In thinking about this issue, we are hampered by the fact that nobody has been able to produce a criterion for distinguishing the inferential from the non-inferential. This Holy Grail is most earnestly sought in the theory of perception, where we want to know whether someone drawing conclusions about the nature of his surroundings on the basis of his sensory experiences is really treating those experiences as premises and inferring from them probable conclusions about how things are in his locality. Those who think that the relevant process is not inferential want to retain the idea that one can *see* that it is raining; one is not reduced to inferring that it is probably raining from premises concerning other things (the nature of one's current sensory seemings, perhaps). This is the sort of picture that Sellars was trying to promote, against those who say that the only possible relation between the experiences and the conclusion drawn in the light of those experiences is inferential. There are two very different pictures being offered here, sure enough. But many feel that until we have a firm criterion for the distinction between what is inferential and what is not, there is really nothing to argue about. The same applies to the practical case that is the focus of our attention. But it seems to me that we can make some progress in this area, despite our lack of a defensible criterion. We do after all have a good model of something that would clearly be inferential. For instance, if

I have a reliable and trustworthy friend who has proved a good judge of what to do in hard cases, I might think, in a new case, that my friend has advised me not to do this, and so it is probably wrong. It is not wrong, note, because my friend has advised me not to do it, nor because my friend thinks it to be wrong. Rather, the thought is that my friend is a reliable guide, and has pronounced against the action, and that therefore it is probably wrong. This is an important contrast. The point here is that the fact that my reliable guide has pronounced against the action is not even supposed to be part of what makes the action wrong. Whatever it is that makes the action wrong is, we presume, my friend's reason for taking it to be wrong. Rather, we *infer* that the action is probably wrong from the fact that my friend thinks it wrong. The contrast here, then, is between the grounds for the wrongness and something that is not a ground but from which the wrongness can, with probability, be inferred.

How would it be if I had thought, 'my friend has pronounced against it, and for that reason I won't do it'? Here my reason for not doing it is not itself among the reasons why the action is wrong—nor do I think of it as such. Rather, what we have here is a piece of practical reasoning, which is laid out on the page, as it were, by specifying the consideration in the light of which I decide to abstain. It is not the moral reasoning we would have if I thought, 'my friend has pronounced against it, and for that reason it is wrong'.

Think of the passage of thought that takes us from the reasons not to do the action to the 'conclusion' that the action is wrong. It would be *possible* to think of this always as an inference to the probable wrongness of the action. But I think of it rather as an attempt to capture in thought the shape of the moral situation. The situation, we suppose, is that the action is wrong and that it is made wrong by certain features, the wrong-making ones. The 'therefore' that lies between the wrongness and the wrong-makers is not itself inferential at all; it is a 'for those reasons' sort of 'therefore', which attempts to capture the idea that the action is made wrong by those features, acting as reasons. Practical reasoning, if it is an attempt to capture the moral nature of the situation one is confronted with, must be an attempt to replicate in thought the structure that the situation presents, which consists in this case in a relation between the wrongness of the action and the features that make it wrong. There is indeed a movement of thought from the wrong-making features to the wrongness made, but it is not one that we should think of as inferential.

I said that it would be possible to continue to think of reasoning whose conclusion is that the action would be wrong as inferential. Many would accept that such reasoning is capable of being semantically valid; in the most favourable cases, a world in which the 'premises' hold is a world in which the conclusion holds. Particularists might have their doubts about that. But I am trying here to avoid any appeal to holistic considerations, and to address the question whether practical reasoning is inference in its own right.

The home ground of practical reasoning is not reasoning to the rightness or wrongness of the action one proposes to do. This is practical in its subject matter, perhaps, but its conclusion cannot be an action. Whatever the relation between 'premises' and conclusion in movements of thought that end with the judgement that it would be wrong to do this, it is not a relation that can hold between the premises and an action. Practical reasoning proper is a train of thought which concludes in, closes off with, an action—or at least a decision to act. So we should avoid trying to understand this sort of reasoning by starting with a conception of moral reasoning and building our account of practical reasoning on that. It may be that moral reasoning is in this sense not practical reasoning at all, *horribile dictu*. So let us think not of the relation between the recognition of the wrong-makers and the eventual judgement that the action is wrong, but rather of the relation between recognition of the reasons not to do the action and the decision not to do it ('so I won't do it'). Here I want to say that there is no possibility that the decision is the conclusion of anything worth calling an inference. First, there is nothing here that is standing as a premise. The idea of there being a premise for a decision is a nonsense, a category mistake involving a cross-classification. Second, in the third-person case we may perhaps be dealing with an inference, as when we say, 'it would be outrageous, and for that reason he (probably) won't do it'. But the 'he won't do it' here has the status of a prediction;[4] in fact we are dealing here with an instance of theoretical reasoning, and one which is surely clearly inferential. (This is not to admit that everything that comes under the theoretical rather than the practical will count as inferential, only that this case does.) In the first-person case, which is the home ground of practical 'reasoning', we distort things if we view the decision as the agent's prediction of how he will behave. When I decide that I will do this rather than that, I am not concluding that something or other is the case about the future, in the way that I decide that it will rain tomorrow. What is going on has to be less like working out a truth and more like acting, since the conclusion of such reasoning can *be* an action.

Of course an agent can say 'I'll probably do that', and sometimes this is indeed an inference. Someone who knows that he is liable to yield to temptation may recognize that he will probably have too much to drink tonight. But this is not the same as making a not very tentative decision to over-indulge. Similarly, someone who says that when he is in Paris this spring he might go to the Louvre *may* be making a tentative prediction; he knows that one of the things he does in capital cities in Europe is to go to see the great collections. But he may mean something rather different: that this is an option to which he remains open, while others are not on that list at all, since he has already decided against them. And we all know that things that are not on that list sometimes get done all the same.

---

[4] Not necessarily, one might say. It is possible to hear this sentence as a third-person version of the first-person one considered above, so that it means 'it would be outrageous, and he refuses to do it, for that reason', i.e 'his reason for refusing to do it is that it would be outrageous, as indeed it would'.

For these reasons I think that practical reasoning proper is not inference. Suppose that this is right: should it affect our account of moral or more generally normative reasoning, or are the two matters so distinct that a decision about one need not influence our views about the other? Technically, I think they are separate issues. But once the inferential paradigm has been broken, flexibility may set in elsewhere. We have two options before us. One is that moral reasoning is inferential, the other that it is more like an attempt to capture in thought the structure of the moral situation. I tend towards the latter, and so view the thought that this action would involve harsh treatment and so would be wrong as the thought that this action, if done, would be made wrong by the harshness of the treatment it involves. The train of thought is: this action would involve harsh treatment and this would make it wrong. At the centre of this thought is a mere conjunction, and the movement or direction in it, which to some will seem symptomatic of inference, to me is merely the sort of direction involved in the wrong-making relation.

So my view is that whether we are thinking of the move from reasons to decision or of the relation between rightness and the right-makers in the case, we should not suppose that what is called 'practical reasoning' is inferential. At this point, its status as reasoning might even be challenged. We are, however, always dealing with reasons here, and drawing our conclusions or making our decisions in the light of those reasons. So there can be nothing wrong with talking of reasoning, since we are involved in the handling of reasons. What would be wrong would be to suppose that all handlings of reasons involve inference.

After all this we still retain considerable flexibility when it comes to writing a more substantial account of practical reasoning. We do not need to say that practical reasoning must be simply a recognition of the reasons in favour of the action and a decision accordingly. Sometimes this is what happens, but not always. Where there is significant choice to be made, we need to consider the reasons in favour of available alternatives, as well as the reasons against each one. And we need to ask, at least on occasion, whether relevant enablers are in place and disablers absent. Further, we must recognize that we are not dealing here always with a balancing judgement of the comparative weights of the reasons for and against. Common though it is to read of the balance of the reasons, and of weight, the matter should not be understood on the model of the kitchen scales. That model is far too atomistic to fit the subject matter of ethics (or of practical reason in general). On the kitchen scale model, each consideration has a practical weight, which it keeps irrespective of what it is combined with—just as a kilogram of butter weighs a kilogram whatever it is added to. A more holistic picture—one that recommends itself to me—has it that the presence of one feature can affect the weight of another. What is more, the two features need not be features of the same action. That one alternative has a certain feature may affect the favouring powers of a feature of another alternative. Judgement may need to pay attention to this sort of thing (which does not mean that no judgements are simple). And then there will be comparative questions to be faced at the end of the process, for once we have understood the claims of each action, in the context of whatever alternatives are available, we then have to decide which claim is the strongest—and this should not be understood on the model of kitchen scales either. As I will argue in Chapter 12, it may be that the mere availability of one alternative can affect the strength of the case in favour of another.

The claim that practical reasoning is not inference is important in its own right and important as a check to over-simple claims in general philosophy. Robert Brandom's generally very impressive inferentialist theory seems to err in this respect. Brandom writes: 'To grasp or understand a concept is . . . to have practical mastery over the *inferences* it is involved in—to know, in the practical sense of being able to distinguish, what follows from the applicability of a concept, and what it follows from. . . . What the parrot and the measuring instrument lack is an appreciation of the significance their response has as a reason for making further claims and acquiring further beliefs, its role in justifying some further attitudes and performances and ruling out others. Concepts are essentially inferentially articulated' (1994: 89). Over and over again Brandom characterizes what he calls 'the game of giving and asking for reasons' in inferential terms.

Now it seems to me to be very attractive to try to understand a concept in terms of what is involved in competence with that concept. And part of that competence, no doubt, is inferential. What is more, as Brandom notes, by stressing the centrality of the inferential we establish a sort of holism. As he claims, 'one must have many concepts in order to have any' (ibid.) This is because one cannot have one concept without knowing its place in the inferential web, and that means knowing which other concepts it follows from, which it entails, and which it excludes or is excluded by.

Actually, however, this is a pretty atomistic sort of holism. A more holistic approach to the game of giving and asking for reasons would allow that the applicability of concept F can bear positively on the applicability of concept G in one context and negatively in another. Brandom does not consider this sort of possibility, but there is no reason why he should not allow it, I think. He does consider something apparently similar, as we saw in Chapter 1. But I suggested there that his appeal to non-monotonic reasoning, as the basis of an account of reasons, does not take us all the way to the more holistic approach that I think would still be consistent with his overall project. (And in Chapter 4 I argued that his attempt to capture the notion of a prima facie reason fails as well.) I have already quoted his example; here it is again:

1. If I strike this dry, well-made match, then it will light. ($p \rightarrow q$)
2. If p and the match is in a very strong electromagnetic field, then it will *not* light. (($p \ \& \ r$) $\rightarrow -q$)
3. If p and r and the match is in a Faraday cage, then it will light. (($p \ \& \ r \ \& \ s$) $\rightarrow q$)

4. If p and r and s and the room is evacuated of oxygen, then it will *not* light.
   $((p \mathrel{\&} r \mathrel{\&} s \mathrel{\&} t) \rightarrow -q)$

Note that Brandom is thinking here in terms of inference (he talks of 'arguments codified in the following conditionals'). But my main claim in this connection is that part of competence with a concept does not seem to be inferential at all; it merely involves knowing what can and what cannot be a reason for applying the concept. It is easy to miss this point if one thinks too much in terms of theoretical rationality—of reasons for belief. Reasons for action do not seem to operate in a purely inferential way—and once we see this, we see that some reasons for belief do not either. Crucially, moving from the reasons why the action is wrong to its being wrong need not be conceived as inference. This is especially clear if one thinks of inference in terms of entailment, for the features that make an action wrong do not entail that the action is wrong; it remains possible that those features be present on another occasion where the context is different and where the action is not wrong. What is more, it seems possible for features that are elsewhere right-making to turn out to be wrong-making here. So wrong-making should not be taken to be the same as entailing the wrongness of the action made wrong. Further, the wrong-making features are not in the business of being good evidence that the action is wrong. Such evidence might be provided by, for instance, the fact that persons more sensitive than one is oneself, or perhaps better informed, do take it to be wrong. The wrong-making features clearly play a different role from this. Further, we do not think 'this would involve casual cruelty and so it is probably wrong'. The probabilifying relation is different from the wrong-making relation. All this is by now familiar.

Still, one might say, if knowing that the action involves unusual cruelty does tell us that it is wrong, there must be some rule to this effect, and any such rule can be understood as a rule of inference. But here I want to say that there need be no such rule. A practical understanding of the concepts of the unusual and the cruel puts one in a position to discern that this action is made wrong by involving unusual cruelty, in a way that does not require one to be following any rule. What you know when you are competent with a thick practical concept such as that of cruelty is not articulable in the sort of way that would be required for it to appear within a rule, whether explicit or implicit. What you are able to do when you are competent with the concept is to tell in new situations what practical difference it makes that the concept is here instantiated in the way that it is. If you don't know the *sort of difference* that cruelty can make to how one should act, you aren't competent with the concept—for it is a practical concept, and competence with it requires an understanding of the *sorts of way* it can function as a reason for action, and an ability to tell in new situations how it is actually functioning. (There is more in this vein in Chapter 10.) But there need be no rule, either explicit and specified in advance, or implicit and only specifiable but not yet specified, that takes one from the features of this context to the conclusion that the action is cruel and so wrong. The matter is too heavily contextual for this. This is a general point about the thick concepts that have a kind of variable practical relevance built into them. To be competent with the concept of lewdness is to be able to tell when lewdness is a reason for action and when it is a reason against,[5] and this sort of ability need not be conceived either as rule-bound or even as capturable in anything worth calling a rule.

The crucial point here, I think, is that what one knows when one is competent with this sort of concept is not articulable in the sort of way that would be required for it to function as a premise in an explicit rule. In a way, I would expect Brandom to agree with this. For he shows few signs of wanting to think of our conceptual competence as computational in any strong sense, and one aspect of computability is articulation. One can only compute the articulable. But his official position is that any aspect of competent action *can* be made explicit as a rule, which can then be criticized, challenged etc. He takes it, after all, that since Wittgenstein has shown that rationality cannot be understood in terms of responses to explicit rules, it must be understood in terms of responses to implicit ones (1994: 23, 25). Rationality and rules seem to go together for Brandom. I am only here concerned to point this out and to suggest that there is available a different picture, in terms of which our passage of thought as we say to ourselves, 'that is wrong because it is casually cruel', need not be conceived as inferential at all. I would rather see Wittgenstein's point, not as arguing that there must be implicit grasp of a rule, but as suggesting that we do not need rules to apply concepts coherently. What it is to go on in the same way need not be capturable in any rule, and what we bring to the new situation need not be an implicit grasp of a suitably context-sensitive rule, but simply an understanding of the sort of difference that can be made by the applicability of this concept, and an ability to apply that understanding to cases that are quite different from the ones in which we originally learnt the concept—an ability that in no way requires either the existence or support of a rule.

My own view of what is going on is modelled on a sort of metaphysical understanding of moral or more generally evaluative judgement that tries to match what it says about the judgement, our side of things, as it were, to what it says about the nature of the situation that our judgement is trying to capture. There is the wrongness of the action, a character that the action has, that is somehow constructed out of wrong-making features combined as they are in the present context. To say that it is wrong because it is cruel is to pick out the cruelty as a constituent part of the wrongness in some way, not to infer the probable co-presence of the wrongness to go with the cruelty. But I do not suppose that you need to buy every detail of this picture in order to deny, with me, that what is involved in the passage of thought, 'this is casually cruel and so wrong', is anything worth calling inference.

[5] As I argue in my 'In Defence of Thick Concepts' (1995).

5. CONCEPTUAL COMPETENCE AND NATURAL PATTERNS

A very different objection is made in a joint paper by Frank Jackson, Philip Pettit, and Michael Smith (2000). In order to be able to refer to this multiple author, I need a general term. Since they all worked in Canberra at the time, I will call them the Canberrans. The objection I have in mind is not this time an objection to holism; the Canberrans admit that holism is a very attractive doctrine. But they think that particularism's strictures on the need for moral principles cannot be defended simply by appeal to holism, and that anyway those strictures must be wrong.

The question raised by the Canberrans concerns whether there is any pattern to the way in which descriptive information determines moral conclusions. They take it that particularists deny, and must deny, the existence of any such pattern. For, if there were such a pattern, say for rightness, we could hope to specify that pattern on the left-hand side of a moral principle, a principle of the right or of the good. If we found that the pattern resisted codification, this in itself is not a terribly interesting result. Particularism is the claim that there neither is nor needs to be any such pattern, not the claim that every such pattern is uncodifiable.

The Canberrans argue, however, that if there is a concept of rightness at all, there must be a pattern that recurs in every case, a pattern in which purely descriptive features are presented. Their argument is semantic. It starts as follows:

We use words to mark divisions. Tables are different from chairs ... wrong acts are different from right ones ... What, then, marks off the acts we use 'right' for from the acts we use 'wrong' for? Or, equivalently, what do the right ones have in common that the wrong ones lack? (pp. 86–7)

The idea is going to be that particularism has no answer to this question. To see why, we need a bit of terminology. Evaluation of every form supervenes on description. We know that if this action is right, there is a right action of the same sort done in any world that is descriptively indistinguishable from the world in which this action is done. There is then a set of world-descriptions, call them D^i, such that where any one of that set is instantiated, a right action is done. We can now continue with the argument. What do the right actions all have in common? Particularists might say that the only thing they have in common is that they belong to the set of right actions. But then what is it to grasp the concept of rightness?:

Grasp of the predicate 'is right' simply consists in a grasp of the various D^i which constitute that set. But this cannot be *all* that unites the class of right actions. There must be some commonality in the sense of a pattern that allows projection from some sufficiently large sub-set of the D^i to new members. If there isn't, we finite creatures could not have grasped ... the predicate 'is right'. So, there must be a pattern or commonality—in the weak sense ... of that which enables projection—uniting the set of right acts. (p. 87)

They go on:

But if there must be a pattern uniting the right acts, either it is a descriptive one, in which case particularism is false, or it is one which cannot be understood in terms of the presence or absence of the descriptive—something unanalysable and non-natural, as G. E. Moore put it when discussing goodness. If this is the particularists' view, however ... the new and exciting thesis that there are no moral principles collapses into the jejune doctrine advanced by Moore ... : moral properties are *sui generis*, and hence are not to be found among the descriptive. (p. 88)

The general idea, then, is that rightness is determined by descriptive features, and there must be a pattern to the way that this is done. There must, that is, be a pattern exemplified by the various sets of descriptive features that determine rightness case by case, and that pattern must itself be descriptive. But if there is such a pattern, particularism is false; for there will be a true moral principle to the effect that wherever that pattern is exemplified, a right action is done.

It seems to me that the Canberrans have indeed identified an aspect of particularism which is both interesting and challengeable. The crucial claim is made in an early article by John McDowell:

[H]owever long a list we give of the items to which a supervening term applies, described in terms of the level supervened upon, there may be no way, expressible at the level supervened upon, of grouping just such items together ... Understanding why just those things belong together may essentially require understanding the supervening term. (1981: 145 = 1998: 202)

The crunch question is whether, where we have a variably grounded property *F*-ness, the component grounds for which function holistically, the various *F* objects *must* be similar to each other in ways that are expressible at the level of the grounds, if competence with the concept is to be learnable by creatures like us. To this question the particularists answer no, and the Canberrans answer yes. Now this question is not itself concerned with the difference between the descriptive and the non-descriptive. The *F*-ness we are talking about might perfectly well be descriptive. Even if it was, the issue between particularists and Canberrans would remain. So the charge that particularism is a form of Moorean intuitionism is really irrelevant. If (*per impossibile*) rightness were a descriptive property, there would still be no principles specifying regular relations between it and the various features that act as grounds for rightness, case by case. At least, this is what the particularist should say.[6]

---

[6] In this respect the Canberrans have been misled by Little (2000). They suppose that the thrust of the position is a distinction between the moral and the non-moral, the claim being that the non-moral is shapeless with respect to the moral and vice-versa. It is true that particularism claims that moral properties have no descriptive shape. But this is best understood as the claim that the relevant similarities are not discernible at the level of the grounds (whether these be moral or non-moral).

One very strong argument in favour of the particularist answer is that we have detailed models of conceptual learning and competence which appear to be coherent and which flesh out the claim that we can acquire competence with a concept without cottoning on to a pattern that is expressible at the level of the grounds. With these models to appeal to, the particularist is in a position to say that our ability to acquire competence with such concepts is more than a mere abstract possibility; we can say something in detail about how this sort of thing might work. I run through two such models in my first attempt to respond to the Canberrans (1999a). They are connectionism and Roschian prototypes.[7] I will not lay out the matter in detail here, however. The real point is just that there is what one might even call empirical reason for supposing that the restriction which the Canberrans wish to impose on us involves an unnecessary pessimism about the ways in which learning is possible. We can do more and cleverer things than they wish to allow.

6. DEFEASIBLE GENERALIZATIONS

The first objections we considered in this chapter were attempts to show that holism is false. The last one was different, however; it aimed to show that even if holism is true, there must be natural patterns for evaluative distinctions, and so there must be a suitable supply of principles taking us from natural distinctions to evaluative ones, even if our ability to formulate those principles may be in doubt. In this final section we look at a different sort of difficulty for holists, and ask whether there is room for a more conciliatory position than any I have expressed so far.

Holism maintains that anything whatever might make a practical difference, or provide a reason, if the circumstances were suitable. It sees no difference, apparently, between such features as being very damaging to one's health and the number of leaves on a tree. It sees no difference between the causation of unwanted and undeserved pain and whether one sets out with the right foot or the left. If there are differences between these things, it can only be that one of them matters more often than the other. But we all think that this is not all that there is to it. The stubborn intuition is that though holism may be right in stressing the possibility of exceptions to all moral rules, still there are rules, and there must be rules for there to be exceptions. What is more, the exceptions are not statistical exceptions, but moral exceptions. These exceptions bear their exceptionality on their face, as one might put it. Where we are dealing with an exception, there is an appropriate attitude, just as the attitude technically called 'regret' is called for when

---

[7] I was much helped by Jay Garfield in my exposition of these models, and his own paper on this topic makes some reference to them too (Garfield 2000, esp. pp. 189n, 191n, 193n).

a reason is defeated. It is hard to say exactly what the appropriate attitude is to a case where, though normally the fact that one is causing unwanted and undeserved pain gives one at least some reason to stop, here it is giving us a reason to carry on. Compunction sounds the right sort of thing, so long as compunction is not taken to be the attitude appropriate to a defeated reason.

This issue should remind us of difficulties faced by internalist cognitivists in the theory of motivation. Such people hold that we are primarily motivated by beliefs, and that desire (if required at all) plays some subordinate role in the motivational economy. In saying this, they make it hard for themselves to suppose that some beliefs have a more intimate connection to motivation than others. But we all think that moral beliefs, for instance, are more tightly connected to motivation than are, say, beliefs about the distance between Australia and New Zealand. The latter, we want to allow, can motivate, and perhaps motivate in their own right; but the former seem to be somehow officially in the motivating business, and it is hard to see how to allow for that in the cognitivist story.

There may be a way out in the motivational case. We seem to be being asked to choose between two views, both of which are blatantly too extreme. The first is that moral beliefs necessarily motivate the believer, and the second is that they have no more intimate connection to motivation than do beliefs about distances on the other side of the world. There should be some way of avoiding either extreme, and there is—or so it seems to me, at any rate. The way out becomes visible when we think about the subject matter of moral beliefs (at least on a certain construal). Those beliefs are explicitly about what we have reason to do. Being so, it is hardly surprising that they can be expected to motivate. If our question is, 'what do we have reason to do?', and we get the answer that we have most reason to do A, it is to be expected that this answer will have some practical influence on us—though of course it still might not. So any belief that can be taken to be explicitly concerned with answering the practical question what to do can be supposed to have an intimate connection to motivation of the sort we were looking for.

But no answer of that sort is available to the holist in the theory of reasons. The features that count in favour of action are the first-order features that give us our reasons, not the fact that they are reason-giving. So the holist cannot make the sort of appeal to a distinctive subject matter that offered the basis of a distinction on the motivational side. Something else, it seems, must be done—but it is hard to see what, if we want to stick to holism.

In a previous work (1993: 26, 103, 230), I suggested a theoretical tool that might be of some help, namely that of a default reason. A default reason is a consideration which is reason-giving unless something prevents it from being so. The idea is that some features may be set up to be reasons, in advance as it were, although it is always possible for them on occasions to fail to give us the reasons they are set up to give. One can express this idea more or less metaphorically. More metaphorically, one could say that some considerations arrive switched on, though they may be switched off if the circumstances so conspire, while others arrive switched off but are switched on by appropriate contexts. Less metaphorically, one could say that if a default reason-giving feature does give us a reason in this context, there is nothing to explain; we only have something to explain when such a feature doesn't provide a reason. With other features it is the other way around; if they do provide reasons there is something to explain, and if they don't there isn't.

This manoeuvre is especially effective when thinking about thick properties. Consider justice. We start off thinking that if an action is just, that is always a reason in favour of doing it. Then, perhaps, a persuasive particularist suggests some very unusual contexts in which it is not such a reason. What are we to say? We can retain at least part of our sense that the justness of an action functions as a reason very differently from more ordinary reasons by saying that it is a default reason. But to be a default reason is not to be an invariant reason. So there might be no true principle of justice; all that is true is that where the justness of an action counts in favour of doing it, there is nothing to explain; in that sense, this is what one should expect to happen. It is only when the justness of the act does not count in favour (or even counts against, if that is imaginable) that there is something to explain.

There is something here, I suppose, though it is all a bit thin. Recent work by Mark Lance and Margaret Little (forthcoming) is more promising. Consider the following generalizations:

Ceteris paribus, lying is wrong-making.
For the most part, pain counts against.
Other things being equal, fish eggs develop into fish.
In standard conditions, red ties look red.
As a rule, cruelty is wrong.
Generally, people say what they believe.

What do such 'for the most part' generalizations say? Like statistical generalizations, they are defeasible. Most sons are as tall as their fathers, but mine are not; young men are by and large more dangerous on the road than are young women, though of course there are many exceptions; as a rule, cruelty is wrong, but it was not in this case. Generalizations like these, which have (and survive) exceptions, are not to be understood as being enthymematic. i.e. shorthand for something much more detailed, which is not subject to exceptions. There need be no way of specifying exactly which cases of cruelty are wrong, or which young men drive no worse than do young women. So we should not yield to the pressure to turn our defeasible generalizations into much more detailed universally quantified ones; the latter would not be exceptionable, i.e. able to survive exceptions, unlike the former.

Unlike statistical generalizations, however, our generalizations are explanatory. If my sons were as tall as I am, this would not be explained by appeal to the fact that most are (though citing that fact might cause us to lose interest in seeking the true explanation). If this young man drives badly, this is not itself explained by appeal to the generality; the direction of explanation goes, if anything, the other way. But if a cruel act is wrong, we might say, this is partly to be explained by the fact that cruel acts are wrong as a rule. So what we want to understand here is the possibility of a sort of generalization that is both defeasible and explanatory. And a sensible way of moving forward is to look for other instances where such defeasible generalizations seem to be available. Lance and Little offer a wide range of potential examples.

Soccer is an eleven-a-side game. Admittedly, not all soccer teams have eleven members. There is five-a-side soccer, for a start, and there are of course informal games that may have any number of players.[8] So the generalization is defeasible. Is it explanatory? In most cases, where the teams do have eleven members each, this is to be explained by appeal to the rule; eleven is the standard size for a soccer team. So far, so good. But what we also want to know is the relation between the standard case, which Lance and Little call the privileged case, and the non-standard cases. What Lance and Little claim here is that non-standard cases bear the 'trace' of standard cases. What they seem to mean by this is that the size of the pitch and of the goal in five-a-side soccer is determined by reference to the eleven-a-side game. The goal is made smaller because otherwise there would be too many goals. Too many for what?—too many for the five-a-side game to be sufficiently similar to the eleven-a-side one. So the nature of the non-standard case is partly explained by the nature of the standard case, and our generalization ends up both defeasible and explanatory, as we wanted.

There is one important respect in which this example is unusual: there is available a determinate account of when a game of soccer is a standard game and when it is not. That account, I presume, is given by the FIFA rules for the eleven-a-side game. What there is not, in this or in other examples to come, is any chance of an equally determinate account of which non-standard games are to count as games of soccer and which are not. Consider, by contrast, the cruelty example. There neither is nor need be a detailed, non-enthymematic account of which cases of cruelty are ones where the cruelty is wrong (given our commitment to holism); nor, indeed, need there be an available account of which cases are cases of cruelty.

So far this is all quite nice. It has the specially hopeful feature that the standard case is a *guide* to the non-standard one. If one is going to play soccer in unusual conditions, one adjusts the rules of the standard game to suit the conditions; otherwise it wouldn't be soccer. It is important to get this notion of a guide into the story, since we want our defeasible moral generalizations

---

[8] I remember that on a reading group I was running many years ago we had an impromptu soccer match between the rationalists and the empiricists. The rationalists were not allowed to move, but they were allowed to pass to each other and to have a strategy; the empiricists were allowed to move, but they were not allowed to have a plan of action. This was no doubt all very odd, but it was recognizably a game of soccer.

to act as guides in new cases, including exceptional ones, even those where things will turn out not to be as the generalization has it.

But yet that may turn out to be the difficulty. The problem here is exactly the idea of a trace. What is the sense in which the non-exceptional case in which his need for help is a reason for helping is a guide to the exceptional one where it is not? What is the sense in which there is a trace of the non-exceptional case in the exceptional one? Lance and Little offer several suggestions about potential asymmetrical relations between the non-exceptional and the exceptional, any of which might prove useful. These suggestions are themselves prompted by further examples, such as:

> *Irony*: to understand the ironic remark, one needs to understand the same remark intended literally. To explain the meaning of the ironic remark, you have to appeal to the meaning of the literal one. The ironic remark is a sort of variation, or riff, on a theme. The theme is there, as a trace, in the ironic remark.
>
> *Fish eggs*: most fish eggs do not develop into fish. When we say that other things being equal they would develop into fish, we are privileging one possible course of events over others, calling it natural, and announcing that if things go *this* way no explanation is to be called for. What calls for explanation is when they don't.

There are various suggestions here:

> *Theme/Riff*: there is a clear sense in which the theme is present in the riff; a variation is a variation *on* a theme.
> *Conceptual Priority*: to understand the exception you have to know the rule.
> *Explanatory Priority*: we explain the exception partly by appeal to the rule.
> *Explanatory Asymmetry*: the privileged case needs no explanation; what requires explanation is the exception.
> *Trace*: exceptional cases carry a trace of the non-exceptional ones.

Of these, Conceptual Priority and Explanatory Priority seem to be caught between saying too little and saying too much, at least in their application to the moral case. It isn't strictly true that in order to understand the case where cruelty is not a reason against, one needs to know the rule. If we demand that, we demand too much. One only needs to know the rule in order to understand the *exceptionality* of the case where cruelty is not a reason against—but to say that is to say too little to be interesting.[9] The Theme/Riff distinction and the Trace idea seem to be the same. They suit the case of irony very well, because there is a good sense in which the ironic remark retains its literal

---

[9] There is also a sort of Epistemic Dependence involved here: our ability to gauge exceptions accurately requires knowledge of the rule. Without that knowledge we will make mistakes, e.g. about how vigorously we are allowed to defend ourselves when threatened. This seems right, but it does not give us a good sense of a defeasible generalization; it could be captured if we thought of the matter as entirely statistical.

meaning on occasions of ironic use. They may not fit the moral cases so well, however. It is not clear that what happens in the non-exceptional case is somehow also present in the exceptional one. With that we are left with the Explanatory Asymmetry, but this we had on the table at the beginning with the original notion of a default.

Matters are never quite so simple, though, and in this case they are complicated by a gloss that Lance and Little put on the notion of a trace. They claim that the exceptional cases carry the trace of the non-exceptional ones in the sense that the former are all necessarily defeasibly like the latter. But it is hard to know what this could mean, beyond what we have already. Whatever it means, it doesn't sound like Theme/Riff any more.

For these reasons, my present view is that we have not advanced far beyond the original notion of a default. But it is worth asking whether, if a richer notion of a defeasible generalization had emerged, this would have been victory for particularism, or defeat. The first point is that holism would have been shown compatible with something much more interesting than the sort of merely possible theory that I considered in Chapter 5.2 as a proof that the argument from holism to particularism is at best indirect. But if that more interesting thing were effectively to be a weaker version of generalism, the discovery that holism is more flexible than we had supposed will be the discovery that particularism cannot be erected on a holistic foundation—or at least, not on that alone.

The Lance–Little idea is that there will be all sorts of morally rich concepts, such as those of cruelty and kindness, of which we will know their 'for the most part' valences. This is very close to one of Ross's accounts of a prima facie duty: an action is a prima facie duty in virtue of being F if being F tends to make an action a duty proper. It is not quite the same, of course, because Ross's account here understands a contribution in terms of what tends to emerge at the overall level. The Lance–Little account, by contrast, understands what we may call a prima facie reason as a feature that *tends* to give us a reason, i.e. tends to make a certain contribution. Still, let us suppose that we know the 'for the most part' valences of all these morally rich properties. We can even suppose that some non-moral properties have such valences as well; for instance, that of causing unwanted pain. With all that in hand, have we got something sufficiently resembling a principled ethic?

A principled ethic must meet certain conditions, which have been emerging along the way:

1. *Coverage*: The moral status of every action must be determined by the principles, in one way or another. (Otherwise the principles would fail to cover the ground.)
2. *Reasons*: Of each action that has a moral status, the principles must somehow tell us *why* it has that status. (Supervenience-based principles would not do this; they are too indiscriminate.)

3. *Epistemology*: We must be able to learn the principles, either from experience in some way or from each other, i.e. by testimony.
4. *Applicability*: The principles must be capable of functioning as a guide to action in a new case; having learnt them, one must be able to *follow* them, or *apply* them.

We could probably continue this list, but as it stands it is enough for now. It will serve to establish that a morality built around Lance and Little's defeasible generalizations will not be a principled morality. It would fail on three of the four counts: on Coverage, on Reasons, and on Applicability. It fails on Coverage and on Reasons because the defeasible generalizations neither determine the nature of exceptional cases, nor (assuming that something else determines that) tell us why the exceptional cases are as they are. And it fails on Applicability because we have seen no way in which the defeasible generalizations will act as any sort of guide to the exceptional cases. On the most charitable showing, we would have said at most that the defeasible generalizations *partly* determine, and explain, the nature of the exceptional cases; but even that we have seen no reason to accept.

I don't mean to suggest that Lance and Little are under any illusions about this—though maybe they award more importance than I think justified to the idea that there is always a trace of the non-exceptional in the exceptional. But the main interest of their work lies in the fact that it promises to establish a middle ground between particularism and generalism. I don't think it succeeds in this. Perhaps in the long term it will be shown that both particularism and generalism occupy extreme positions of some sort and that the true view lies between them. But we are not yet seeing how this could be so.

As things stand, then, we have not found a way of moving beyond the notion of a default reason. This notion gives us some answer to the worries outlined at the beginning of this section. One weakness with that answer, though, is that it introduces a step in what might really need to be a matter of degree.

7

Competing Pictures

The previous chapter considered direct objections to the holism of reasons and thereby to the particularism that springs from it. In the present chapter the boot is on the other foot; I consider and reject various positive alternatives to the particularist picture of moral rationality. The authors of some of these alternative pictures are broadly sympathetic to the broad thrust of particularism as I present it. In one way or another, however, they attempt to pull back from what they see as an exaggerated version of the position; they take it that I have gone just too far, in this way or that. My aim is to see whether, given what we now have in hand, it is possible to avoid going the whole hog. Of course my general conclusion will be that it is not. But I will also consider some opposing pictures which are less sympathetic.

Perhaps the main focus of criticism of a view that, like mine, tries to make do without any appeal to principles at all is that the arguments it appeals to do not take us as far as that. It is all very well to stress the variability of reasons and to insist that we abandon any position that is at odds with that variability. But this does nothing to show that there are no invariant reasons. We can allow, then, that rationality itself does not require that all reasons be invariant, and to this extent particularism may be allowed to be sound. But there may for all that be a reasonable supply of invariant reasons, and it may be thought that this supply is important for the possibility of ethics.

It is this last point that will turn out to be crucial. I may allow the possibility of invariant reasons, in ethics as elsewhere, without allowing that in the absence of such things moral thought and judgement could not be thought of as rational. On the picture I want to promote, the occurrence of invariant reasons should be viewed as something of a surprise, an odd excrescence, almost, on a generally particularist canvas. It is as if we have a broadly holistic world-view, with dashes of atomism here and there.

1. IMPROVING ON ROSS

The alternative I am considering is propounded by McNaughton and Rawling (2000), and in effect by Little (2000) also. McNaughton and Rawling hold that if we think of the matter in terms of principles taking us from the non-ethical to the ethical, particularism is the truth. There neither are nor need to be principles of this sort. But there are other possible principles of an intra-ethical sort, ones that take us from the applicability of one essentially normative concept to the applicability of another. These, they maintain, can be found in reasonable supply, and, what is more, the supply of such intra-ethical principles is essential to ethical thought and judgement. Take justice as the central example. Without a conception of justice (and maybe another one of fairness), we might well think that moral thought could not proceed at all. And it is not just that we need to know what justice is and why it matters; we also need to know that an action or institution is *always* the better for being just. Equally, if an action would be just, that is *always* a reason to do it. This is an example of the sort of thing that McNaughton and Rawling are after. If they are right, then there will be a sound contributory principle, which we might perhaps express in the form 'just actions are right', or 'one ought to act justly'. This principle takes us from the applicability of the essentially ethical concept of justice to the applicability of the essentially ethical concept of the right.

McNaughton (1996) in particular notes that it has been common in discussion of these issues to distort the position of W. D. Ross. I have broadly taken Ross to maintain that we know by intuitive induction of any feature that counts in favour in one case that it would count in favour wherever it is to be found. It was then easy for me to find counter-examples to this view. That it is raining is sometimes a reason to stay indoors and sometimes a reason to go out; that she is already pretty upset is sometimes a reason to stop, sometimes a reason to go even further. McNaughton's point is that Ross never said otherwise. Ross in effect distinguished between derived and underived reasons, and supposed that only the underived ones were invariant. If a feature stands as a reason in the case before us, that feature will either be relevant in its own right, as it were, and so have an underived relevance, or it will be relevant only because of some relation to something whose relevance is underived. Thus, for example, that I did not treat him as I treated her is a feature of blatantly variant relevance; sometimes it counts in favour of my action, sometimes against. Where it is relevant, however, it will be so because justice required that I treated both of them in the same way (or for some other such reason, of course). Justice is a feature of invariant relevance, then, and the possibility of variant reasons only makes sense against a backdrop of invariant ones for the variant ones to derive their relevance from.

I think it is fair to say that McNaughton and Rawling never offer any reason for supposing that variance is impossible without invariance. This is, of course, what is really needed. Otherwise the dispute will descend to examples, when for the particularist the point really is why we need the invariant at all. Nonetheless, things clearly *could* be the way McNaughton and Rawling propose, so let us admit the possibility of their picture and see how

things stand once we start to try to apply it across the board. We could start
by trying to run Ross's own account. According to Ross, prima facie duties
are of six distinct types. Those types are:

1. duties grounded in previous acts of one's own: (1a) fidelity, (1b) reparation;
2. duties grounded in previous acts of others: gratitude;
3. duties of justice;
4. duties of beneficence to others;
5. duties of self-improvement in respect of virtue or intelligence;
6. duties of non-maleficence to others (i.e. avoiding or diminishing harm to others).

Of these, I am admitting pro tem that justice is an invariant reason. But the
others seem to be examples of *types* of reason rather than of invariant reasons
themselves. What I mean by this is that an action could be right because
it is just; this makes perfectly good sense. But no action will be right simply
because it is a response to previous acts of others, or indeed of one's own.
This disposes of the idea that Ross's first two categories are of the same sort as
his third. As for beneficence and non-maleficence, though Ross does indeed
suppose that any act of those sorts is for that reason a prima facie *duty*, he is
surely wrong about this. There are many acts that would benefit others that I
have no particular duty or reason to do, and in many such cases the act would
not even be for the better. If someone does not deserve a benefit (or rather
'undeserves' it), giving her that benefit is not something one has a prima facie
duty to do; and the same *mutatis mutandis* applies to those who, by their own
acts, have lost a certain immunity to harm. Similarly, an act that is a duty to
oneself is not a duty *for that reason*. In all these cases (Ross's categories (1),
(2), (4), (5), and (6)) we are dealing with categories of duty and not with
invariant reasons. In fact, the only one of Ross's seven categories that bids fair
to play the role required by McNaughton and Rawling is justice, the one we
were trying to use as a model for all the others.

Would things look better if instead of considering the general headings we
looked beneath them, at the next level? In the case of the first heading, we
have duties to do what we promise and to make reparation for harm done. I
would have thought it obvious that one does not always have even a prima
facie duty to do what one has promised to do, and the same goes for making
reparation for harm done. Matters do not change in this last respect if we
think only about making reparation for a wrong done, for just as there are
cases where there is no reason to make reparation for a harm done, there will
be cases where even though the harm was a wrong, there is no reason to make
reparation for it. The same surely applies to fidelity and gratitude. The point
here is that Ross's general category is clearly the wrong place to look for an
invariant underived reason, and once we delve into the category we immediately come across reasons that show no signs of being invariant. It may of
course be that fidelity and gratitude are default reasons—a possibility that

McNaughton and Rawling do not consider. The use of the notion of a default might well give them much of what they want here, but within a more determinedly particularist position.

What about justice, though? Here I recognize the pull of the idea that we are not just dealing with a default, and that justice always counts in favour. There are only two possible grounds for doubt that I know of. The first is that there are many actions we could do and which would be just, but which we have no reason to do; this, however, can be dealt with by saying that it is really injustice, not justice, that is the invariant reason. The second was suggested to me by Christine Swanton. In certain contexts such as ordinary family life the question whether what one proposes to do would be just or unjust 'does not arise'; it is, as it were, the wrong question to ask. It is not that the domain of the just/unjust distinction excludes family life entirely. If that were true, it would be as nonsensical to ask whether my distribution of the breakfast cereal this morning was just as it is to ask whether today's weather is just. Family decisions can indeed involve justice, but the inappropriateness of approaching ordinary family life in the way that one approaches public institutions reveals that the role of justice as a reason can vary according to context.

My own view is that this is probably right. But suppose that it is not. What we would then have is a concept that plays an invariant normative role as a reason-giver. This would, however, do little or nothing to show that there is a decent supply of similar concepts. McNaughton and Rawling tend to suggest that once the point has been made about justice, one can say the same about all thick concepts (p. 260: 'we concur with Hare that thick moral terms are univalent')—but in the next breath they allow that some concepts, such as that of lewdness, are variant. This last point was first made by Simon Blackburn (1992) as a point against cognitivist conceptions of thick terms as picking out concepts of a special sort, ones that involve, as he put it, an 'indissoluble amalgam' of description and evaluation. I suggested in my (1995) that cognitivists could continue to think of thick concepts in this sort of way so long as they accept that the evaluation involved could vary from case to case; the example of lewdness was exactly the one on which the discussion focused, the idea being that lewdness is sometimes just what is called for, though more often it is out of place.

Allowing this, McNaughton and Rawling comment rather strangely that lewdness does not have 'the stature of justice' (p. 262n). More to the point, perhaps, would be the possibility that justice is not a standard thick concept at all. It is notable that Samuel Scheffler, in his review of Williams (1985), suggested that justice is unique in standing somehow between the thick and the thin (Scheffler 1987). My own view is that almost all the standard thick concepts, such as those of integrity, fidelity, gratitude, reparation, and so on, are of variant relevance, as I have already suggested above. I want to allow that without a reasonable supply of thick concepts, moral thought and judgement are hamstrung; this is a point that McNaughton and Rawling rightly think to be important. Admittedly it is hard to produce a decent argument for it, but, as I said in Chapter 5, the general idea must be that the thick concepts give a certain shape to what is thrown up from below, and in this way both affect the store of reasons given us by the lower-level natural facts and in some way prepare things for overall judgement, which will amount to the predication of a thin concept such as that of wrongness. However, the fact—if it be a fact—that thick concepts play this central role does not require them to be of invariant relevance. Centrality is one thing and invariance another, and I want the first without the second.

In response to this suggestion, McNaughton and Rawling take the line that each of these concepts has constant relevance under certain specifiable conditions.[1] They write:

We suggest that a moral principle may draw attention to a feature that is always relevant, and relevant in the same way, under certain implicit conditions. In our example, provided that one's promise is not given under duress and is not an undertaking to do something immoral, then it supplies one with a moral reason to act so as to keep it. We don't normally spell out these conditions when articulating the principle, both to keep it simple and because the principle is, as it were, written with the standard case in view. But the list of conditions is not open-ended, and it is knowable in advance. It has a rationale. The conditions are inherent in a proper understanding of the nature and role of promising in the fabric of our moral life. ... Even if our account of the conditions is not complete and someone were to come up with an ingenious counter-example requiring supplementation or amendment to the principle, we can be confident that the needed amendments would be variations on the kind of theme we have already seen. (pp. 269–70)

Now it is obvious why they should want to say this, but not so obvious that it needs to be true. My own view would be that a person who understands the nature and role of promising in the fabric of our moral lives is certainly in a position to judge (not infallibly, of course), of any marginal case, whether promising plays there the reason-giving role which it normally plays. But this capacity need not be seen as the application of an implicitly understood set of formulatable conditions. (I agree with Scanlon and Wallace here; see below.) What we know when we understand the role of promising, etc., is that by appeal to which we judge the appropriateness of suggested 'amendments'.

---

[1] In this they differ from Margaret Little, who writes 'Thick moral features differ from non-moral ones precisely because, so identified, they are guaranteed of carrying a given valence of moral significance (part of what it is to *count* as a moral feature, to earn the status as a moral feature so identified, is to count as a moral reason of a given direction)' (2000: 289). She adds that 'invariant valence here is an implication of the proper model of moral internalism', a remark which I either do not understand or do not accept. This means that Little only takes a holist view of the relations between non-moral and moral features; indeed she takes particularism just to be the claim that moral concepts are naturally shapeless. Though I think that the moral is indeed naturally shapeless, I do not think that this is all that particularism amounts to; for otherwise it would begin to look as if it were just a rather heavy-handed application of the fact/value distinction.

It therefore cannot be that we approach such decisions with the question already 'implicitly' answered. True enough, 'the needed amendments would be variations on the kind of theme we have already seen'. But this only means that once one understands the rationale underlying the concept of a promise, one is aware of the *sort* of contribution that promising can make (its practical purport) in a variety of cases in such a way that there need be no dramatic surprises—without this doing anything to show that what one knows is articulable in the sort of way that McNaughton and Rawling seem to be requiring.

Note that McNaughton and Rawling are not suggesting that the original 'principle' that one should keep one's promises turns out to be shorthand for a longer principle that includes the various qualifications and exclusions that are required to save the principle from refutation by counter-example. They accept my view that the principle should be understood as specifying the relevant reason, and that one's promise was not made under duress is not itself part of the reason for keeping it. The reason is that one promised, and that the promise was not made under duress stands only as an enabling condition. So what McNaughton and Rawling are offering is genuinely a form of Ross-type intuitionism whose principles have the sort of direct simplicity that Ross supposed. We will have to deal later with those views that defend themselves by complicating their contributory principles in the hope of beating off all possible counter-examples.

Ross talked of derived and underived duties. McNaughton and Rawling talk of primary and secondary reasons. The basic claim is that there cannot be secondary reasons, variable ones, unless there are primary, invariant ones; the secondary ones depend on a sufficient supply of primary ones, of which there must be enough to cover the ground. But, first, we have not yet seen why this should be so. Second, how well would such a claim fare when applied to the aesthetic? Is there a sufficient supply of invariant aesthetic reasons? Here, my own view is that there is little sign of any such thing. As I would say of moral reasons, there may be some aesthetic concepts of invariant relevance—the imaginative, for instance; though when I consider suggestions like this I always feel they depend on a lack of imagination on someone's part. But it seems very improbable that all aesthetic reasons depend on invariant ones. There just aren't enough to go around. And there seems to be no need for them anyway. So why should morality not be like this?

2. VIRTUES AS GUARANTEES

McNaughton and Rawling offered their suggestions from a perspective that is intended to be largely friendly to particularism. Similar suggestions, however, are made by Roger Crisp, and his intentions are not so friendly at all. As we saw in Chapter 6, Crisp (2000) introduces a conception of an 'ultimate reason', defined as a feature whose presence *guarantees* that there is something to be said for the relevant action. A by now familiar problem with this demand is that a guarantee that there is a reason for doing the action need not itself be a reason in favour of doing it, so that in moving from our original account of the reason to the guarantee, we move from something that is a reason to something that is not.

Up to this point in his paper, it looks as if Crisp is intending to defend some form of complex Rossianism, and my discussion of his views in Chapter 6 took them in those terms. There are contributory reasons, Crisp seemed to be saying, which need far more complex specification than we might have originally thought if they are to stand as ultimate, though still only contributing reasons. But that is not what Crisp is really after at all. For what he offers as his own candidates for ultimate reasons are such things as justice, dishonesty, prudence, and benevolence. He calls these 'virtues'—though I myself would prefer at this stage merely to think of them as supposedly invariant thick properties, thus still aligning Crisp to some extent with McNaughton and Rawling. Now I have already suggested that thick concepts are not all invariant as reasons. Crisp's virtues, by contrast, are intended to be invariant. But—and this is the crucial point here—they are also guarantees of overall rightness (not just of the existence of a reason). For, given the unity of the virtues, if an action is just, it is necessarily right overall, according to Crisp; and the same is true of each of the other 'virtue-related' thick properties. Justice cannot 'require' us to do an action that is not right; it would not be just for an examiner publicly to expose the girl who, given her problems at home, failed to prepare properly for her test and was driven to cheat. In this case 'speaking out, because it would be going wrong within the sphere governed by justice, would be a kind of injustice' (2000: 45). So we see that Crisp's virtues are not only invariant reasons, they are also guarantees of overall rightness. This is no longer a form of Rossianism at all. There are no ultimate contributory moral reasons that are overwhelmed by reasons on the other side, and every ultimate contributory consideration on the winning side can stand alone as a guarantee.

Crisp does speak of stronger and weaker ultimate reasons (p. 47), but I don't see that he has left himself the space to do this. If all are guarantees, how can one do more than another? What he needs is a way of saying that certain considerations favour action even if the action is ruled out for other reasons; this would give him a conception of competing and of contributory reasons, and he could perhaps hope to construct a notion of the strength of a reason on that basis. And he does at one point suggest such a thing. He writes:

But this is not to say that we should not make room for conflict here, of a kind which will issue in deliberation itself. The *considerations* that favour speaking out are real enough, and they do indeed conflict with those favouring keeping quiet. We can capture their force using counterfactuals. Had the girl not been facing problems at home, justice would have required you to speak out. (p. 45)

But what I want to know is why this shows that *as things stand* (the problems at home, etc.) speaking out is favoured by anything at all. In the case as he describes it, it seems to me perfectly possible to maintain that there are no ultimate reasons for speaking out as things stand, and if there are no ultimate reasons for doing so there are, for him, no reasons for doing so (since all reasons rest somehow on ultimate reasons). The fact that if things were different I would be required to ϕ because of feature G does nothing to show that as things stand feature G favours ϕ-ing. (These remarks are intended to echo earlier claims that attempts to understand the role and nature of contributory reasons by appeal to subjunctive conditionals are bound to fail.)

Still, that is the picture. Responding to it, first, I do not accept the unity of the virtues in the sense that Crisp gives to that term—a sense that is required if each is to stand as a guarantee. Nor do I accept the supposed need for a guarantee that drives him to say what I think of as very implausible things, such as that there can be no reprehensible kindness (p. 45n), no brutal honesty (p. 38n), and no cases where dishonesty is required (p. 38). Nor do I accept the idea that prudence is an ultimate reason. Crisp suggests this in a peculiar passage where he writes:

In an ordinary case, it may be that doing the same thing as we did last time will save both of us time. It may sound grand, but it is nevertheless the truth, that our ultimate reason for doing the same thing as we did last time is that our lives will go better for us if we do. (p. 38)

The sense of 'ultimate reason' that is at issue here seems to be the one in which we would say that at the end of the day the basic reason for doing the same thing again is that our lives will go better if we do (a rather different sense from the official definition). This chimes with Ross's sense that justice is a basic, or underived, reason, while other prima facie right-making properties are only derived, and hence variable, reasons. But in this sense of 'ultimate' as 'underived' it seems to me that Crisp has misidentified the relevant reason. For the reason why my life will go better if I do this must be the feature that favours doing it, for instance that it would be quite amusing. Maybe that feature would not be able to favour the action if my life would not go better for my doing it. But this subjunctive conditional does not show that the real, basic, ultimate reason for doing it is that my life will go better if I do. The reason for doing it (that it would be quite amusing) is the reason why my life will go better if I do it. Yet again, the search for a guarantee has taken us away from the grounding reason to something that is not in fact the reason for doing the action at all.

3. EXPANDING THE REASON

Crisp wanted to turn the applicability of a thick concept into a guarantee, in the light of a disputable conception of the unity of the virtues. There are other attempts to provide guarantees, however. Crisp thought the simple fact that an action was honest could act as a guarantee of its rightness. Other approaches allow that nothing as simple as this could stand as a guarantee, and seek therefore to complicate the supposedly contributing feature until we reach something of invariant relevance. Derek Parfit has suggested to me in conversation that my counter-examples to supposed invariant reasons can all be coped with by importing the nature of the counter-example into the reason. So I might point out that if I make a promise to someone who has deceived me about the relevant circumstances, this does not mean that I have any reason to do what I promised. But the response is that in other cases the reason is not that I promised, but that I promised and was not deceived. The point can be put in terms of principles by saying that the relevant con-tributory principle is not, 'If you promised to do it, you should do it', but, 'If you promised to do it and were not deceived, you should do it'. In a non-moral case, I might point out that the fact that nobody else is there is sometimes a reason to go there and sometimes a reason not to go there, and claim therefore that this consideration is of varying valency. The reply is that the reason is more complex than that. There is the (larger) reason to go there given by the complex consideration that one is in no danger and there is nobody else there and a little solitude would be good for the soul (or whatever), and another such reason not to go there grounded in the complex consideration that there may be bears and that there will be nobody else there to provide help if necessary. If we complicate all our reasons in this sort of way, no provision of counter-examples, however rich, can serve to dislodge a principle-based conception of moral rationality, or a generalist conception of practical rationality as a whole. So what is all the fuss about?

As Parfit sees things, there is a sort of spectrum of complexity, and what the provision of counter-examples shows is merely that defensible con-tributory principles cannot be at one end of the spectrum, where we would find Crisp's principle, 'If it is the only honest course, you should take it'. At the other end of the spectrum is the sort of thing that Frank Jackson seems to contemplate, namely the sort of 'principle' that has an entire world-description on its left-hand side. Such an object is blatantly incapable of serving the purposes for which principles are usually required (e.g. guidance, or the specification of a reason for doing something). But somewhere in between these two extremes we will be able to find a stable resting place. On the way to that stable point we may have to admit that many of our familiar principles are merely stop-gap versions of something rather harder to for-mulate and of which we may find it quite hard to suppose we have a truly adequate conception. But this is the nature of progress—in particular, of theoretical progress, which is sometimes presented as moral progress.

It is important to realize that this method of expanding in the hope of assimilating all counter-examples is available both to those who think of the eventual principles as decisive (in the sense discussed in Chapter 1) and to those who are merely looking for contributory principles. Either way, my response to it can be seen in what has gone before. I want to say first that there is no reason to embark on this process of complication, and second that the process itself is grounded in a fallacy.

On the first point, the fact that this consideration would not be a reason in a different situation does nothing to show that it is not a reason here, and there is no acceptable notion of a complete, entire, or ultimate reason by comparison with which the status of this consideration as a reason here can be undermined. Nor should we allow thoughts about 'complete' explanations to unsettle our thought that we can specify the reasons present in this case, that is, the features that favour doing the action in this situation, in a way that is not directly affected by the question whether there might not be another case in which those features do not play the role they play here. (That question may of course play an epistemic role.)

On the second point, the process of complication is grounded in the agglomerative thought that if a consideration c is a reason only under the condition that p, the 'real' reason in the case is not c but $c + p$. But this is a fallacy. It involves failing to distinguish from other possible relations the specific normative relation of favouring—a relation in which c can stand to our action when $c + p$ does not. Whatever relation $c + p$ stands to the action, it will for certain be different from the one that c stands in (see Cullity 1997: 116–17).

Of course, what we do get, if we complicate our principle, is something that is vulnerable to fewer counter-examples, and we might hope that eventually this process will come to a stable conclusion. But the eventual result will not serve one of the main supposed purposes of principles, namely that of telling us why we should do the action, that is, what makes the action right. And it will not support another leading thought in this area, that without principles moral thought and judgement are impossible. For there is no reason why, without stable stopping points for the expansion, the rationality of moral thought and judgement would suddenly be in doubt.

None of this does anything to show that every feature that speaks in favour of an action is somehow to be simple.

4. MAKING IT SPECIFIC

A familiar model of moral thought has it that there are various right-making and wrong-making properties, and that where we get one of each in play at once we have a conflict, and that the resolution of that conflict involves balancing something or other (the kitchen-scales model, roughly). It is perfectly proper to object to this model on more than one count, but especially for supposing that the only way to resolve conflict is by balancing.

Henry Richardson suggests (1990, 2000) that another and a better way of resolving a difficulty lies in a process which he calls 'specification'. We begin from a situation in which it seems to us that there are reasons both for and against. But instead of gritting our teeth and plumping for one side or the other, we might reconsider the nature of the 'principles' or reasons at issue. One of Richardson's examples is the standard lawyer's dilemma of whether to say something false and defamatory about a supposed rape victim in court in order to get his client acquitted. The idea is that we start from two principles (which Richardson calls 'norms') that are in head-on conflict:

1. It is wrong for lawyers not to pursue their clients' interests by all means that are lawful.
2. It is wrong to defame someone's character by knowingly distorting their public reputation.

These norms conflict, and one way (but not the only way) of making progress is to adapt those norms so that they become:

1*. It is wrong for lawyers not to pursue their clients' interests by all means that are lawful and ethical.
2*. It is wrong to defame a rape victim's character by knowingly distorting their public reputation.

This form of adaptation is called specification. The point is that in a way we retain the previous norms (1) and (2); the new norms (1*) and (2*) are recognizable successors of the old ones. The main advantage that this procedure has over simply trying to resolve the issue by balancing the claims of the client and of the rape victim is that balancing may appear to be essentially arbitrary, there being no form of rational defence of our eventual decision. The specification procedure is rational throughout, supposedly, and in particular it does not involve simply abandoning the norms that revealed the difficulty. So we can see how it is that contingently conflicting norms still 'hang around' even after the conflict has been resolved by specification.

We intend the more specified norms somehow to stand alongside the original norms rather than to replace them. Interestingly, Richardson supposes that to be revisable in this way a norm must start with a phrase like 'Generally speaking' or 'For the most part'. For otherwise, he says, the more specific norm would either be otiose, being logically implied by the initial one, and so could hardly be said to 'stand alongside it', or it would be incompatible with the initial one and hence replace it, since it stands as an implied exception (1990: 292). Of these two possibilities the first is exemplified in the relation between (2) and (2*) above, and the second is exemplified by the relation between (1) and (1*). But if we start our norms with 'For the most part', or something like that, we get neither result.

This is all very well, but the fact is that if we start our original norms with 'For the most part', we lose the sense that they can conflict in a particular case. Richardson's account of the original conflict between (1) and (2) was run in terms of what he called a 'Peripatetic syllogism' (p. 281) of the following form:

(i) For all actions x, if Ax then x is (is not) permitted (obligatory).
(ii) Aa.

Therefore,

(iii) Action a is (is not) permitted (obligatory).

And conflict arises from our two principles (1) and (2) by deriving from them, according to this inference schema, the propositions that it would be wrong for the lawyer to defame the rape victim and that it would be wrong for the lawyer not to defame the victim. But if the form of the Peripatetic syllogism is really:

(i*) Generally speaking, of an action x, if Ax then x is (is not) permitted (obligatory).
(ii) Aa.

Therefore,

(iii) Action a is (is not) permitted (obligatory),

we need to ask some questions about the form of this inference. It is clearly not a syllogism of any ordinary sort. One special worry is that something of the form of (i*) is not well suited for the purposes of subsumption. Something else must be going on, but until we know what 'Generally speaking' is supposed to mean it is impossible to be sure what sort of 'derivation' we are engaged in.

    However this may be, I am not at all disposed to say that nothing of the sort that Richardson has in mind is ever appropriate. I would, of course, wish to recast his talk about norms and represent the matter in terms of reasons. Once we get our reasons right, we may find that we don't have the conflicts we originally thought we had. In the case of (1), it may be that the lawyer's relation to her client is a reason for her to take any available means to get an acquittal, but only on condition that those means are both legal and ethical. If we are dealing here with enabling conditions, it may take a specific case to reveal to us that the lawyer–client relation is not a reason to do this rather than that if doing this is unethical. This is what one might call the 'specification' of a reason, and I have no need to insist that it can never happen. However, I don't suppose, any more than Richardson does, that all conflict can be 'resolved' by this means.

    There are others who do suppose this, as I mentioned at the end of Chapter 1. Scanlon seems to think that there can be no such thing as a conflict of moral reasons. He supposes that what looks like a conflict between principles is really a relation between inadequately specified principles. I have already criticized this view, in Chapter 2. But it is propounded in a certain context, which has an independent significance for my purposes. Reading his (1998), one would be forgiven for thinking that Scanlon is a straightforward generalist. He writes:

Since she accepts the judgment that, given G, she has reason to help her neighbor, Jane is also committed to the view that anyone else who stands in the relation described by G to someone in need of help has reason to provide it. This is an instance of what I call the universality of reason judgments.... [which] holds that if I have a reason to do something because it will satisfy my desire, then anyone else who has that same desire (and whose situation is like mine in other relevant respects) also has this reason. (pp. 73–4)

And later we read:

To justify an action to others is to offer reasons supporting it and to claim that they are sufficient to defeat any objections that others may have. To do this, however, is also to defend a principle, namely one claiming that such reasons are sufficient grounds for so acting under the prevailing conditions. (p. 197)

Let us suppose that G, in the first passage above, is a specification of the reasons that Jane recognizes—the considerations that Jane takes to favour her helping her neighbour. Scanlon's own view is that such a specification is never more than shorthand for the true content of a moral principle. He writes: 'their succinct verbal formulations turn out on closer examination to be mere labels for much more complex ideas' (p. 199), and that 'in making particular judgments of right and wrong we are drawing on [a] complex understanding [of the point of having a constraint on, say, the breaking of promises], rather than applying a statable rule' (p. 201). The idea is that hardly any principles are capturable in an exact formulation. But if this is the case, how can it be that in making a particular judgement, we are committing ourselves to a principle? We might, I suppose, be committing ourselves to the existence of some principle or other, but surely not to this rather than that principle, since on Scanlon's own showing we need have no very clear idea of what we are committing ourselves to, and this raises a doubt about whether we have really committed ourselves to anything at all.

The most probable reply to this is that a moral judgement does commit one to a principle, but it will be a vague or inexact principle. Gleaning ideas from various remarks of Scanlon's, we might say that a judgement such as 'this act of throwing your snails and slugs into your neighbours' garden is wrong because it subverts their horticultural purposes' commits one to an inexact principle of the form 'an act that subverts one's neighbours' horticultural purposes is generally or normally wrong, and always wrong in circumstances relevantly similar to these'.

The first thing to say here is that even if there is a variety of cases in which in making a moral judgement one does indeed specify as a reason a consideration that one takes to be *normally* sufficient, it cannot be that in all cases one commits oneself to the normal sufficiency of one's reason. For there will be many an unusual case concerning which there is no suggestion that the feature doing the work here must normally have the same effect elsewhere. So it cannot be the case that a moral judgement, with reasons specified, per se commits the judger to the normal or general sufficiency of those reasons.

What then about the notion of relevant similarity? It is common ground between me and Scanlon that the considerations that favour an action may only do so in a certain context. They may, in that context, be 'sufficient' (that is, good enough to make the action actually right). But this does not show that they will always be sufficient, nor even that they will count in favour of the action at all in other contexts. Suppose now that we take a conception of the context itself and ask whether this at least is true, that wherever that context recurs these considerations will favour similar action. Is there a notion of context such that the considerations *in that context* can be guaranteed to play the same normative role as before? Obviously it depends on how widely we cast the net of 'context'. We might take it to mean 'all the prevailing conditions whatever' (see Scanlon 1998: 197, quoted above). But this, though it might retain the truth of the universality of reason judgements, retains it on pain of rendering such judgements only trivially, not substantially, universal. For if we cast the notion of context that wide, no context is repeatable. Does the notion of relevant similarity provide the more restricted notion of context that we are looking for? It depends what is to be included in this notion. It is obviously important, for one's particular judgement to *commit* one to the principle, that it commit one to condemning any action that damages one's neighbours' horticultural purposes in circumstances of a certain sort. There has, we might say, to be some hard-edged content to the commitment. But there neither is, nor needs to be, any available specification of the relevant sort. The matter is reserved for judgement, quite properly. The question will then be this: must it always be possible to determine whether we are dealing with a relevant similarity or not, independently of any decision on whether the action concerned is right or wrong? If the question whether a similarity is relevant or not cannot always be determined in advance of the moral judgement we are supposed to be committed to, the notion of relevant similarity will not be able to play the role here required of it. We may indeed be committed, should we judge the circumstances to be relevantly similar, to condemning the action in the new case. But our initial judgement cannot *commit* us to judging, of any different circumstances, that they are relevantly similar. At least, it cannot do this *on pain of contradiction* (or of *logical inconsistency*).

The underlying weakness of Scanlon's proposal, from my perspective, is that it requires principles of relevant similarity: principles that establish under what conditions one situation is relevantly similar to another. But I doubt that anyone thinks that such principles are available. I have never seen one suggested, and I never expect to.

So far I have been reading Scanlon as holding a general doctrine of the universality of reason judgements, which, as quoted above, says that if I have a reason to do something because it will satisfy my desire, then anyone else who has that same desire (and whose situation is like mine in other relevant respects) also has this reason. But he holds this while allowing that a feature that normally counts in favour of a (sort of) action may on occasion not count in favour at all, in a way that is to be explained by special features of the context in the unusual case. How does he manage to hold these things together? Only, I think, by persuasively reinterpreting his own doctrine of the universality of reason judgements. In public discussion of his (2000), he said this:

As I understand the universality of judgments about reasons, it is a purely formal claim, something close to a tautology. If I claim that R is a good reason to do A for one person but not for another, then I am committed to the claim that their circumstances differ in some way that explains this.

Scanlon goes on to call this commitment 'pretty trivial'. Now this version of the universality of reason judgements is one that the particularist can happily accept—quite unlike the one in the passage first quoted above (1998: 73–4). Scanlon seems to have moved here. However—and this is the crucial point—he has moved on reasons in general, but not on moral reasons. He continued the discussion from which I am quoting by saying:

In my book, I did not discuss principles in connection with the universality of judgments about reasons because there seemed to be little work for principles to do here. But things are different in the moral case, where principles have a significant role. Morality is crucially concerned with cases in which we want people to act in certain ways and in which we want to have reliable expectations that they will so act. It responds to these wants by specifying principles by which people are to govern their actions. In order for these principles to do their jobs... they must have some identifiable shape.

The considerations that prevent ordinary practical reasons from being specified in principles that have 'some identifiable shape' seem to me to apply with equal force to moral reasons. I am also influenced by what I see as the general unattractiveness of holding that moral reasons function in quite different ways from others, given the lack of the sort of distinction between the moral and the non-moral that would make such a significant difference even possible. I think, however, that though Scanlon agrees that there is no such difference between the moral and the non-moral, he thinks that there is one between the features that are concerned with what we owe to others and those that are not. And he claims that we find principles at work within the more limited area of what we owe to each other, because they are required for certain practical purposes. I now turn to consider this idea directly.

5. MORALITY AS A PRACTICAL TOOL

Scanlon is not alone in trying to admit holism as applied to ordinary reasons and then to try to carry on as before when it comes to ethics.[2] His pragmatic rather than logical justification for doing so is echoed by Brad Hooker's claim (2000) that we need principles to keep society together; without principles we will not know what to expect of each other in the social sphere. So there had better be some, and those dangerous particularists who suggest that principled ethics is a strange philosophical imposition on an area that would do rather better without it have failed to see the practical purpose served by principles. Hooker is not as cautious as is Scanlon about the notion of the moral that he is using, and is therefore more vulnerable to the worry that his approach requires a suitable distinction between the moral and the non-moral, and that none is available. Onora O'Neill (1996) suggests that we need principles for conflict resolution; if we have no agreed principles, there will be no common ground to work from. One might say in response to this that much conflict is actually caused by principles, so that if there were no allegiances to principles there would be less to fight about. However, O'Neill's suggestion is not that moral thought and judgement are principle-based, but rather just that we need to have, or to construct, some common ground if we are to resolve serious practical conflict—and the sort of common ground we need is general, since it must be prior to the circumstances of any particular conflict, for only so would appeal to it be capable of resolving a clash.

In saying these things, these writers seem to think of morality as a sort of social device, a human institution that has got set up for a purpose, a bit like the National Trust or the World Bank. Nobody thinks of ordinary reasons in that sort of way, but the moral ones are quite different.

My response to these suggestions is that for the purpose of predictability, we can perfectly well rely on people by and large to do what is right in the circumstances. We don't need principles to tell them what to do, or to determine what is right, or to tell us what they are likely to do, any more than we need principles of rationality to be in place before we can begin to rely on people by and large to act sensibly. Contributory principles are not very good at telling us what people are likely to do, anyway; they will only tell us which considerations people are likely to take to make a difference to how they should behave, which is quite another thing. Hooker contrasts two people, the particularist Patty and the Rossian generalist Gerry, and asks which of them would be more predictable in their actions. This contrast is between two people who only differ in their meta-ethical views, but they do live by those views. Suppose that they have both made the same

---

[2] Another interesting but very different example is Bernard Williams (1995a: 232–3).

promise in the same situation. Hooker writes that 'whether or not particularism is likely to lead agents to make moral mistakes, the Rossian generalist seems in the circumstances more likely to keep the promise' (2000: 21). But if the particularist Patty is making no mistake in not keeping her promise, that means that morality does not require her to keep it. If so, it does not require Gerry to keep his either. If he does so, it may even be that he is wrong to do so, because he has no reason to keep his promise and may have considerable reason to do something else—reason which he takes to be overridden by the non-existent reason to keep the promise. It seems, then, that Patty and Gerry will only differ in their behaviour in cases where it is certain that Patty will do the right thing, and not at all so certain that Gerry will. At this point, it seems to me that the value of predictability is very much overrated.

Perhaps Hooker's claim is intended as the empirical point that particularists are more likely to break their promises because they lack the extra motivation supplied by adherence to a principle. And so far as this goes, it is true. But there is something pretty even-handed here. The most we can say is that the particularist is more likely to break the promise when he ought not and the generalist more likely to keep it when he ought not.

As for conflict resolution, it is true that if we can find no common ground we will in many cases be unable to achieve peaceful and consensual resolution of conflicts, and that gives us a considerable incentive to establish something that is not to be challenged and by appeal to which disputes can be sorted out. But the idea that the basic principles of morality have been arrived at by this route, quite apart from the idea that they constitute some sort of basic common element in our divergent thoughts about how to behave, strikes me as quixotic. The sense in which all agree that justice is important is far less significant than the substantial disagreements between us about what sorts of things are just and what unjust. The common stock of terms by appeal to which disagreements can alone be resolved—terms like 'just', 'fair', and 'equal'—are exactly the ones in which disagreements are formulated. To use an old distinction: we have common *concepts* of justice, fairness, and equality, perhaps, but widely divergent *conceptions* of these things. Agreed 'principles of justice' would be agreements on which things are just and which unjust, formulated in advance of the particular case. Though we can make laws about permitted and required forms of behaviour, laws to which all contestants are antecedently bound, and hope to resolve conflicts thereby, this is a far cry from getting agreement in advance about which things are just and which unjust, which fair and which unfair, and so on. There is no reason to suppose that such agreement is possible, and no reason to suppose that if it is not possible the whole enterprise (if it is an enterprise, which I doubt) of moral thought is thereby subverted. It seems to me, therefore, that the model of an antecedently accepted legal system by appeal to which conflict is to be resolved should not be applied to ethics.

6. SEEING THE POINT

The odd thing is that as well as the Scanlon of specifiable moral principles and of specification as the method of conflict resolution, there is a quite different Scanlon who thinks that our moral thought cannot be captured in any precise way. There are two ways in which this comes out, one weaker and one stronger. The weaker way is that our principles contain phrases such as 'too soon', hard enough', 'large cost', and so on. These phrases cannot be replaced by specificities, and hence any principle that contains them cannot really be 'fully specified', if we give the appropriate sense to the notion of a full specification. The consequence of all this is that the application of any such principle requires judgement, and is not mere subsumption. All this is true and more or less uncontentious in the present context.

The stronger way is rather different and much more contentious and interesting. As we saw earlier, Scanlon claims that in making particular judgements of right and wrong we are drawing on a complex understanding of the point of having a constraint on, say, the breaking of promises, rather than applying a statable rule. When we understand a principle, we do not know some truth, it seems; it is rather that we see the point of a prohibition or constraint. To do this is to understand why there should be a constraint on actions of the kind in question, and to understand the structure of the constraint itself. In the case of all the standard moral principles, we do in fact have a shared understanding of the relevant values, and this is what explains why we normally have no difficulty in agreeing on what counts as a permissible exception to an acceptable general rule.

So far, so good, I would have said. But Scanlon goes further. We might agree that we are here dealing with an exception to a sound general prohibition, and move on. But Scanlon seems to think that such agreement is to be expressed in a more specific formulation of the principle, one which explicitly provides for the right kind of exception. 'We then use our understanding of the reasoning behind this principle to specify it further' (2000: 308). This seems to me to be at odds with the sound suggestion that our understanding of a certain value is not to be expressed in a formula, but is rather something in virtue of which we can agree on most 'central' questions, including what we might call ordinary exceptions to standard principles, and debate constructively on many more peripheral questions, the protagonists on each side understanding perfectly well what drives those on the other.

Here my diagnosis is that Scanlon is being driven in two directions at once by two distinct aspects of his position. He wants to have explicit formulations to work on because he wants to have something that can stand as a distinct object of disagreement in a certain sort of public forum, where objections to principles are raised and assessed by people all of whom are interested in reaching principles which nobody can reasonably reject. He may not think that we commit ourselves to such explicit formulations every time we make a judgement about reasons (by the universality of reason judgements); I discussed this above. But he does think that morality needs to provide explicit formulations if it is to serve its purpose of getting people to act in certain ways and helping us to form reasonably firm expectations about how they will act. On the other hand, he takes the view that in most cases we are quite unable to come up with a formulation that will serve our purposes, saying that, 'it is unlikely that I could formulate a principle to back this up' (1998: 198). It is because of this that he makes heavy play with the need for judgement and interpretation, and stresses a shared understanding of the point of a value, rather than a common grasp on a statable rule. One side of this drives him to think in terms of more and more complex formulations, as each principle contains more and more exclusion clauses specifying its relation to all other principles (i.e. saying clearly which one trumps the other in cases of 'apparent conflict'). The other side drives him to stress our ability to apply a shared but rather formless grasp on the point of a value to determine the issue in a hard case.

There are two aspects of this part of the story that seem disputable to me. The first is that we are said to be able to elaborate our principle in the light of our understanding of a moral rationale, an understanding which consists in a grasp on the point of a value (or of a constraint), and a grasp on the structure of that constraint (ibid: 201). But a grasp on the structure of a constraint seems to be the very thing we were trying to explain; the *explanandum* was our ability to agree in many cases on what is and is not a permissible exception to a prohibition, say, and it looks as if this is what is meant by the 'structure' of a constraint. Second, one might reasonably doubt whether we do really have a 'shared sense of what the point of freedom of expression is and how it is supposed to work', in virtue of which those 'who understand freedom of expression will agree on a wide range of judgments about which of these involve violations of the First Amendment and which do not' (ibid: 200). I myself don't think I do have a sense of what the point of freedom of expression is, even though I do sense that this freedom is important. I can certainly allow that it does have a point, but I have no very clear idea what that point is. And I imagine that most others are no better off than I am.

Despite this, I find the general idea of reliance on a shared but unspecifiable sense of the practical relevance of something (a concept or feature, presumably) both attractive and important. But I would want to insist that such a feature can speak in favour of action on some occasions and against it on others. If so, it would be hard to think of the feature as supporting a principle, exactly.

Scanlon is not the only person to stress a notion of 'seeing the point'. James Wallace argues interestingly against Ross's account of what we know when we know that we have a prima facie duty to tell the truth:

If all I know about truth-telling as a practical consideration is that we have a reason to tell the truth, I do not understand about truth-telling. . . . One has a fuller or lesser knowledge and understanding of truth-telling as a practical consideration depending upon the extent of one's understanding of the importance of truth *in various areas of life*, why it is important, and how it is to be compared in importance with other considerations that pertain in these areas. (1996: 22)

For Wallace, as for Scanlon, it seems that a grasp on the importance of truth, or of kindness, or of honesty, is not a grasp on a statable proposition, but someone who has that grasp is nonetheless in a position to see which instances of departure from the truth are defensible and which are not. In that sense, there is not really a principle, 'you should tell the truth'; rather, the ways in which truth is important explain both why we should generally set ourselves to speak the truth and why it is permissible on occasions to be, as a senior English civil servant once memorably put it, 'economical with the truth'—by which he did not mean simply less forthcoming. Wallace puts these ideas together with remarks about the ways in which we go about handling conflict and developing our moral perspective in response to experience. He says, in ways that should remind us of Henry Richardson's notion of specification, that we modify a norm or principle in the light of novel situations within an established practice, or as we move to a new practice, and we do this in such a way as to *preserve the point* of the original norm.

The mistake in all this, if there is a mistake, is to try to think of seeing the point as having a grasp on an incompletely specified principle. Practical knowledge of the importance of truth need not be conceived of in this way. It is only if we have an antecedent commitment to the existence of principles that we should ever have supposed that something that is perfectly complete in its own nature is actually an incomplete form of something else.

7. ARISTOTELIAN TELEOLOGY

So far, then, I have considered the following suggestions:

1. There is a good supply of invariant reasons, consisting in the applicability of thick concepts. Particularists can allow intra-ethical principles such as, 'One should always be sensitive to the needs of others', even though they should not allow principles that link non-moral concepts to moral ones. There can be no variability without a core of invariability.
2. Not only do the central thick concepts stand as invariant reasons, but they also guarantee the rightness of any act that they favour.
3. Particularism should allow that we have a supply of moral principles, though these can never be completely specified, and may have to be pretty complex.
4. Whatever particularists may say about the logic of reasons, morality is required to provide a good supply of defensible general principles, for the

sake of preserving social order, increasing the predictability of the behaviour of others, and resolving conflict.
5. What is known by someone who understands the importance (the practical purport) of a moral concept is at least partly expressible in a formula, even though it will outrun any formula we can come up with.

I end by considering a very different account of what a principle might tell us. One of the main ways in which particularists try to put pressure on generalists is to ask them what it is that a moral principle says that has any chance of being true. The main answers we have considered have been that a principle tells us that all actions of a certain sort are actually right (or actually wrong), or that a principle specifies a feature (perhaps a thick moral feature) that always counts in the same way wherever it crops up. But there is another answer, which has so far not appeared at all. I associate this answer with Thompson (1995), Irwin (2000), and Garfield (2000). It involves a rather surprising appeal to Aristotelian biology.

Aristotle, it seems, gave his own account of what is said by certain laws in biology. Take the claim that tigers have tails. What does this claim say? It might say any of the following:

1. All tigers have tails.
2. Most tigers have tails.
3. The species of tiger is a tailed species.
4. Tigers have tails (understanding this as a non-statistical generalization, if there is any such thing—see H. Lewis 1977).

The Aristotelian suggestion is that it says rather:

5. A tiger without a tail is a defective one of its kind.

This would be compatible with no tigers actually having tails, perhaps because we have cut them all off to make aphrodisiacs. Here we have the idea that even scientific laws can be normative. If so, we can perhaps hope to apply this model of a scientific law and what it tells us to the moral case. But how exactly might this work? Take a specimen moral principle: one should look after one's ageing parents. What does this say? On the analogy above, it looks as if this principle should be saying that an action of failing to look after one's ageing parents is a defective one of its kind. But this looks utterly unpromising. Perhaps then we should look rather at the agent, and think of the principle as saying that an agent who fails to look after her ageing parents is a defective agent. But is this any better than what we started with? I cannot see that it is. If our worry about the initial principle was that it is not always wrong not to look after one's ageing parents, or that one does not even always have some reason to look after one's ageing parents, such worries seem to apply equally well to moral principles conceived in the Aristotelian way. An agent who fails to look after her ageing parents may not be a defective agent.

Instances of such non-defective parent-neglecters come in two sorts. First, there are those who have an even more pressing duty to do something else; our agent may have such a duty to look after her handicapped brother, which her parents can no longer do, and she cannot look after everybody. Second, there are those who have no duty to look after their ageing parents; our agent's parents may have abused her dreadfully throughout her childhood. This is just normal stuff, entirely predictable by now, but it seems that the Aristotelian suggestion about what moral principles or laws tell us is as vulnerable to such attack as is any other.

8

Knowing Reasons

1. BASIC NORMATIVE FACTS

As I have presented it in this book, particularism is a view in moral meta-physics: it is a view about the ways in which actions get to be right and wrong. For me, this way of looking at things has meant a change of perspective over time. I used to think that particularism was a position in moral epistemology, and to suppose that I was therefore working in a sort of hinterland between pure ethics and pure epistemology—a hinterland that was very sparsely populated. But it now seems to me that the real battleground lies in moral metaphysics. We cannot avoid epistemological questions, however, even if we wanted to. But even so I will be suggesting that once the metaphysical issues have been sorted out, the epistemic ones do not add many further problems.

This sort of talk about metaphysics raises worries that have probably surfaced already along the way. The language of this book has been unashamedly realist. I have spoken freely of moral properties, of moral truth and of moral facts, of features that make actions right or wrong, and so on. Admittedly, I have not explicitly addressed the thorny issue of the exact nature of the realism that I have been assuming; nor have I asked what sort of objectivity we can appropriately ascribe to ethical facts and beliefs. (I did some of this in *Moral Reasons*, ch. 10.) I have been leaving those things aside because I wanted to focus as far as possible on the narrower topic of the rights and wrongs of particularism itself. But talk of metaphysics inevitably raises the question whether those who are not ethical realists can be particularists.

The realist *language* which I have been using should not really be a stumbling block, since it is characteristic of non-cognitivists to maintain that they can perfectly well talk of ethical truth, facts, and properties without signing up to the sort of realism that is involved in taking such talk, as they see it, too seriously. The more important question is this: why shouldn't the non-cognitivists agree with the holism of reasons, and adopt whatever con-sequences follow (however loosely) from that? As I see it, there are two issues to bear in mind. The first is whether non-cognitivists are committed to a naturalistic conception of rationality that is at odds with particularism's claim that moral considerations are naturally shapeless. I have already discussed this issue elsewhere (see my 1993: ch. 5.5 and 1995: sect. 7), and have nothing further to add here. There is a second issue, however, which is whether non-cognitivists are capable of giving a good sense to the notion of a contributory reason. If, as I suggested in Chapter 4, they are not, and if particularism is, as I have been suggesting, largely driven by what one finds when one gets the behaviour of contributory reasons right, a non-cognitivist could only become a particularist at the cost of a peculiar sort of theoretical instability.

When I said above that particularism is itself a view in moral metaphysics, however, this was not supposed to mean that it is a *form* of metaphysical realism. What I meant was only that particularism is a view about how actions get to be right and wrong; it is a specific way of understanding how this works. There are of course other particularists than me, and they will have their own way of thinking about these things. But the picture that I have presented in this book has the following distinctive features, which will each play their part in the epistemic story to come.

First is the holism of contributory reasons for action, and of right-making features. Second is the distinction between playing a normative role and enabling something else to play that role. Third is the claim that to be a contributory reason for action is to stand in a specific normative relation to some response or other, be it action, belief, feeling, attitude, or emotion. Fourth is the claim that there are no independent overall qualities of rightness and wrongness; these supposed qualities are to be understood more in terms of verdicts on the way in which the reasons present in the case 'come down'. Fifth, moral judgement is not conceived as a form of inference from premises to conclusions; to say, 'that would be cruel, and so it would be wrong' is to say, 'that would be cruel, and would be wrong for that reason'. Sixth, practical reasoning is not inference either; the movement of thought from 'that would be cruel' to 'I shall not do it', like that from 'that would be wrong' to 'I shall not do it' is a movement from a relevant consideration to a decision to be implemented either later (if the action is to be delayed) or straightaway (if it is not).

These proposals dictate in large part the form of our moral epistemology. The basic, ground-level moral facts are facts about what is a moral reason for what, and our moral epistemology will therefore be merely an application of a more general epistemology of reasons. The epistemology of reasons is, I maintain, the epistemology of the normative (which is not the same as normative epistemology). The basic reason-facts which we are to come to know are particular; their purview is initially restricted to the particular case. We need to be able to come to know these non-general facts, or to acquire justified beliefs about them; and our knowledge of them will be our basic normative knowledge.

The holism of reasons dictates a non-atomistic approach to such basic normative knowledge. To recognize an instance of favouring, more is required than just gazing at it in a receptive frame of mind. We need to bear in mind the presence of enablers, the absence of possible disablers, the absence of disablers for the enablers, and so on. This complicates the picture. We also need to bear in mind that we have to evaluate the role of this feature in context. It is no use trying to run an isolation test, thinking about the feature in abstraction and asking how it would operate in that artificially barren environment.

These features complicate the picture, and one might worry that they complicate it to such an extent that we have already ruled out the possibility of responsible judgement. Given that the cycle of enablers and disablers may continue indefinitely, are we ever going to be in a position to determine how things actually are in the world of reasons? This sort of worry needs to be firmly put aside, on pain of driving us to overall moral (and other) scepticism. Competent moral judges do not need to be aware of everything that just *might* make a difference in order to determine whether it does or not; they don't even, I would claim, need to be aware of everything that does make a difference, any more than the competent chess player needs to be aware of all the indefinitely ramifying contributions of the different aspects of the position in front of her in order to reach a responsible judgement about what move there is most reason to make. We don't have to know everything before we can make a start at all.

So what we are trying to do is to establish what reasons are present in the case before us. The ability to do this is a sophisticated one, which children develop as they grow up; presumably it is one for which some form of training is virtually essential. If we want to know what it is like to have that ability, we could start by asking what it is that competent judges bring to a new case. Of course, one thing that they bring is their experience of similar cases. But then we want to know how that experience is brought to bear on new cases, most of which will not be exactly similar to anything we have come across before. The particularist will say here that our skills in reason-discernment are not rule-based, meaning by this that we do not extract rules for the operation of reason-giving features from the cases we have come across and then try to subsume new cases under those rules. Reasons do not behave in the sort of invariant way that would be necessary if we were to place such rules at the centre of our epistemology of reasons. Rules of this sort, even if they could be found, would be at best a dispensable crutch for judgement.

This tells us something about how not to conceive of our ability to determine reasons in a new case, but it tells us nothing about how we should conceive of it. We were asking what we bring to a new case, and casting this question as asking in what way we bring our experience to bear as we move to a new judgement. Particularists conceive of the knowledge brought to a new case as much more like knowledge-how than like knowledge-that. That is, it is a skill of discernment, not knowledge of a set of true general propositions discovered by thinking about previous cases and applied somehow to new ones. In terms that will be used in discussion of practical and semantic purport in Chapters 10 and 11, to know the practical purport of a concept is to know the sorts of difference that its applicability can make to how one should respond. But knowing this is just being able to tell the differences made case by case, in a way that is informed by one's past experience but not articulable in propositional terms. The competent judge is not the person in command of general truths about the behaviour of reasons, all extracted from experience. She is a person who can tell a difference when she comes across it.

Looking now not so much at what we bring to a new case as at what we need to determine about that case, we can say that we need two interlocking skills. The first of these is the ability to discern which features are playing the favouring and disfavouring roles here; our knowledge of this sort seems to be propositional, to be true knowledge-that, though this does not make it any the less practical. The second is the ability to put this first sort of knowledge to use in determining how the various contributors combine here to give an overall answer to the practical question what is the thing to do. Though there are two distinct skills here, both of which issue in knowledge-that, I would say that we have both or neither. The ability to discern the 'rational weight' of individual features of the situation would not be comprehensible in a creature incapable of using the resulting knowledge in practical decision. And a creature capable of determining what is overall right and wrong without any sort of sensitivity to the reasons at play is equally incomprehensible.

It is with this combination of abilities that we are able to discern the salience of those features that are salient in a situation, and the overall evaluative shape of the situation. I think of the overall evaluative shape of a situation as the demands that it makes of us, demands that are built out of the various favourings to be found in it, in non-additive ways. Our competent moral judge can tell when a feature is operating normally (if it is a default reason), when one feature's contribution is intensified or diminished by the presence of another, when the presence of one feature affects the sort of action that another feature favours, and so on. In tracking these matters, we track interlocking saliences on the way to overall judgement. Deliberation is the first-person version of this process, but the process itself is not essentially first-personal.

2. IS THERE A MORAL SENSE?

We do not have or need a special *moral* sense, since moral reasons are not relevantly different from other reasons. Do we, then, have a sort of *normative* sense which renders us capable of discerning instances of normative relations such as the favouring relation? If so, it will have to be very broadly conceived, since it will be what renders us sensitive to (i.e. capable of discerning) reasons wherever they crop up, theoretical reasons as well as practical ones. My own view is that, though we can indeed discern reasons across the board, our ability to do it is not sensory; it is not sensibility that issues in the recognition of reasons (though sensibility may be required along the way). It is rather our capacity to judge that is at issue. We might, I suppose, conceive of judgement in general as a *response* to recognized reasons; if that was all that there is to be said, recognition of reasons would have to be prior to judgement. And it is, indeed, prior to *overall* judgement. But just as there is (an application of) judgement in the move from the contributory to the overall, so there is (an application of) judgement in the recognition of the contributory. To recognize that this feature favours that response is to judge that things are so.

Is this capacity to judge a purely cognitive capacity? The cognitive is contrasted with the sensory and with the appetitive. We have decided that the capacity to judge is not sensory (whether we approve of some general distinction between cognitive and sensory or not). It may not be sensory, but that capacity might still be appetitive. There are various views about this, particularly among those who are in the business of constructing alternatives to the received view of motivation and the nature of intentional action. We find there an interesting division of opinion about how to relate the recognition of reasons to other things—to motivation, for instance. All wish to allot practical significance to the recognition of a reason. All wish to find some account of the role of desire that can stand as a sensible alternative to the post-Humean view that desire is the dominant partner in the belief–desire pairings that are a sort of 'rational cause' for intentional actions. And all wish to give an account of what motivation itself is and where it comes in the overall story. There are, then, three apparently distinct things to be accommodated: desire, motivation, and the recognition of a reason. How are we to map these three elements relative to each other?

Consider the views of Scanlon (1998), Garrard and McNaughton (1998), and myself (1993, 2000b). For Garrard and McNaughton, to be motivated just is to recognize a reason, and vice versa. For Scanlon, to desire is to recognize a reason. (This is not quite fair, but I am working with a rather broad brush here, the breadth of which will not affect the point I want to go on to make.) On the view that I favour, to desire is to be motivated. So each of us effectively seeks to collapse the original triad into a pair. Now the relevance of this to the present context is that on either of the views that I reject, the recognition of a reason is not purely cognitive. If to recognize a reason is to desire, then it has a cognitive element and an appetitive one. If to recognize a reason is to be motivated, then again it has an appetitive element. If either of these views was right, then, we would have established a priori that the recognition of reasons is not a purely cognitive matter. However, it seems to me that there is a simple reason why, if we are to collapse three into two, we should do it in my way rather than in either of the other two ways.

Here is the objection as it applies to Garrard and McNaughton. Motivation comes in degrees. One can be more or less strongly motivated. The recognition of a reason does come in degrees too, but they are not degrees of the same thing. A very clear recognition of a negligible reason will generate motivation, perhaps, but not much; the motivation it generates will be easily defeated by a muddier recognition of a much larger reason. Nor is there any other sense in which degrees of motivation should track degrees of recognition.

The same objection can be levelled against Scanlon, at least at the outset. Desire comes in degrees, and the recognition of a reason comes in degrees, but they are not degrees of the same thing.

Here we surely see an advantage in my suggestion that to desire is to be motivated. It is *very* appealing to identify degrees of desire with degrees of motivation (but see Humberstone 1990). Suppose that this is right. To confirm my claim that it gives us reason to turn three into two in my way rather than in the others, however, we need to pursue the details of Scanlon's position. Scanlon does not in fact *identify* desiring with recognizing reasons. He only says that recognizing a reason is an element in desiring. In fact, it is even weaker than this, for he speaks of a tendency to recognize something as a reason. We might reasonably think that this *tendency* can come in degrees, and that those degrees could be mapped onto degrees of desire without strain. So it is, I allow, possible that Scanlon's position escapes the objection that seems effective against Garrard and McNaughton.

My own position here is very close to that of Joseph Raz, who claims that 'a desire is an endorsement of a reason that is independent of it' (1986: 141). In saying this sort of thing, we are taking it that there is a distinction between recognizing a reason and endorsing it; this is where my view differs from Scanlon's. Endorsement of a reason is motivational in a way that mere recognition is not. We might suppose, therefore, that the distinction between recognition and endorsement returns us to the view that the sort of judgement that consists in the recognition of a reason is purely cognitive. But now the question arises why this should matter. What we want here is to find a natural relation between the recognition of reasons and motivation. It would be enough for this purpose to announce that the recognition of reasons is itself an intrinsically motivating state, in the sense that I gave to the notion of the 'intrinsically motivating' in *Moral Reasons* (ch. 2.2). The idea here is that, even if it is possible to be entirely unmoved by a reason which one recognizes as such, there is what we might call a natural connection between the recognition and the motivation. It is not merely that someone who claimed to recognize reasons but who never took the slightest notice of any of them in practice would be providing us with sufficient evidence for rejecting his claim. It is more that, once we acknowledge that there being a reason for ϕ-ing consists in there being something to be said for doing so, it becomes unintelligible to suppose that those who think in terms of reasons should generally suppose nonetheless that such things are irrelevant to the question what to do. To think in terms of reasons at all is therefore to be motivationally disposed in one way rather than another, and this is all that is needed to establish that, even if the recognition of reasons is itself a purely cognitive matter, it is not for that reason deprived of what we might call intrinsic practical relevance.

3. THE MODAL STATUS OF BASIC MORAL FACTS

The modal status of basic moral facts might affect their epistemology. There seems to be a choice: either the facts are necessary and knowledge of them is a priori, or they are contingent and knowledge of them is a posteriori, if not empirical.

On the particularist account, a consideration that is a reason may depend on the presence of suitable enablers and the absence of potential disablers if it is to enjoy that status. It follows that the proposition we know when we recognize a reason is not necessary but contingent. The feature that we are focusing on does favour responding in this way rather than that, but it might not have done, and would not have done if the surroundings had been different. There is nothing necessary here. And this is true whether we are dealing with default reasons or not. Whether a default reason is *here* a reason at all is a contingent matter, since it depends on the context.

So far, so good. But what does this tell us about the epistemology of the moral? There are two reasons why we cannot just announce that, since basic moral facts are contingent, our knowledge of them must be a posteriori. The first of these is the tendency to identify a posteriori knowledge with knowledge that cannot be gained without appeal to empirical evidence, where empirical evidence is understood as the evidence of the senses. This is unfortunate, since we have already decided that we have no moral sense, and no reasons-sense either; it is not sense but judgement. A standard way of handling the distinction between a priori and a posteriori knowledge is to define the a posteriori first, and then take all other knowledge to be a priori. On this approach, if we are worried about the absence of a moral sense, we might announce that basic moral knowledge must be a priori.

But to know that an action was wrong, or that there is a reason for him not to do what he is doing, we need to have all sorts of genuinely empirical knowledge about the situation. Is this enough to show that basic moral knowledge is a posteriori, being empirical? This is where the second reason referred to above comes in. In Chapter 3.4, I introduced a distinction drawn by Marcus Giaquinto, between positive and negative dependence. Giaquinto suggests that a belief that would be abandoned if experience becomes awkward for it need not for that reason be thought of as a posteriori. Such a belief is only negatively dependent on experience. A belief is only a posteriori, he claims, if it is positively dependent on experience, that is, if experience is its ground. Suppose that this is right. What is the ground of our basic moral knowledge, of our basic knowledge of moral reasons? Such knowledge is knowledge that certain facts stand in a normative relation to something else. Knowledge that there is an instance of that relation before us is not itself grounded in a posteriori knowledge of the facts that stand on the left-hand side of the relation. The moral knowledge may *require* a posteriori knowledge of those facts, without itself being a posteriori. It may not itself be empirical, even if we need the evidence of our senses to get it.

This point tends to undercut the thought that, since it does not concern situations unrolling before our eyes, much of our moral knowledge cannot be empirical. We can decide not to do an action because to do it would be wrong. We can decide that there was good reason for Napoleon not to invade Russia. The facts that lie on the left-hand side of the normative relations involved here are beyond observation, in the one case because many of them are true subjunctive conditionals, and in the other because they lie so far in the past. But if straightforward knowledge about the reasons presented in the situation before us is not shown to be empirical by the way in which it depends on empirical knowledge of that situation, these points about less straightforward cases become less worrying.

Suppose we allow that knowledge of basic moral facts is not empirical, since it is not grounded in the evidence of the senses. Does this establish that it is a priori? If so, we seem to be stuck with the view that contingent truths can be learnt in a way that is not sensitive to the different ways in which things might be and sometimes are. Saul Kripke (1971) showed us that we can have a posteriori knowledge of necessary truths, but he did not show us how to get a priori knowledge of contingent ones. There is a suspicion that too few options are on offer here. The decision that basic moral knowledge is not empirical was only based on the fact that such knowledge is not *grounded* in the deliverances of the senses, moral or otherwise. But particular cases can reveal to us facts about reasons, even if facts available to the senses are not acting as grounds for them. After all, we sometimes learn from a particular case that a feature which previously we supposed to be of no moral relevance at all can on occasion make a moral difference. An adolescent who had always thought that the way in which adults insist on being tactful is just a sham might learn from a particular case that it is not. Is this enough for it to count as a posteriori knowledge? Perhaps the idea that it is a priori should not really alarm us, once we realize that this merely means that experience is not its ground; with this realization comes recognition that a priori knowledge of contingencies may not be so very incoherent after all.

I admit that it sounds alarming to say that knowledge of basic moral facts is a priori. Where Kant taught us to think that only necessary universal truths can be known a priori, our basic moral facts are particular and contingent.

And things are made worse by the fact that we expect a priori knowledge to be gained by examination of the interrelations between concepts, or between meanings; we expect it to be conceptual knowledge, or knowledge of analytic truths. But nobody could suppose that knowledge of a basic moral fact is gained purely by examining one's concepts, nor by thinking about the meanings of words. In fact, there doesn't seem to be a *method* of acquiring that sort of knowledge at all. So not only is such knowledge a priori, it is not the sort of a priori knowledge that we are used to. However, there are companions in guilt, and once we realize this, most of our worries will subside. There are unmysterious examples of a priori knowledge that not only require antecedent a posteriori knowledge, in the sort of way that knowledge of basic moral facts does, but is also acquired using no method at all, so far as one can tell. Consider our ability to assess similarities. We have four things, *A*, *B*, *C*, and *D*; and we can ask whether the first two are more similar to each other than are the second two. Let us say that *A* is a house designed by Frank Lloyd Wright, *B* is a house designed by Le Corbusier, *C* is an apartment block by Frank Lloyd Wright, and *D* is an apartment block by Le Corbusier. Is *A* more similar to *B* than *C* is to *D*? Are the two houses designed by these architects more similar to each other than are the two apartment blocks? In order to answer this question we need a posteriori knowledge of the independent natures of the four buildings; but that knowledge is not itself enough. Nor would it be enough to have listed the points of similarity and dissimilarity on either side of the two comparisons. The difficulty is that some similarities are more telling than others. No list of points of similarity will suffice for a judgement about which of those points is the most telling in the present comparison. The matter is reserved for judgement, perfectly properly, and that judgement is one for which there is no method; but such judgements can yield knowledge. So here we have a more or less perfect analogy, and one which, I would claim, takes the mystery out of the situation. If this sort of knowledge of comparative similarities can be thought of as a priori, so can knowledge of basic moral facts.

4. IS THIS FOUNDATIONALISM?

There are basic normative facts, but our knowledge of them, when we can get it, is not basic knowledge in the sense given to that term by epistemic foundationalism. In fact, there are all sorts of ways in which the picture I outlined in section 1 above is non-foundationalist.

Let us call a belief in a basic fact a 'basic belief'. First, it is possible for one such belief to be appealed to in confirmation of another. My suspicion that feature *F* stands here as a reason against action *A* may be confirmed by noticing that on another occasion, which differs from this one in various telling ways, that feature is operating differently. So basic moral beliefs are not to be thought of as epistemological atoms. There is such a thing as mutual support (and its opposite) at the basic level.

Second, it is possible for a basic belief to be confirmed or weakened by a non-basic belief. That one action is wrong overall (which on my account is a non-basic matter) may be a reason to suspect that elsewhere a certain feature is not functioning as a favourer. So our two skills are mutually reinforcing. Overall judgements can confirm judgements about contributions; confirmation does not always flow from basic to non-basic.

Third, the *ordo essendi* need not be the same as the *ordo cognoscendi*. Although facts about what favours what are the basic normative facts, they need not be the ones we first discern, or by recognition of which we become aware of non-basic facts. A competent chess player is capable of discerning directly the overall weakness of a position, before turning to look at what it is about it that makes it weak. I have used that example before. For another, rather closer to home: an argument can smell bad to the trained philosophical nose, long before the owner of the nose gets anywhere near a diagnosis of what has actually gone wrong. These are cases where we are capable of direct discernment of a resultant feature; the metaphysics of resultance do not show this to be impossible. So it should be possible first to discern that an action is wrong, and only later to come to recognize what is wrong with it.

Fourth, recognition of instances of favouring presupposes possession of concepts whose domain of application does not lie at the favouring level, but elsewhere. First, one needs the concept of the overall (allowing for the moment that there are separate concepts of this sort) if one is to grasp the concept of a favourer. Second, one needs knowledge of which conditions are conducive or antipathetic to sound moral judgement. Third, one needs at least an implicit understanding of the ways in which disabling and enabling conditions work. Some such knowledge lies, admittedly, at the basic level; but some does not. When I first introduced the notion of an enabler in Chapter 3.1, I suggested that some enablers govern the relation between favourers and overall judgement. The example I gave there concerned the way in which the fact that I have no more pressing duty enables my having promised to make keeping that promise my duty.

The point that basic knowledge requires concepts whose domain of application does not concern basic facts is an intentional echo of Wilfrid Sellars's attack on the Myth of the Given. As Sellars sees things, foundationalists think of basic knowledge as presupposing no other knowledge. But he argued that possession of the concept 'looks red' requires possession of the concept 'is red'. He also argued that possession of colour concepts, of the sort evinced in judgements about what colour something looks, requires one to know which conditions are and are not appropriate for telling what colour something is by looking at it.

Sellars has a further point, whose application to the moral case is less straightforward. As he sees things, foundationalists miss the fact that experiences, as he puts it, 'make claims' about matters that lie beyond themselves, namely about reality. The experience we have when something looks red to us is not a simple epistemological atom, sufficient unto itself; it somehow contains the claim that things are one way (the red way) rather than another. This is an interesting idea. In the moral case, we might think that a reason for action 'makes the claim' that the action is overall right—a claim that may be defeated if there is a better claim made on the other side. This sort of talk about claims needs to be distinguished from the sort of thing I said in characterizing the evaluative or normative shape of a situation as the claims that it makes on one. The latter are not claims 'that the action is right'; they are claims on one to do the action. But there seems to be no reason why we should not use the notion of a claim in these two different ways at once. If so, Sellars's point gives us a further way in which our talk of basic moral facts is no sign of foundationalist leanings.

5. IS THIS COHERENTISM?

This is a rather more shapeless question than the one which the previous section addressed, because there is rather less agreement about what is required if one is to count as a coherentist. Two tenets often mentioned in this connection are:

1. Only a belief can justify another belief.
2. Everything that is justified is justified in the same sort of way.

There is no reason to think of particularism as committed to the first of these (nor to suppose that such a commitment is the price of not being a foundationalist, in my view). More interestingly, I see little reason to accept this first tenet. First, if actions can be justified by appeal to features other than beliefs of the agent, why cannot beliefs be too? One can sometimes justify one's action by showing that one didn't know some relevant fact. Perhaps the point is supposed to be that the appeal is to beliefs of the justifier, not of the agent. In my own case, then, I might appeal to something I now believe (but did not at the time of action), namely that there is a relevant fact which I did not know. Note, however, that this means that the thing appealed to in justification (the *justificans*) is a belief only in the sense of a thing believed, not in the sense of a believing; it is a supposed fact, not a mental state of the person doing the justifying. The point seems only to be that this supposed fact must be believed by the person who offers it as *justificans*. Turning now from the justifier to the thing to be justified (the *justificandum*), again we should ask whether we are thinking of beliefs in the sense of things believed, or in the sense of believings, i.e. mental states. With the *justificandum*, one would suppose it to be the latter, because the idea of justifying a thing believed is incoherent, whatever account one gives of the things we believe.[1] One can verify a thing believed, or check it, or defend it; but one cannot justify it, if by that is meant do to it what one can do to the believing of it or to the believer for believing it. The notion of justification needs control here. Even if one can justify both the doing of the action and the thing done,[2] one can only justify the believing, not the thing believed. So the first tenet above must be taken to mean that only a thing believed by the justifier can justify a believing. Why has this been so often asserted, and with such confidence? Partly, I suspect, because people have had in mind the case of self-justification, that is, of a person trying to justify himself for having believed what he did believe. How, for such a purpose, could someone appeal to something that they did not believe? This rhetorical question in fact applies even to third-person justification. But we should note that the idea that successful justification and increases in coherence go together is not really applicable any more, since the justifying belief does not necessarily belong to the same person as does the belief to be justified (and vice versa). And it is not even obvious that I can only appeal to things I believe when justifying someone's actions, or their believings. If the thing I appeal to succeeds in doing the justifying for which I am appealing to it, it would be irrelevant for someone to complain, should they find out that I myself did not believe it. It is the truth of what I appeal to that matters, we may suppose, not whether I who appeal to it actually believe it.[3] Overall, I suggest that we can safely leave aside this supposed first mark of coherentism.

We need to ask rather similar questions of the second supposedly coherentist tenet above. Suppose that I make a basic moral judgement and am asked to justify 'it'. What am I being asked to do? The worry that it does not make sense to talk of justifying a thing believed might perhaps be circumvented by understanding justification in terms of defence: one can defend oneself for believing, and one can also defend the thing one believed. (These are rather different sorts of defence, no doubt.) In these terms of defence, then, there seem to be three things I can do. The first is to defend the judgement made, in the sense of showing sufficient reason to believe it to be true. Here it is enough if I manage to show that there is *now* sufficient reason; I don't officially need to show that there *was* sufficient reason when I came to believe it. The second, as before, is to defend my having made the claim, or accepted it *in foro interno*; I may be able to do this even though I cannot do

[1] Are they propositions, states of affairs or something else—or nothing at all? See White (1972).
[2] And this is dubious too. I would rather distinguish justification from verification, for things believed, and justification from 'rectification' for things done. It is not the thing done that is justified when, though it was wrong, one can be defended for having done it.
[3] There may of course be a suggestion that it is *morally* wrong to appeal to something which one does not oneself believe, but that, I would say, is quite a different matter.

the first, since it is not impossible to have been justified in making a claim that turned out to be false. The third is to show that I had a right to make it, or that I was in a position to judge. In each case we are thinking of justification as an activity of defence after the fact. Though one can, and does, ask oneself 'what would I be justified in believing here?', this may mean no more than 'what would I be able to defend myself for having believed?'. If it does mean more, it comes suspiciously close to 'What is true here?'.

The last two of these three possibilities are nothing much to do with the rights and wrongs of coherentism. I establish a right to judge by showing a combination of general skills and particular opportunities. I need to show, for instance, that I can at least normally recognize (a sufficient range of) the reasons present around me and what it is that they favour in context, that I am suitably sensitive in general to the presence or absence of enablers and disablers, intensifiers and attenuators, and that I am generally sensitive to the sorts of ways in which reasons on different sides combine to yield an overall answer. These are the skills of the competent judge, and to them we need to add the required opportunities to gather the information relevant in the case before me. I don't think that the second supposedly coherentist tenet has much to say about this side of things.

Nor, I think, does it have much to say about what is going on when, having (let us say) made a mistake, I defend myself for having made it. Such defence might, as I suggested above, amount to pointing out that someone intentionally deceived me. Coherentists might claim that rational defence of this sort must consist of an attempt to establish that in adopting the beliefs one did, one was seeking maximal coherence between the various pieces of real and supposed evidence available to one. But, though that is true of some instances, it will not be true of others. I might, for instance, defend myself— justify myself, that is—for having made the mistake I did by pointing out the stress I was under and that I was very tired and had a great many things to do all at once, so that normal criteria should be to some extent put in abeyance in my case. There doesn't seem to be anything here for coherentism (in terms of the second tenet) to get its grips on.

Things are different when we are thinking about justifying a claim in the sense of showing good (not merely apparent) reason to believe it (here: the thing claimed) true. This is not quite the same as showing the reasons why it is true. Reasons for believing something may not themselves be reasons why the thing to be believed is true. If my normally reliable friend tells me something, that she has told me it is (probably) a reason for me to believe it true, but is unlikely to be among the reasons why it is true. To draw this contrast one has to think of 'the reasons why it is true' along the lines of 'what makes it true'. In moral cases, what makes it true that I ought to do this will be such things as that I promised, i.e. the favourers. Now if we are doing epistemology, we are not specially concerned with the reasons why the thing claimed is true, unless those count among the reasons for believing it to be true, which is our official topic. And on that topic I have already claimed that one can defend a basic belief (which here is being understood as showing sufficient reason to believe a basic fact) either by appeal to another basic fact, or by appeal to a non-basic one. Is such a claim itself a sign of coherentism? This surely depends on what is supposed to be going on in such appeals.

But we can approach that issue with several preconceptions. The first is that the core of the distinction between foundationalism and coherentism is that foundationalists suppose there to be two quite distinct ways of justifying something, one appropriate for what they nominate as 'basic beliefs' and the other appropriate for the rest; coherentists, by contrast, suppose that all justification is of the same sort, at bottom. The question then is whether we are thinking of moral justification as all being of 'the same sort'. It seems wrong to suggest that since one can defend a belief about reasons in one case by appeal to a belief about reasons in another, or by appeal to a belief about the overall in another, we are dealing here with justifications that are not of 'the same sort' in the relevant sense. Presumably, for coherentists, what makes apparently different justifications still of the same sort is that they show a significant common feature. And there are two main views about what that feature is. The first view is that justifications revolve around increases and decreases in 'explanatory coherence'. The second is that they revolve around inferential relations. Could either claim be made of the justifications we are here discussing, namely the ways in which we can defend a basic reasons-claim by appeal to how things are reasons-wise in another case, or by appeal to how things are overall elsewhere? This seems to me to be the crucial question.

Not all would agree that this is the crucial question. Some who discuss moral justification, and even some who call themselves coherentists, take as their model of coherentism John Rawls's notion of reflective equilibrium (see e.g. Sayre-McCord 1996). That model is inapplicable to the topics of the present chapter, because for reflective equilibrium (whether wide or narrow) one is required to establish a stable balance between particular judgements and general principles, and this is something that no particularist is going to see any need for. Perhaps one should rather say that in this way we might establish in very short order that no particularist is a coherentist—in such short order, indeed, that the conclusion would not be of very much interest. More to the point, I think, is what things look like when Rawls turns from what he calls narrow reflective equilibrium (which is as characterized above) to 'wide' reflective equilibrium, where we are supposed to establish a stable balance between particular judgements, moral principles (as before), and pretty well anything else that might prove relevant (psychological, social, physical, metaphysical, whatever). At this point it seems that to be a coherentist is merely to think that justification is achieved when one gets the best balance, the most stable fit, between all conceivably relevant considerations. On this account, it would be hard not to be a coherentist, but the rights and wrongs of coherentism as a significant epistemological theory have ceased to be interesting. Particularists would just turn out to be people who had their own version of the input to wide reflective equilibrium.

So the crucial question is whether the sorts of appeal to other cases that particularists would wish to allow are to be thought of as attempts to increase either explanatory or inferential coherence. What we are interested in is what is involved in the attempt to defend basic claims, claims about what is a reason for what in a particular case. My suggestion is going to be that it is possible for another case to be *revealing* in a way that makes no use of inferential relations, and which we are not required to interpret in terms of an increase in explanatory power—though I will allow that the latter is at least possible.

As far as the inferential goes, it is always going to be an uphill struggle to think in inferential terms of the ability of one case to help us see how things are in another. Of course, this point depends on having some sense of what is to count as inferential and what is not. And since nobody seems to have much of an answer to that question, we are left rather groping in the dark. Perhaps the main 'inferentialist' proposal to be considered should be that someone who moves in this sort of way from a judgement about one case to a judge-ment about other should be understood as thinking, 'it is thus and so there; so probably it is so and thus here'. But that need not be what is going on. I would say that one case can help us see how to understand another without there being any such relations of probabilification between the two.

It seems much more plausible to think in terms of explanation than of inference. Suppose then that, when challenged, I defend a claim about a favourer by pointing out, or painting, a range of analogous cases in which changes in favouring go along with changes elsewhere. I might, for instance, defend the idea that I have at least some reason to send my uncle a birthday card by pointing out the strength of the reasons I have to send cards to my father, to my uncle's new wife, and to my wife's cousin. The strength of the reason to send my uncle a card seems to lie somewhere on a spectrum, so as nicely to match the strength of family connection. This looks like a sort of confirmation. And one could think of it as increasing explanatory relations, since it would be harder to explain the absence of any reason to send my uncle a card than it is to explain its presence, given the relative strength of the reasons to send the other cards.

Suppose, to take another case, that you make a certain claim about the contribution of a distinctive architectural feature to the building of which it is a part. When challenged, you might point first to a case where a very similar feature makes a quite different contribution, and second to a case where a rather different feature makes a very similar contribution. The idea here is that the way things are working in those further cases can provide some support for your account of what is going on in the first case. This is the sort of justification that we are at present considering. Is there any link to explanation? It is not as if the further cases explain what is going on in the first. They help one to see what is going on there; they are revealing. As such, they act as reasons to believe your original claim. Perhaps it is like this: given the further cases, it would be harder to explain the falsehood of your original claim than it is to explain its truth. But no explanation of the truth of the first claim has yet been offered, or is in the offing. The point must then be that it would be harder to explain your being right about the further cases and wrong about the original one than it is to explain your being right about them all.

Some structure of this sort seems to be present whenever appeal to further cases acts as confirmation for a hypothesis about how things are in the case before us. If so, particularism can make some claim to an epistemology of a broadly coherentist style. But whether it can or not, the phenomena of which I have just given a broadly coherentist interpretation would still be there. The main point, from the particularist perspective, is that a range of further cases can act as confirmation for a belief about how things are in the case before us. If this is interpreted in terms of an increase in explanatory interconnections, then we have a form of coherentism. If not, we don't—but nothing much would thereby be lost. The question is more a problem for coherentists than for particularists. At worst, particularists would merely have to hold that they do not have to choose between foundationalism and coherentism.

6. SCEPTICAL CHALLENGES

In this section I consider the possibility that particularism is especially vulnerable to sceptical challenge. That it is vulnerable to sceptical challenge is undisputable; so is every other option in moral philosophy. The real question, then, is whether particularism has greater weaknesses in this respect than do its rivals. I maintain, of course, that it does not. In doing so, I will consider three possible difficulties. But first I want to elaborate a little on the relation between particularist and other moral epistemologies.

The epistemological structure of particularism is so different from that of Kantian approaches, given the inability of the latter to capture the role of contributory moral reasons, that I won't devote any time to comparing the two. A more fruitful comparison is with Ross's theory of prima facie duties. Ross's view is that moral knowledge starts when we become first aware that certain features make a difference to how we ought to behave. Our first such knowledge is of a feature that makes a difference in a particular case, but we learn immediately from this that the same feature will make the same difference in every other case in which it is present. We do this by a process called 'intuitive induction', which is broadly similar to the way in which we learn the validity of logical principles such as *modus ponens* from instances.

Here, what we learn is a necessary truth, whatever we think of the modal status of that from which we learn it. That is, even if there is no necessity in the particular case, we move from that to a necessary general truth.

There are obviously things to be said about this hopeful bottom-up epistemology, and I have already said some of them. Given the supposed starting point, is it really possible to move upwards to knowledge of necessary general moral principles in the sort of way that Ross suggests? I doubt it. What I want to stress here is that Ross's starting point is the same as that of the particularist. The only difference between them is that Ross is trying to get more out of that starting point. He wants knowledge of basic moral facts (as I have been calling them) to generate knowledge of necessarily true universal propositions, in a way that has nothing to do with inductive generalization. It is fair to say that he doesn't suppose that the latter knowledge is actually in play when we move, in a given case, from what we discern at the prima facie level to our overall decision about what to do. That move, he thinks, normally bypasses our general moral knowledge altogether; we go straight from recognition that these or those features matter morally in the present case to some judgement about how the reasons come down overall, i.e. to what we have most reason to do in this case. Nonetheless, it is obviously important for Ross that we can acquire knowledge of these general truths, partly because he supposes that in the absence of those general truths there could be no such thing as moral thought or moral reasons, and partly because he is not at all keen to allow that, though there must be such truths, we are incapable of recognizing them.

The particularist, by contrast, is not looking to extract anything of that sort from what he maintains is available to us case by case. All that the particularist says it must be possible to recognize is the basic moral facts of the cases we come across, that is, the reasons that they throw up. Since Ross and the particularist start from the same point, but Ross needs to extract much more from that point than the particularist does, I would say that particularism stands at a natural epistemological advantage.

Not everyone would agree with me about this, however (a phenomenon to which one becomes only slowly inured). So I turn to consider three ways in which, irrespective of this supposed advantage over Ross, it might be held that the particularist cannot suppose that one moral judgement has an epistemic advantage over another. (I will leave aside the question whether the supposed difficulties are also difficulties for Ross, as I suppose them in fact to be.)

The first supposed difficulty is that according to particularism there can be no way in which the epistemic status of one judgement can be altered by appeal to another. Everything is the way it is, and nothing has anything to do with anything else. Whatever is a reason in one case may perfectly well be no reason at all in others, and so there can be no sense in appealing to other cases in support of one's view of how things are here. All one can do is to look as hard as one can at the present situation; everything else is technically irrelevant.

The first thing to be said here is that the difficulty may not be quite so severe as that. Particularists claim that the move from what we say about one case to what to say about another is never automatic. But that does not show that appeal to one case can do nothing whatever to reinforce one's tentative judgement about another. I claimed earlier in this chapter that one may find other cases instructive or suggestive, whether one is considering simply what features are acting as reasons there or looking at how things stand there overall. The sceptical challenge is that this was just bluster, and that the effect of an extreme holism of reasons is an extreme epistemological atomism. The right response to this, I think, is going to be an appeal to examples, lest we find ourselves adopting trenchant theoretical positions without much consideration of how things actually happen. One that I used above is the example of an adolescent who suddenly realizes that tact can matter. The idea here is that our adolescent, having stoutly maintained that his parents' talk about the need to treat people tactfully is just a lot of adult irrelevance, comes across a case where he finds it hard to deny that an action that was tactless was somehow the worse for it.[4]

So far, this is standard particularist moral epistemology; we are dealing, let us suppose, with an epistemological atom. But now our adolescent has realized that tact can matter, and did in that case. And this might well lead him to reconsider some earlier cases of which he had previously maintained that the tactlessness of what he did was not a moral defect. Having now seen that this might be a mistake, and having an example of the sort of situation in which tactfulness does matter, he may come to see that in at least a range of those earlier cases he has reason to change his mind. In others, however, he might stick to his previous view, namely that though what he did was indeed tactless, it was none the worse for that. Tactfulness, he may yet maintain, is still often overrated by adults, or rated when it ought not to be rated at all. But there is a range of cases about which he now admits that he was wrong, and another range about which he sticks to his previous view. And he might think that the status of his unchanged view of the latter situations is improved by his now growing sensitivity to the distinction between the situations in which tactlessness matters and those in which it doesn't. Given that he is learning to tell that difference, he may think that his judgements are becoming sounder than they were. This is an increase in defensibility, in justification.

The matter need not only be handled at the contributory level. It may be that our adolescent first noticed the importance of tact in a case where he said to himself, 'this feels overall wrong', and then, trying to work out what made

---

[4] I should say, in a bizarre form of self-defence, that the adolescent I am talking about here is, or was, myself.

it wrong, found the only possible explanation in its tactlessness. Reached in this way, I would claim, the judgement that the tactlessness of the action counts against it is more defensible, more justified.

These are the sorts of things that particularists should say in response to the complaint that on their approach no one judgement can affect the epistemological status of another.

My second sceptical challenge is the claim that particularism renders moral knowledge unattainable. This claim derives from the holism of reasons and the ever-widening circle of enablers and disablers, enablers for enablers, enablers for disablers, disablers for enablers for disablers, and so on. Given all this, one might say, it is going to be impossible ever to know how things actually are with respect to any one feature. No matter how much one knows, there will always be something more that one doesn't know, but whose truth or falsehood makes all the difference.

I alluded to this challenge in the first section of this chapter. The difficulty with it is that it is in danger of appealing to a conception of what is required for knowledge that is so exhaustive as to render knowledge almost universally impossible. The claim seems to be that the following argument is sound:

1. If it were the case that p, it would (or at least might) not be the case that q.
2. S does not know whether p.
3. So: S does not know that q.

I would say that if, to know the truth of p, one has to know the truth-value of everything whose status would or might affect the truth-value of p, one could never know anything at all. The question then is whether we can find something short of this general requirement—something which is independently defensible, which does not have this disastrous effect and which could be brought to bear on the epistemological status of particularism. I think that the answer to this question is yes, but that what we find is something that undermines the sceptical challenge rather than the particularism it challenges.

G. E. Moore faced the same sort of difficulty as the one I am here raising for particularism. In his case it took a consequentialist form. Since we can never know all the consequences of what we in fact do, let alone all the consequences of all the alternative actions that we don't do, how can we ever know whether what we do is right or wrong? Moore felt that he had to allow that we don't. This would, however, only be a weakness if some other moral theory is in a better position. What would a moral theory be like if it is not to be vulnerable to this sort of attack? Presumably a finite list of absolute principles that are incapable of conflicting with each other would do the trick—provided that the principles themselves are epistemically manageable. By this I mean that an absolute principle that says, 'Do whatever has the best consequences', is not manageable, while one that says, 'If you have promised, do what you promised to do', is manageable. The problem for such a theory will be to let the consequences in without ending up facing Moore's problem.

For even if other relevant features are epistemically manageable, the fact that this one is not will destroy the whole thing.

There is a way of dealing with this problem. This is to restrict the relevant features to those recognized, or believed by the agent concerned. A consequentialist can take this line; there is even some evidence that J. S. Mill took it.[5] If he did, his view is that only the actual consequences of an action can make a difference to whether it is right or wrong, but that not all actual consequences do make such a difference, only those that were actually intended, or perhaps predicted, by the agent. The choice between those intended and those predicted is relevant to the doctrine of double effect, but makes no difference for our present purposes. Either will suffice to block the general sceptical argument that I am considering.

What we are dealing with here is a sort of epistemic filter through which a consequence must pass if it is to affect the rightness or wrongness of the relevant action. I have argued elsewhere (2000b: ch. 3) that we do in fact need such a filter, but I think that the one I have been imputing to Mill is not the right one. First, as a non-consequentialist I allow other things than consequences to be relevant; so my filter will let through some things that are not consequences. Second, and more important, I think that the restriction to those aspects (let us call them) that are actually recognized or intended by the agent is too charitable. Agents will too easily get off the moral hook if we do things this way, for aspects that they should have recognized but didn't, through carelessness or inattention perhaps, will not be allowed to affect the morality of what they subsequently do. We would do better to relax the filter so that more things get through than those actually recognized or intended. How far to relax it is certainly a problem, though as a particularist I am happy to maintain that there need be no general answer. But something like this might be right: all and only aspects that the agent is capable of recognizing and/or at fault for not recognizing or for not being able to recognize can pass the filter and so affect the morality of the action.

If anything like this is right in general, it will give us a general answer to my second sceptical challenge. Even if the ramifications of possibilities go on for ever, in a way that takes them far beyond what any agent could possibly recognize (as I am allowing, for present purposes, that they do), this will not make it impossible for agents to determine which of the available alternatives is in fact right.

My third sceptical challenge requires no such tortuous epistemological manoeuvrings. The thought here again concerns what resources we have available to us, should someone disagree with our identification of a reason in the present case. It is all very well saying that different cases can be revealing, so that some progress can be made by considering a suitable range of other

[5] See the last two sentences in the long footnote to paragraph 19 of ch. 2 of his *Utilitarianism* (p. 65 in the 1998 edition by R. Crisp).

possibilities. But suppose that this does not work, either because the present case is so unusual that no such range can be found, or because our objector disagrees with us about them as strongly as she did about the first case. We now seem to be stuck. Is this a defensible epistemic position?

Of course, if we can point to some way in which we are better situated, epistemically, than is our objector, this might reassure us; for it would offer a way of explaining the objection away, as grounded in some misconception of what is going on, or some grasp less adequate than ours. Perhaps we have had more opportunity to discover relevant facts, or can somehow show that we have more of the skills of a competent epistemic judge. But perhaps we can't show this. We have, it seems, reached an impasse, in a way that is, epistemically speaking, not very comfortable. It is not, after all, as if it would be satisfactory just to say that there are two defensible views of the situation, ours and hers, and that so long as our view is defensible, that is enough. (As it is often said, we might be satisfied with showing that our view is at least justified, even if we have to abandon our claim to knowledge.) The sad fact is that there is a crucial respect in which choosing views is not like choosing actions (though the two are very similar overall). The difference is that, where I recognize two equally attractive courses of action, I have the right to do either of them. But where I recognize that another view, another belief, is just as good, just as defensible as my own, I seem to have to abandon my adherence to my own in favour of a temporary agnosticism. If I can't find some way in which my view is better, I lose the right to say that it is the truth.

There may be no general answer to this difficulty. But so far as that goes, particularism need be no worse situated than its competitors. So why should this difficulty be thought of as especially damaging for particularists? I think it is because particularists tend to deny the existence of any substantial general theory of what it is to be a reason. If there were such a theory, it would offer an independent court of appeal in our present difficulty. Suppose, for instance, the following theory of reasonhood:

> That it is the case that p is a good reason for A to ϕ if and only if there is some E such that, if fully rational and perfectly informed, A would desire that E and, given that p, ϕ-ing subserves the prospect of its becoming or remaining the case that E.

I don't suppose that this theory is the truth, but it may not be so far off either. If we changed the 'if and only if' to 'only if', for instance, we would get a more defensible theory that would still be of some use. And if anything like it were available, we might be able to make progress with our objector. For it might be the case that either her reasons or ours would fail to pass this test. What we would have found, effectively, is a reason why whatever is a reason is a reason: a sort of meta-reason. Particularism, at least in my hands, has seen no need to suppose that any such meta-reasons are there to be found. I am tempted to echo Prichard here: our sense that something is a reason is absolutely underivative and immediate, and can be given no independent theoretical support.

My point would only be that there are plenty of non-particularist positions that make similar claims. All are in the same boat, if only they are minimalists in the theory of reasons. Particularism as such is perfectly compatible with the existence of a general theory of reasons which tells us the reason why our reasons are reasons, though in my view no such theory is in fact available. All I would say, then, in answer to my third sceptical challenge, is that it is one to which all sensible positions are going to be equally vulnerable. Particularism, on this point at least, does not make things any worse than they were already.

PART III

Holism in the Theory of Value

9

Intrinsic and Extrinsic Value

1. SIX ISSUES ABOUT INTRINSIC VALUE

G. E. Moore set the scene for subsequent debate by claiming that something can be of value either in itself, intrinsically, or as a means to something else that is of value. Value, on this account, was either instrumental or intrinsic. If nothing had intrinsic value, nothing could have value at all. So the search was on for the sorts of thing that had intrinsic value. How are we to tell whether something has intrinsic value, then? The answer is that we apply a sort of isolation test. We ask whether that thing would retain its value if it were the only thing in the universe. Applying this test, Moore announced that personal affection and aesthetic appreciation had far greater intrinsic value than anything else; indeed, they may be the only bearers of intrinsic value (1903: 188). Pretty well everything else that has any value at all—all good actions, for instance—has it because it stands as a means to one of these two.

Moore's views were almost entirely wrong, and few people nowadays defend them in their original form. There are six issues that I need to raise for the sake of what is to come below, in which I will be trying to present an alternative picture.

The first point is that not all non-intrinsic value is instrumental. It is possible to have value because of a relation to another valuable thing that is not the means–end relation. (It may even be possible to have value because of a non-instrumental relation to something else that either has no value or whose value is irrelevant to *this* relation.) Rae Langton (forthcoming) gives the lovely example of a wedding ring, which has value because of a symbolic relation in which it stands to something else that is valuable, namely one's marriage. The ring is clearly not a means to the marriage; one can, I suppose, imagine cases in which a ring does serve to cement a marriage, but this is not one of them. So here we seem to have found something that is not of value of itself (as we are supposing), has no instrumental value either, but still has value of some sort. It looks, then, as if Moore simply missed a significant form of value by understanding the extrinsic as the instrumental. There may, however, be more to the matter than this. The supposed simple mistake may turn out to be the sign of a more far-reaching confusion.

The second issue is whether there is such a thing as instrumental value at all. There are two angles to this question. The first is the assertion of Ross and Prichard that having value merely as a means is equivalent to having no value at all, but being a means to that which has. A thing does not become *good* just because without it we will lose something else that is good. So to have value only as an instrument is merely to be an instrument to that which is of value. Ross wrote: '[W]hatever value [the act] has independently of its motive is instrumental value, i.e., not goodness at all, but the property of producing something that is good' (1930: 133; cf. his 1939: 127).

I have some sympathy with this claim, though in order to make it we seem to have to set our faces against the buck-passing account of value. On the buck-passing account, after all, to take something to be valuable is to take it that we have reasons to protect it, promote it, etc.; and clearly, if an object *A* is the only means to another valuable object *B*, we will (take ourselves to) have reason to protect *A*, conserve it, or whatever, and this will have the immediate consequence that we will take it to be of value. So buck-passers will see no difficulty in the notion of instrumental value. The worries of Prichard and Ross stemmed, we will then say, from their tendency still to take goodness as a distinct normative property or character which some things had and others didn't; this is not a picture that the buck-passers would recommend.

But there is a different approach to this issue, which is taken by Christine Korsgaard in her paper 'Two Distinctions in Goodness' (1983). Korsgaard suggests that there is a distinction between valuing something for its own sake and valuing it as a means to something else, just as Moore said. But, she claims, there is no such thing as instrumental value; value is either intrinsic or extrinsic. As she sees things, the distinction between instrumental and non-instrumental is a distinction, not between types of value, but between ways of valuing something. To value something for its own sake is to value it, not intrinsically, but as an end; to value something for the sake of something else is to value it instrumentally. If so, it seems that Ross and Prichard are right and the buck-passers wrong. For it looks as if the buck-passers are talking about valuing, and we are admitting that there is such a thing as instrumental valuing, valuing something as a means. But we can give the buck-passers this without allowing them the conclusion to which they are committed, that there is such a thing as instrumental value.

I leave this issue here for the while, and turn to the third one that I want to raise. Many writers have supposed that Moore's isolation test for intrinsic value cannot be defended. The question whether an instance of aesthetic appreciation would still have value if it were the only thing in the universe is just too bizarre to stand as an appropriate test. Further, we may say, many things that could not stand alone as the sole inhabitants of the universe can have intrinsic value, such as a happy marriage. Marriage is a social institution, and requires a social setting—quite a specific setting, in fact. This fact does nothing to show that marriages can only have extrinsic value—let alone that they only have instrumental value, of course. Generally, then, total abstraction from any possible setting is not the way to determine what sort of value we are dealing with.

There are, however, other forms of the isolation test than Moore's, and these may not be so easily seen off. The point that some valuable objects can only exist in a social context will remain important, I think, but there are at least less bizarre forms of loneliness test, as one might put it, than Moore's. Noah Lemos suggests the following:

> p has intrinsic value iff p is intrinsically worthy of love, that is, iff p is necessarily such that the contemplation of just p by x requires that x love p and not hate p. (1994: 12)[1]

He calls his approach 'intentionally isolationist', since the isolation is in intention rather than in supposed reality. My own view about this is that it requires a rather more detailed account of what is included in and excluded by the notion of 'the contemplation of just p'. Berkeleian worries about abstraction seem appropriate in this connection.

The fourth issue is how to place Lloyd Humberstone's distinction (1996) between the question whether a property is itself intrinsic and the question whether something has that property intrinsically or extrinsically. The idea here is that an extrinsic property, such as that of being in the same room as Prince Charles, can be had intrinsically. Prince Charles is, however, the only person who has it intrinsically; everyone else has it extrinsically. Value, then, or being valuable, might be an intrinsic property that can be had extrinsically. If this distinction is sound, we need two criteria, not just one. We need one for the distinction between intrinsic and extrinsic properties, and one for the distinction between having a property intrinsically and having it extrinsically. While waiting for the arrival of such criteria, we might start out by supposing that neutral value, that is, value as traditionally conceived, is intrinsic, while agent-relative value (should there be any such) is extrinsic. Something that has instrumental neutral value has an intrinsic property extrinsically; but there can be instrumental agent-relative value, and this will be an extrinsic property held extrinsically.

Langton and Lewis (1998) propose a non-intentionalist variant of Moore's isolation test, under which a basic intrinsic property is one that is *independent* of isolation and accompaniment, where this means that something can (1) have that property and be isolated, (2) have it and be accompanied, (3) lack it and be isolated, and (4) lack it and be accompanied. Is this an account of what it is for a property to be intrinsic, or of what it is to have a property intrinsically? It looks as if it is the former; agent-relative value would fail this

---

[1] Lemos intends p here to stand for a state of affairs rather than for a concrete object, which gives me some difficulty, since I am much more used to loving and hating individuals than I am to loving and hating the state of affairs of their existing. His view about states of affairs and indeed his version of the loneliness test are both taken from Chisholm (1976 and 1981, respectively).

test, but neutral value would pass it. *Being valuable* is a property that a thing can have and lack whether it is isolated or accompanied. We would then want to know what it is to have that intrinsic property intrinsically. Given Humberstone's distinction, that is the question that is my main focus in this chapter. Two answers suggest themselves. The first is that something's value is intrinsic (in the sense that the thing that has that value has it intrinsically) when that value is grounded in intrinsic properties. The second is that a value is intrinsic when it is grounded in properties held intrinsically.

The fifth issue I want to raise is whether intrinsic value is essential value. Moore certainly supposes so:

> The part of a valuable whole retains exactly the same value when it is, as when it is not, a part of that whole ... We are not then justified in asserting that one and the same thing is under some circumstances intrinsically good, and under others not so. (1903: 30)

Lemos calls this the Thesis of Universality, and he defends it. But it seems to me to be ambiguous. The matter turns on whether an object is capable of changing in respect of its intrinsic properties. I would have thought that there is absolutely no reason to deny this possibility; shape is intrinsic, and objects change their shape often enough. If so, objects that retain their intrinsic properties might be expected to retain their intrinsic value (though I will shortly deny even this), but where their intrinsic properties change, their intrinsic value may perfectly well change accordingly.[2] Moore writes elsewhere:

> [I]t is impossible for what is strictly one and the same thing to possess that kind of value at one time, or in one set of circumstances, and not to possess it at another; and equally impossible for it to possess it in one degree at one time, or in one set of circumstances, and to possess it in a different degree at another, or in a different set. (1922: 260–1)

One may presume that the word 'strictly' here is doing a lot of work. Moore held, as we have seen, that value is a consequential property, that is, that a valuable object is valuable because of other features that it has. If so, he may not be meaning to suggest that an object is literally incapable of altering in respect of its intrinsic value, but only to say that so long as it retains its 'basic' intrinsic properties, and in that sense remains 'strictly one and the same thing', it must retain the original intrinsic value. This amounts to saying that if the ground for intrinsic value remains the same, the same intrinsic value must result, which sounds sensible enough (though I will, as I say, shortly deny it). If we do not understand Moore as saying this, then surely what he

---

[2] Of course all this talk of objects changing in respect of their intrinsic qualities may not really get a grip on Lemos's picture, since he thinks of the bearers of value as states of affairs, and it is not clear that a state of affairs can change, in the relevant sense—if there is a change we get a new state of affairs, not the old one in a different form. In the text I am assuming that we can perfectly well suppose that things other than states of affairs are good and bad—such as people, for instance.

says is false.[3] And whatever he is saying, it looks as if he is committed to the view that an object that changes its shape is no longer 'one and the same thing' that it was before.

Finally, what is the relation between valuing something for its own sake and taking it to have intrinsic value? Korsgaard seems to suggest that these are very different, for she maintains that the 'for its own sake' locution is properly contrasted with the instrumental, both being forms of valuing, and that the intrinsic is properly contrasted with the extrinsic, both being forms of value. Taking something to have intrinsic value looks, however, like a form of valuing. Is it possible, then, to value something for its own sake but not to take it to have intrinsic value, or vice versa? This question is worth asking partly because of claims made by James Wallace in his *Moral Relevance and Moral Conflict*. He inveighs very soundly against Moore's isolation test, and then writes:

Economic theory *is* intrinsically interesting ... [but] it is interesting because it illuminates an extremely important dimension of human social behavior, because it is an application of certain sorts of theorizing to such social phenomena, because it can exemplify certain qualities that are excellences in theories ... and, no doubt, for other reasons too. (1988: 112)

The idea here is that this sort of value is intrinsic value but that it is a value that economics has not for its own sake but because of relations in which it stands to other things—as Wallace puts it, 'because of its place in human life generally' (p. 111). Someone who finds economics important (and Wallace is really more concerned with the important than with the valuable) will take it to have intrinsic value, as I think Wallace is suggesting, but will not be valuing it for its own sake, and will not be supposing that it has value 'in itself'. Indeed, he suggests that to value economics for its own sake or in itself would be 'most eccentric ... the furthest thing imaginable from a deep appreciation of the value of economic theory' (p. 113).

I have, then, raised six issues, by way of setting the scene:

1. Is there non-instrumental extrinsic value?
2. Is so-called instrumental value a form of value?
3. Can any form of the isolation test be defended? If not, what is the criterion of the intrinsic?

---

[3] Moore does seem at one point to commit himself to a general identification of the intrinsic with the essential. He writes: 'I personally find the taste of caviare pleasant; but I believe that some people do not find it pleasant; and I see no reason to suppose that an experience of mine, which was a tasting of caviare, might not be exactly like an experience of another person, which was a tasting of caviare, and that yet my experience might be pleasant to me, while his exactly similar experience was not pleasant to him. If so, then the property which I assert to belong to my experience when I say that it is pleasant, cannot be an intrinsic property of that experience; and it seems to me that one of the properties which we frequently are ascribing to an experience, when we say that it was pleasant, is, as in this case, a purely external property—a property which it is quite conceivable that that experience should not have had' (1942: 588).

4. How are we to handle the distinction between a property's being intrinsic and being had intrinsically?
5. Is intrinsic value essential value?
6. What is the relation between valuing something for its own sake and taking it to have intrinsic value?

2. INTRINSIC VALUE FOR HOLISTS

I now want to lay out my own conception of intrinsic value. In what follows, the phrase 'intrinsic value' is to be understood as meaning 'value had intrinsically'; I allow that being valuable is an intrinsic property; my question is what it is for something to have that property intrinsically. I start from the thought that value is (always assuming it to be a property at all) a consequential or resultant property. This gives us the distinction between the value of an object and the ground[4] for that value—the features in virtue of which the thing is good, the ones that 'make it' good. It also gives us the distinction between the ground for value and enabling features, those required for the ground to be able to play its grounding role, but which are not playing that role themselves. The idea of an enabler has application right across the domain of the normative, and so applies to value as much as to reasons. (We will see some examples shortly.)

    Given that value, or goodness, is a grounded or resultant property, it seems reasonable to understand intrinsic value as value that is grounded in a distinctive way. And the obvious way for a value to be grounded if it is to count as intrinsic is for it to be grounded in intrinsic properties of the value-bearer and in them alone. There are of course various forms of non-intrinsic value. Value can be grounded in non-intrinsic properties of the valuable thing, and I see no reason to deny that it can be grounded in properties of other things, in relations to other things, and even in the values of other things to which the value-bearer is related. But intrinsic value is special.

    This account requires us to offer a criterion of an intrinsic property (that is, in the present context, a property that is had intrinsically). In the previous section we saw two possible ways of understanding value had intrinsically: either as value grounded entirely in properties of the value-bearer that are intrinsic or as value grounded entirely in properties that the value-bearer has intrinsically. Properties that an object has intrinsically are either properties that are not themselves resultant properties (and so have no ground) or are

---

[4] I will use the term 'ground' in what follows to refer to what plays the role in the theory of value that is played by favourers in the theory of reasons; I do this because it is hard to think of the features that make something good as favouring that thing, exactly. There is nothing in the theory of value very like the favouring relation that holds between reasons and action. But I don't mean to deny that there is good-making as well as right-making.

grounded entirely in properties that the object has intrinsically. A property that an object has intrinsically is thus one that is, as we might put it, eventually grounded in ungrounded properties of that object. This requires, of course, that there are no ungrounded properties had extrinsically.

But if this picture is defensible, it follows immediately that intrinsic value, despite being special, can vary even when the ground for that value remains fixed. Where there are grounds, there may well be enablers, and the enablers for intrinsic value can perfectly well be extrinsic features of the valuable object, or even features of other things. Intrinsic value, on my account, counts as intrinsic because of the nature of its ground; it need not, for that reason, be utterly insensitive to variations elsewhere. So intrinsic value, as I see it, is variable. It is not merely that it is not essential; it is not even persistent. What is more, even value that is grounded in essential properties can vary, as I see things; like any other value, it will vanish if enabling conditions fail or disabling conditions obtain.

How important is it that there should be intrinsic value? Would it be possible for there to be value if there is no intrinsic value? Moore, as we saw, says not. But on my account it is perfectly possible. Since that which has extrinsic value is not in general to be understood as that which is a means to a valuable end, nothing throws us back from the notion of extrinsic value to that of intrinsic value.

Korsgaard offers an argument to the effect that if there is to be conditioned value, there must be unconditioned value (1996: 259). And this looks like an argument that there must be intrinsic value for there to be extrinsic value, an argument that is of the same basic structure as the argument that if there is to be instrumental value, there must be non-instrumental value. The argument is that to 'justify' a conditioned good, we must pass through conditioned goods to an unconditioned one before our justification can be termed complete, that is, if it is no longer to rest on something conditioned whose condition has not been shown to be present. Conditioned value is value which obtains only under a certain condition, a condition other than the presence of the ground for that value. As far as that goes, I applaud; in my terms, we are here thinking of value for which there are enabling conditions as well as ground. But there is absolutely no need to go on to suppose that the condition for a good must itself be a good, and so long as we do not make this mistake Korsgaard's regress cannot even get started. Suppose, for instance, that object A is good only under condition C. Must the obtaining of condition C itself have value? If it *must*, this value will only be a value because it is required for the value of A. It is not that the value of A is somehow dependent on the value of C—things are the other way around. The value of A is only dependent on its being the case that C, not on C's being valuable, and this generates no threatening regress from conditioned to unconditioned value. So Korsgaard's argument fails.

Let us now consider some potential examples of the various categories made available by this account of the intrinsic and its relation to extrinsic. The most

interesting category is that of intrinsic value which has an extrinsic enabling
condition and so is capable of failing even though its intrinsic ground persists.
It is harder than one would expect to find effective examples of this; the one
that follows adapts a suggestion that I owe to Frances Kamm. Remember that
enablers are supposed to enable an already existing feature to have a certain
value. We are looking for examples where what is enabled is not the presence of
the valuable feature, but the value of a present feature. (This is why it can be
misleading to think of enabling conditions merely as necessary conditions for
value; the notion of a necessary condition is too indiscriminate.) There are
some jokes about people that it would be cruel to tell in their presence, but
delightful to tell in their absence. In these cases, I would think, their presence is
part of the ground for the cruelty; it is part of what makes telling the joke cruel
rather than delightful. So here we are not dealing with enablers at all. But there
are other jokes which are only amusing if their butt is present, and which, in
that case, are amusing to everyone present, to the butt as much as to everyone
else; if the butt of the joke were not there, that would take all the fun away. But
that the butt of the joke is present is not part of what makes the joke funny. It is
a feature in the absence of which the joke would lose its humour. Humour is
a value, or of value. So what we have here is an enabling condition for a value.
And the value is intrinsic, but the enabling condition is extrinsic, since it is
not an intrinsic feature of the humour that the butt of the joke is present.

Before turning to extrinsic value, we should perhaps ask whether there is
any unconditioned intrinsic value. In my terms, this means whether there is
any intrinsic value for which there are no enabling or disabling conditions. It
is no part of my brief to argue either that such a thing actually occurs or that
no such thing is possible, though a broadly holistic approach to value should
lead one to doubt any proposed candidate. My general line, then, is just that
no good candidate suggests itself to me. I am not persuaded, for instance, that
pleasure or, more generally, prosperity are goods independent of context.

Consider, in this connection, the views of Lemos, who defends what he
calls the *thesis of universality*:

any part of a valuable whole retains exactly the same intrinsic value when it is, as
when it is not, a part of that whole. (1994: 40–1)

He defines *intrinsic value* thus:

p (a state of affairs) has intrinsic value iff it is intrinsically worthy of love = the
contemplation of just p by x requires that x love p and not hate p. (Ibid. 15)

The defence of the thesis of universality is run by appeal to two main
examples: pleasure at an evil e.g. the pain of another, or one's own wickedness,
and the prospering of the wicked. Take the latter first. Let us consider
this in the light of the essential link between reasons and values. We will allow
no value that is not essentially linked to reasons. We start by expounding
various theses which we wish to preserve in our analysis. First, we have

sufficient reason to prevent the wicked from prospering and no reason to promote their prosperity, and so the prosperity of the wicked is not a good (because of the link between reasons and values). Second, prosperity is 'unfitting' to the wicked, which is to say that it is wrong that they should prosper (by definition of what it is for something to be in this sense unfitting). Third, that it is not good that the wicked should prosper does not show that their prosperity is not a good *for them*. So, fourth, it is possible that though their prosperity is a good for them, it is not good that they should prosper. This conclusion fits the pattern of the reasons. For they may have sufficient reason to preserve their prosperity, though we have no reason to do so, having indeed sufficient reason to prevent them from prospering—which is where we started.

We cannot hope to argue here that prosperity is not a good for the wicked. For we can define what is to count as prospering for the purposes of the argument simply in terms of something that is *allowed* as a good for the wicked. There must be some such thing, e.g. health or comfort. Health is a more tricky one, because it is not clear that we have reason to prevent the health of the wicked. Let us allow, then, that comfort is a good for the wicked, so that they prosper to the extent that they are comfortable. We are saying that their comfort is something which *they* may have sufficient reason to preserve, but that *we* have no reason to do so; indeed, we have sufficient reason to prevent it where we can.

What does this have to say to Lemos's main argument? The argument is that if we claim that it is not good that the wicked should prosper, we presuppose that their prosperity is a good—for otherwise their having it would not be inappropriate to their being wicked. We are allowing this, but only in terms of the distinction between what is a good for them and what is good. In terms of this distinction, that they should prosper is a good for them, but not good. It is not good that they should have this thing that is a good for them.

Is this an admission that Lemos is overall right—that we are dealing here with an instance of the thesis of universality? For him, what we have is their prospering, which is good, and their wickedness, which is bad, and the whole of which these are the parts, which is bad. (This is a Moorean organic unity; I reserve discussion of such things until the next chapter.) For us, we have their prospering, which is good for them but not good given that they are wicked, and their wickedness which is bad. Since our position seems plainly coherent, there is no argument here in favour of the thesis of universality. Further, only our position is capable of respecting the link between values and reasons.[5]

So I turn to the other sort of example, that of pleasure at the pain of another. Lemos writes:

If Brentano and Ross are right, we may say that the property of *being pleased that someone is suffering* is not an intrinsically good-making property, that is, the fact that

---

[5] I owe at least part of this argument to Brad Hooker.

something has it is not intrinsically good. But if *being pleased that someone is suffering* is not an intrinsically good-making property, it hardly follows that the property of *being pleased* is not or that it is only a prima facie good-making property. These are, after all, distinct properties, since someone can have the latter without having the former. Similarly, if the fact that *someone's being pleased that someone is suffering* is not intrinsically good, it follows that some pleasures are not intrinsically good ... But we cannot infer from these claims that *someone's being pleased* is not intrinsically good or that it is only prima facie good. ... It is simply mistaken to infer from the fact that some pleasures ... are not intrinsically good the conclusion that *someone's being pleased* is intrinsically good in some contexts and not in others, or that the property *being pleased* is not an intrinsically good-making property. (1994: 46–7)

What is going on here? Lemos's position is driven by his conception of intrinsic value, perfectly properly. That conception, however, is disputable. It rests on the notion of 'the contemplation of just *p*'—a notion that Lemos took, like much else, from Chisholm. Applying this to the example in hand, where someone is pleased that someone else is suffering, we can, if we like, contemplate merely the pleasure, and we can contemplate the more complex state of affairs which includes what they are pleased about. Understanding the intrinsic in this way, it seems to me, we have no real reason to dispute that the mere fact that they are pleased is of intrinsic value. But by my lights this is a merely paper victory for Lemos. There is no reason for anyone to deny that if one contemplates merely the part of the whole without consideration of larger contexts in which it might be placed, one would always think of that part as having the same value; there would be nothing to cause one's assessment of value to vary. But the question whether it is of intrinsic value here is not the same question as whether if we contemplated it alone we would take it to be of value (or love it, in Lemos's terminology). The whole point of the organic, in the eyes of those antagonistic to Moore's position, is that to isolate something for contemplation is exactly to consider it out of relation to its present context. But to show that if we were to consider it out of any relation to its context we would always ascribe to it the same value does nothing at all to show that it has that value in any context in which it appears. Lemos has been misled by his 'isolation in intension' test for intrinsic value.[6]

Let us now turn to extrinsic value. This sort of value is value grounded at least partly in the existence and/or nature of other things than that which has the value. The obvious examples are those of rarity and originality. An original suggestion has merit partly because it has not been made before, which I take to be an extrinsic feature. Something that has the value of rarity has its value partly because of the relative absence of other similar objects.

---

[6] Quite apart from this, one could argue that someone's being pleased should not be understood as a part of someone's being pleased that someone else is suffering. But that argument would get embroiled with Lemos's peculiar understanding of the part/whole relation, and it is better to keep out of that.

Can there be extrinsic value grounded at least partly in the value of other things, rather than just in their existence and 'nature'? I can see no reason why not. Someone does me a favour and I repay it in kind. Part of the ground for the value of my action seems to be that they did me a good turn, and that I am doing the same for them in gratitude. This is apparently a case of extrinsic but not yet instrumental value. An example of something grounded in an instrumental relation to other goods might be effective brakes for one's car.

Finally, I consider the relation between valuing an object for its own sake and supposing that it has intrinsic value. I think that Korsgaard is right to claim that one can value an object for its own sake and yet suppose that its value is entirely extrinsic. This is because an extrinsic feature of an object is still a feature of that object; its extrinsicness does not mean that it is a feature of some other object instead. When I value an object for its own sake, the features for which I value it need not, therefore, be intrinsic. An example here might be Wallace's example of valuing economics; but Wallace took it that to value economics for its extrinsic features is exactly not to value it for its own sake.

There is an issue here about how to handle the 'for its own sake' locution. Langton (forthcoming) argues that we have three categories: what is valued for its own sake, what is valued for the sake of something else, and what is valued as a means to something else. I would rather have two categories: what is valued for its own sake, and what is valued but not (wholly) for its own sake. The latter category might have more than two sub-categories. It might be that an object is valued partly because of some relation in which it stands to another object, but not valued either for the sake of that other thing, or as a means to it. The 'for the sake of' locution seems to suggest that the 'other thing' must be conceived to be of value, as it certainly is in the means–end case; and there seems to be no reason why it should always be necessary for this to be so. We have already seen a non-instrumental case of a relation to an object of value: Rae Langton's wedding ring. What is needed is a non-instrumental relation to a second object whose value, if it has any, is irrelevant to the value of the first. In the Vatican in Rome there is a display of the smallest and the largest books in the Vatican Library. We might say that we value the largest book for being the largest. Its being the largest is an extrinsic feature. Are we valuing it for its own sake or for the sake of something else, or neither? I would say, first, that we are not valuing it for the sake of those other things; the value, if any, of the other smaller books is irrelevant to the way in which the relation between the biggest and all the rest can give the biggest one the rather peculiar value it has got. Are we valuing it for its own sake? I suspect at this point that there needs to be no determinate answer. We are valuing the huge book for its size, sure enough. But the value we are dealing with here is more to do with comparative size than absolute size (in a totally relative sense of the comparative/absolute distinction). It may then be that we are valuing it for a relation in which it stands to certain other things, and this suggests that there are indeed valuable things that are neither valuable for their own sake nor for the sake of something else.

10

Are there Organic Unities?

1. ORGANIC UNITIES: HOLISM IN THE THEORY OF VALUE

In the previous chapter I developed a conception of intrinsic value under which the intrinsic value of an object can vary according to context, even where the intrinsic ground for that value remains unchanged. This was in the service of a broadly holistic conception of value, to go with the holistic conception of reasons on which, in the moral sphere, ethical holism depends. I now turn to consider Moore's theory of organic unities: organic unities are those 'wholes' whose value may be either more or less than the sum of the values of their parts. One would think that holists should view Moore as a friend in an unfriendly world. His conception of organic unities seems to be pretty well just what holism has been suggesting in the theory of reasons. But this is an illusion. Even Moore's claim that the value of the whole is not necessarily identical with the sum of the values of the parts is not holistic, because it implicitly allows that the parts cannot change their value as they move from whole to whole. At least, it allows this for intrinsic value. Moore would of course allow that what he calls 'extrinsic value', by which he means only instrumental value, can vary according to circumstances. But he insists that a part retains its intrinsic value as it moves from whole to whole. So his theory of organic unities combines two claims:

1. Parts retain their intrinsic value regardless of variations in the context.
2. Parts may contribute either more or less value to a whole than they themselves have there.

The argument for (1) consists not in an investigation of actual examples, but in an appeal to supervenience. The intrinsic value of the part supervenes on the intrinsic properties of the part, and these, we are to suppose, do not change as the part moves from whole to whole. If so, Moore argues, the same intrinsic value must be present wherever the part is to be found. As far as (1) goes, then, Moore's position might be called invariabilist. The variabilist bit, to the extent that there is one at all, is (2). Moore is committed to (2) because he thinks it possible for the value of the whole to differ from the sum of the values of its various parts. This, together with his acceptance of (1), drives him to say that a part can contribute to the whole either more or less value than it has there.

If one wants, one can avoid this talk of the part 'contributing' value to the whole, which I use partly because it reminds one of talk of contributory reasons. The point can be made in terms of an asymmetry of explanation. The whole can, say, be more valuable than it would otherwise have been in a way that is to be explained by appeal to the presence of the part, but *not* by appeal to the value of the part. If you look at the value of the part, you might easily be misled as to the value that it contributes to the whole.

Now I think we should be wary of the idea that a part can contribute to a whole more value than it has actually got *there*. This idea may not appear incoherent immediately, but I think that it cannot be sustained—at least, not within the context of Moore's overall position. For within the terms of that position, such a claim severs the necessary connection between value and reasons. When I say it 'severs the necessary connection between values and reasons', I am going to have to speak cautiously, because there are various conceptions of that connection, and the point that I want to make is intended not to depend on any particular one of them. The general idea is that where there is value, there are reasons of certain sorts—reasons to protect, promote, cherish, respect, tend, approve, defend, and so on. So to say that a part with no value can contribute value that it has not got commits one to saying, it seems, that though there is no reason to preserve the part as a part, there is a reason to protect the whole; and that reason derives from the presence of the part. Now this does sound incoherent. Surely we do have reason to protect the part *here*, if it is contributing value. So its presence is of value, it would seem, on pain of breaching the link between values and reasons.

This point does not depend on, though it is congenial to, the buck-passing conception of value. On this conception, as we have seen, to be of value is to have reason-giving features (and vice versa). The nature of the part does give us reason to protect its presence here, and this is just what it is for the part to be of value here, on the buck-passing view. But that view is not the only alternative on offer; a slightly different view would have it that wherever there is value there are reasons, but that to be of value is not itself to have reason-giving features. This view need not be thinking in epiphenomenal terms, but simply in terms of a necessary co-presence. And the point here is that even on this weaker view the argument of the previous paragraph seems sound. It would only be undermined by a position that maintained that there need be no connection between values and reasons.

If Moore's position is unsound in this way, why did he adopt it? The position rests on two claims, both of which I take to be mistaken: a *local* doctrine of supervenience for intrinsic value, and the claim that all non-intrinsic value is instrumental. Both of these claims are made in the following passage concerning the relation between an arm and its body:

Thus we may easily come to say that, *as* a part of the body [the arm] has great value, whereas *by itself* it would have none... But in fact the value in question obviously does not belong to *it* at all. To have value merely as a part is equivalent to having no value at all, but merely being a part of that which has it. Owing, however, to neglect of this distinction, the assertion that a part has value, *as a part*, which it would otherwise not have, easily leads to the assumption that it is also different, as a part, from what it would otherwise be; for it is, in fact, true that two things which have a different value must also differ in other respects. Hence the assumption that one and the same thing, because it is a part of a more valuable whole at one time than at another, therefore has more intrinsic value at one time than at another, has encouraged the self-contradictory belief that one and the same thing may be two different things, and that only in one of its forms is it truly what it is. (Moore 1903: 35)

The argument here, as far as supervenience goes, is that if you allow a part more intrinsic value in one context (whole) than in another, while retaining its intrinsic nature, you are committed to the claim that an object can change its value without changing in other respects, and this involves denying the supervenience of value. It is this notion of supervenience that is at the bottom of Moore's invariabilist claim that parts retain their intrinsic value regardless of variations in the context.[1]

What is at issue here is the proper conception of supervenience. Moore's version is a sort of local supervenience: that an object cannot change in intrinsic value unless it changes in other respects. There is, however, a more global conception of supervenience: that an object cannot change in intrinsic value unless there are other changes somewhere, without these needing to be changes in *that* object. How are we to decide between these two conceptions? I think that Moore's commitment to the first is to be explained by his failure to distinguish two quite different relations, that of resultance and that of supervenience. Here I briefly rehearse considerations which should now be familiar. The resultance relation relates a value to its ground—to the features that generate that value. The supervenience relation relates a value to something far more extensive than the ground for that value. The subvenient *base*, as it is usually called, contains all the features that diminish the value as well as those that add to it, and it contains also every other feature (of the value-bearer, but perhaps also of other things) that can in any circumstances make a difference to the ability of the features in the resultance base (i.e. the features that act as ground for the value) to play their special role.

I argued in the previous chapter that, once we see the distinction between these two relations, we see that there is room for an object to change in intrinsic value even if intrinsic value is grounded in intrinsic features of that object and

---

[1] Though the argument is phrased in terms of parts and wholes, it is not restricted to that context. We could run the same argument in terms of objects in their context, in a way that increases in scope as we widen and weaken the notion of a context. The widest and weakest notion of a context is just that of the object's world.

the object remains unchanged in respect of those intrinsic features. For the *ground* of value does not contain every 'relevant' feature; there are other forms of relevance than being a ground. There may be other features, not themselves intrinsic to the object concerned, but which are required if the intrinsic ground is to be able to generate the relevant intrinsic value. These further features may not even be features of the object concerned. A change in those further 'enabling' conditions will be able to affect the intrinsic value of the object without necessarily altering the intrinsic features that ground that value.

This means that intrinsic value is not essential value, for two reasons. The first is that intrinsic properties need not be essential properties; this is true anyway, irrespective of the present matter, and I mention it only to ensure that it is on the table. The second is that an object can remain intrinsically the same while its intrinsic value changes. The intrinsic value of an object is thus capable of being affected by context. This generates a conception of intrinsic value that is available to the holist and thereby to particularism. And it also undermines Moore's argument for his invariabilist claim that the intrinsic value of the part must remain unchanged as it moves from one whole to another; that argument rests on an over-narrow conception of supervenience. So we have now rejected that invariabilist claim and rejected the argument for it.

But there is more explanation to be done. We have not yet considered the possibility of value that is neither intrinsic nor instrumental. It is by ruling this possibility out that Moore's position becomes vulnerable to the complaint that it breaches the necessary connection between values and reasons. For otherwise Moore could perfectly well say that a contributing feature will, in virtue of its contribution to the whole (a non-intrinsic matter), have a form of value that we can think of as extrinsic. What is at issue here is his assertion that to have value merely as a part 'is equivalent to having no value at all, but merely being a part of that which has it'. (Note that this assertion is a perfect analogue of Ross's claim against the concept of instrumental value, that to have value merely as a means is equivalent to having no value at all, but merely being a means to that which has it.)

Re-reading the long quotation from *Principia Ethica*, printed on the opposite page, one might well wonder whether I have really got Moore right on this point. Is it true that he denies the possibility of value that is neither intrinsic nor instrumental? We have now come across two types of value of that sort: symbolic value, that of a wedding ring, and value as a part, which is what is involved in organic unities—as I understand them, at least. There may be others, too. Now the final sentence in that quotation is explicitly about *intrinsic* value. We might therefore suppose that the crucial earlier sentence, the one that claims that to have value merely as a part is equivalent to having no value at all, is implicitly intended only to concern intrinsic value. If it were, Moore would be denying that a feature's intrinsic value can be affected as it moves from whole to whole. I might point out, in defence of my way of reading this passage, that the language here and in the next sentence is pretty trenchant. More effective, however, is the fact that nowhere in *Principia Ethica* does Moore ever suggest that features can change their value (other than their instrumental value, of course). He is always careful to avoid such remarks and to say that the whole is more valuable for the presence of the part.[2]

It may be that Moore's antagonism to extrinsic value is itself partly to be explained by appeal to his conception of supervenience, which we have already rejected. But if it is not, there seems to be nothing else to hold it in place. And its loss is significant, because it will deprive Moore of the claim that underpins the entire structure of *Principia Ethica*, that unless something has intrinsic value nothing has any value at all. For it could perfectly well be that all value is extrinsic, so long as some of that extrinsic value is non-instrumental value.

The distinction between intrinsic and extrinsic value is to be run, according to me, in terms of the relevant grounds (the difference between two styles of resultance base). Extrinsic value is value that is partly grounded in extrinsic features of the valuable object, or else grounded in features of other objects, or else grounded in relations between the valuable object and others. A book can become more valuable if the only other extant copy is burnt. The value that is increased is neither intrinsic nor instrumental.

Once we accept a notion of extrinsic value, we are in a position to respect the necessary connection between reasons and values and hold that a part cannot contribute value that it has not got. If a part contributes value, it must have at least as much value *as a part* as it contributes. To put the point in terms of explanation rather than of contribution, if a part is an element in the ground for the value of the whole, rather than playing some other role, perhaps as an enabling condition, the value of the whole must be explained partly by appeal to the value of the part, not merely by appeal to its presence. Note that to say this is not to say that every part of a valuable whole must contribute to that value. There may be parts that are required for the whole to exist—to come together, as it were—but which do not contribute any value to the whole. As such, they stand as enabling conditions for the value of the whole; and as such, they are of value (because we have reason to protect them). But that value is not contributed to the value of the whole. So, we might say, every necessary part of a valuable whole will be of value, though not all such parts contribute their value (or all their value) to the value of the whole.

In the previous paragraph, I said that if a part is an element in the ground for the value of the whole, rather than playing some other role, perhaps as an enabling condition, the value of the whole must be explained partly by appeal to the value of the part, not merely by appeal to its presence. Should we take

---

[2] See §§18 (last paragraph), 55, 57, 117, 119, 121, 122 (second paragraph).

the distinction between grounds and enabling conditions to be at odds with this claim? Could we not say that a part that has no value can be a vital enabling condition, making it possible for other valuable features to be the ground of the value of the whole?[3] The point here is that even if those enabling conditions contribute to the explanation of the value of the whole, they do not do so by way of contributing to that value in the way that the grounding features do. Still, the features that enable the ground to function as such can surely be expected to be of value in this context, because they play a positive role in the construction of value, and we therefore have obvious reasons to preserve them etc. It remains true that no feature contributes to the whole any value that it has not got in that context. But it is also true that some features that have value in that context do not contribute that value to the value of the whole. Their value cannot be put towards the value of the whole. In that sense, the value of the whole is not identical to the sum of the values of all the parts. But the value of the whole is identical to the sum of the values of the contributing parts, as we might put it. Any part, then, that contributes value must have that value to contribute; but some valuable parts do not contribute their value to the whole, even though their presence is necessary for the whole to have the value it does.

In fact, the idea of uncontributed value has other applications than this. A feature can have intrinsic value which it does not contribute to every 'whole' of which it is a part. Suppose that Geoffrey has value as a husband, as a father, and as a colleague. He will probably contribute the latter value to the value of his department, but not to that of his family—and vice versa. The diamonds on a simple dress may be intrinsically valuable (let us suppose), but they may also make things worse; the main charm of the dress is its simplicity, and the diamonds don't fit. This possibility, I think, disposes of a worry raised by Philip Stratton-Lake (2000: 129–30). He argues that the idea of a feature that is of intrinsic value making the whole worse by its presence is incoherent. 'It cannot be sustained', he says, 'because it cuts off intrinsic value from any reason-giving relation.' This seems wrong to me. Stratton-Lake is thinking that the fact that the diamonds are of intrinsic value should show that we have some reason to welcome and protect them (i.e. keep them on the dress) even though their presence makes things worse. But there cannot be a reason to keep in place something whose presence makes things worse. And if there is no such reason, the intrinsic value of the diamonds is shorn of its normal link with reasons—just the sort of worry I am dealing with. The reply to this is that the intrinsic value does indeed give us reasons to protect and preserve the diamonds whose presence makes things worse; it is only that we do not have reasons to keep them on the dress, and we do have independent reasons

---

[3] This question is relevant to the buck-passing debate. Intuitively, one would have thought that some classic enabling conditions for value are themselves absolutely valueless. For instance, that I am able to choose not to do this action is a feature that enables my doing it to have value that otherwise it would not have had, though my having that ability seems to be absolutely valueless.

to take them off it, since the dress becomes more valuable when we do. So in a case where something of intrinsic value makes matters worse by its presence, what we should do is to preserve it, but remove it from the present context.

We can check the overall picture that is emerging here by asking whether it avoids what are sometimes called 'share of the total' problems. Suppose, rather unrealistically, that we have ten equally contributing parts, each of which is necessary for the others to contribute. How is this contributed value to be distributed among the parts? We do not want the sum of the value we find in the parts to be greater than the value contributed to the whole, any more than we would wish, where ten people contribute to saving a hundred refugees on a sinking boat, to credit each of them with more than a tenth of the total. But in our imaginary case, the reasons we have to protect each part are as strong as if that part contributed all the value, apparently leaving nothing for the other contributing parts to do. For the loss of any one part means the loss of all the value. This seems to mean that there is too much value floating around, with each part being worth as much as the whole. But that is a mistake, and the distinction between enabling conditions and contributing parts is capable of exposing what is wrong. Our view is that nothing can contribute value that it has not got, but that parts may have value which they do not contribute to the value of the whole (like the diamonds on a dress that make no contribution to its value, which derives entirely from its simplicity). Now even though each part is such that, without it, all the value would be lost, this does not mean that each contributes all the value. No: the loss of any one part means that all the other parts lose value, and the value lost is divided equally between them, according to their equal contribution. There is nothing here to show that each part is as valuable as the whole.[4]

There is, however, a further objection to our picture. Surely we should distinguish, for each organic whole, between the parts and the 'arrangement' of the parts. We need not go so far as to maintain (in broad agreement with metaphysical idealists) that the parts of this whole *could* not be present elsewhere, in a different context. Now once we have drawn this distinction, we can allow that the arrangement of the parts makes its own contribution to the value of the whole, and in this way say that the sum of the values of the contributing parts need not be identical with the value of the whole, while still holding that features cannot contribute value that they have not got. In terms of explanation, part of the explanation of the value of the whole runs by appeal to the way in which the parts are arranged, configured, here. We should not, on pain of a regress, think of the arrangement of the parts as itself a part—for otherwise the now increased set of parts will need a new 'arrangement' and so on ad infinitum. So the arrangement is not itself a part. But it can affect the value of the whole in such a way that the value of the whole need not be identical with the sum of the values of the parts. All that we

---

[4] Thanks to Don Garrett and Geoff Sayre-McCord here.

have, now, is that the value of the whole must be the sum of the values of the contributors, whether those be parts or 'arrangement'.

There is a reply. The new suggestion returns us to an account under which a part can contribute value that it has not got, and thus to a breach of the link between reasons and values. Suppose, for the purposes of illustration alone (and we should be wary of all this talk of parts and wholes anyway, which seems to me to apply to jigsaw puzzles much better than it does to morally testing situations and actions), that all the parts but one are in place, and we add the final part. (This might be the last chapter of a book, for example—should I ever get that far.) In doing so, we put an 'arrangement' in place, and we are currently supposing that the arrangement itself makes a contribution to value that is beyond that which is contributed by any part. So our idea is that by adding the part, we effectively add the arrangement, and that in doing so we add two distinct value-contributing elements. But now remember the link between reasons and values, and consider the reasons we have to 'protect' this final part. It looks as if, where the value of the whole is awaiting the arrival of this final part, the part itself is worth protecting, not only for the value that we are supposing it itself to be contributing, but also for the value supposedly deriving from the arrangement that its presence enables. But if so, it is the more worth protecting, and this means that though the arrangement is itself a source of value, it is not an *independent* source, since all the value that it contributes sinks down to the part whose presence is the last link in the arrangement.

This reply needs adjustment in two respects. The first of these is the rather arbitrary restriction involved in talk of adding the 'final' part. The second is that we are in danger of forgetting the relevance of the distinction between contributing and enabling (or the less metaphorical distinction between two forms of explanation). We need to readjust the terms of the debate in both these respects. But when we have done so, two possibilities seem to remain. The first is that the value supposedly added by the arrangement is in fact distributed among the contributing parts. After all, the arrangement is not here to be conceived as a valuable thing of a rather abstract sort; it just is the parts so arranged. So arranged, we may suppose, they each have more value than they would have had otherwise, and this increase in value accounts for the value supposedly contributed by the arrangement. The arrangement itself, on this account, contributes no value, and so we retain the thesis that the value of the whole is identical with the sum of the values contributed by the parts. The second possibility is that though each part is indeed more valuable in the whole than it would otherwise be, since we have more reason to protect each part to the extent that it is required for the whole, that aspect of the value of each part is not itself contributed to the value of the whole, but is rather derived from the value of the arrangement, for which it functions more as an enabling condition than as a ground. On this second account, the arrangement itself, though not a part, is still a contributor.

I see no way of deciding conclusively in favour of either of these positions, though I confess to a sense of unease in the attribution of value to so abstract a thing as an arrangement. But this, of course, in no way undermines the differences between Moore's view and the one I am propounding here. They remain as follows. First, on Moore's account a part can contribute more value than it has, even in that context. On my account this is impossible. Second, Moore's account depends on a local conception of supervenience, which I reject. Third, it also involves the denial of extrinsic value *other than* instrumental value, which I also reject.

With respect to the first of these, it now appears that the holist will want to say that no feature can contribute value that it has not got, but that some features, though they have value, fail to contribute that value to the value of the whole. There is the familiar explanatory asymmetry at issue here. Of the enabling conditions, we can say that they are of value here because the whole is better for their presence. Of the contributing features, we can say that the whole is better for their presence because they are of value here.

Holism, then, has a distinct picture of an intrinsic value, and more generally cannot accept Moore's conception of an organic unity, despite what one might have thought at the outset. We have moved away from Moore in four respects. We have abandoned his local version of supervenience; we have allowed a non-instrumental conception of extrinsic value; we assert that a feature cannot contribute value that it has not got; and we allow that intrinsic value is variable.

2. DEFAULT VALUES

At this point some will see a difficulty. The picture we are now offering suggests that there is nothing constant in the realm of value, or at least that if there is something constant, that itself is some sort of anomaly. Everything appears to be, at least in principle, context-dependent. If one wants to know whether some feature is of value here, one cannot get one's answer by looking to see how it behaves elsewhere. No matter what it does elsewhere, it might be doing something different here. So there are few props for judgement, and one might reasonably wonder whether we are really able to cope if things are as variable as that. Doesn't judgement require some sort of regularity to work on or from?—some sort of rules, even? It should surely not be surprising that rationality is normally thought of as requiring rules of one sort or another. Think of the way we learn a language, and of what it is that a competent speaker knows. We learn rules, syntactic and semantic, and without these rules language would be impossible—unlearnable, unspeakable, and uninterpretable. And the same goes for value. Without the right sort of regularity, value judgement would be no better than guesswork, and probably worse.

There are, however, two distinct forms of holism in the theory of value—extreme and moderate. The extreme form announces that no feature has any value other than that which it acquires as a result of its relation to a context. Features *bring* no value with them, we might say. They have value in a context, but only in a way that is to be explained by other aspects of that context. The moderate form of holism allows the possibility of what we might call 'default value'. By this I mean that it can accept a distinction between those features that bring no value to the situation, though once there they acquire a value that they can contribute to the whole, and those features that bring a value with them, though once they are there that initial value can be wiped out, or even reversed, by other features of the situation. In this sort of vein we might distinguish between features such as, 'that the train is about to leave', which in a certain context may increase the value of running, but in others does nothing of the sort, and features such as, 'that this is causing needless pain', which seems to be already set up so as to diminish the value of a whole of which it is a part, even though, if holism is right, there may be contexts in which it does not do that. The idea, then, is that some features come switched on already, as it were, though they can be switched off by other features; others do not come switched on, but they can be switched on by a suitable context. We might think of this notion of a default value as retaining something of what was contained in a pre-theoretical notion of intrinsic value, shorn of its invariabilist tendencies. It is, of course, simply the analogue of the notion of a default reason, introduced in Chapter 6.6.

The point of all this is that with default values of this sort, rationality has something rule-like to work from. There is something that the competent judge can bring to the new situation; one is not reduced to starting from scratch again each time. So the possibility of defaults palliates the sort of pure variabilism that threatens to turn value judgement into mere guesswork.

Another way of expressing the idea of a default value is in terms of explanation again. If a feature that has a default value does contribute that value to a whole of which it is a part, there is nothing here that is specially in need of explanation. If it does not contribute that value, there must be some special explanation of why that is so. The reverse is true for other features. If they do contribute some value in this case, there must be some special explanation of why that is so, how it comes about. If they do not contribute value here, that is only to be expected, and no special demand for explanation is in place.

Now it seems to me that, as we saw in the case of default reasons, there is nothing in holism that would justify our adopting the extreme position. If that is so, particularists who ground their position on holism should allow the possibility of default values, while stressing of course that a default value is nothing like an unvarying value. I presume, further, that a default value will be an intrinsic value, but of the holistic, not the Moorean, sort. It is worth pointing out, in this connection, that a default value is not the same as a normal value—a value that a feature has in most contexts, or in normal contexts in some other sense of 'normal'.

It seems possible that the notion of a default value is at least part of what is needed to answer a challenge raised by David Bakhurst. Bakhurst points out:

> [A] good person might set herself against actions of certain kinds, and do so in a profound and meaningful way, while retaining a holist appreciation of the complexities of predicting moral relevance and acknowledging that features which somewhere make actions abhorrent may elsewhere be morally inconclusive. The holist needs an account of moral commitment. (2000: 172ff.)

Such an account would contain two elements. First, it would show how it is possible to be committed to the fight against torture, say, even while one admits that torture is actually called for on occasions. Second, it would show how it is possible for someone rationally to select one or two of the admittedly many abhorrent types of act (as we might put it) to be those that she is especially concerned to help eradicate. The first of these is the one that the notion of a default value can be used to address. One can suppose that torturing has a default disvalue, and work to eradicate it as such, while admitting that default disvalues can, on unusual occasions, be overturned. Someone like this would indeed be, as Bakhurst demands, 'antecedently attuned' to the presence of torture. The second element in the notion of commitment requires different treatment. The worry is that the sort of selection involved in commitment of this sort is necessarily mismatched to the structure of the reasons thrown up case by case. To set oneself wholly against torture seems to require that one should do the anti-torture thing even when there is something that is actually more important waiting to be done instead. Why is it, then, that commitment does not involve a distortion of the reasons? It is not only the holist who needs an answer to this question, however, and I do not think that holism makes the question harder to answer.

In conclusion, it is worth comparing the structure of Ross's conception of duty with the structure of Moore's conception of value, which Ross officially accepted (though he held that there were not many significant instances of organic unities). One might have expected Ross to accept that a feature that in context is a reason for action may not contribute that reason to the overall reason for that action that is presented by the situation conceived as a whole. This would be the straight analogue of one thing that Moore said about value. Perhaps, however, common sense prevailed. Translated into the language of reasons, Moore's view begins to betray more openly the sort of incoherence that, as I suggested, it has already in the language of value. For instance, Moore might end up having to say that the painfulness of the punishment is a reason against punishing (intrinsically, that is) but that it gives us greater reason to inflict it (or something like that). Ross accordingly held that duty proper is, as we might put it, a straight function of the rational contributions made by relevant aspects of the situation. But he does, of course, accept the analogue of Moore's view that a feature that is of intrinsic value in one case is of the same value in every case. This is his generalism, the claim that a feature that grounds a prima facie duty in one case will play the same role wherever it occurs.

As I noted in Chapter 7.1, Ross reserves his generalism for underived prima facie duties; derived duties are as variable as the holist could wish. The distinction between underived and derived in Ross's overall picture is the analogue of Moore's distinction between intrinsic and extrinsic. The underived and the intrinsic are invariant; the derived and the extrinsic are variable. Neither picture, however, makes any room for a notion of a default. The sort of variability that holism insists on is not at odds with defaults, so long as we do not confuse the default with the invariant.

3. A DIFFERENT CONCEPTION OF ORGANIC UNITIES

Kagan (1988) wants to deny two theses:[5]

The Ubiquity Thesis: if a factor makes a difference anywhere it must make a difference everywhere.

The Assumption of Independent Contributions: the contribution made by a given factor is affected only by variations in that factor.

The strange thing is that Kagan wants to retain something fairly traditional: 'The universal nature of fundamental moral principles implies that the role a genuine factor plays must be universal as well' (p. 13). How does he offer to do this? He does it by distinguishing between the role of a feature and the effect of the presence of a feature (or the difference made by its presence). The *role* played by the presence/absence of oxygen is always the same, since the fundamental laws of chemistry do not vary from case to case. The *effect* of the presence/absence of oxygen will vary from case to case.[6] By analogy, therefore, the role played by the presence/absence of a 'genuine feature' will always be the same, since the fundamental laws of morality do not vary from case to case. The effect of the presence/absence of the feature will vary from case to case.

If one wonders how to apply the distinction between role and effect to the moral case, one is helped to see what Kagan is after by his distinction between additive and non-additive 'governing functions'. Governing functions are the

---

[5] The following discussion of Kagan's position could have been placed in Chapter 7, since his views concern the behaviour of reasons just as much as they do that of value. I have held it back until now in order to be able to draw certain parallels between his views and those of Moore.

[6] So Kagan allows the chemical analogue of non-monotonicity, but supposes that it must be built on a bedrock of universality, that is, invariance. This makes his position an interesting variant on Brandom's.

rules governing the ways in which various moral factors go to determine the moral status of an act, and these rules remain the same from case to case. If the rule is additive, so that $V = x + y + z$ (here V is the value of the whole, and x, y, and z are values of the parts), we get the two theses displayed above. If the rule is $V = x.y + z$, we get neither of them—for where $x = 0$, y does not contribute, but where $x = 1$, it does.

Kagan views his position here as a version of Moore's doctrine of organic unities. And one can see why. For Moore suggests that the effect of the presence of a feature may vary according to what other features are also present, but also supposes that something is held constant, namely the value of each intrinsically valuable part and the governing function that takes one from values of parts to their effects on the values of wholes. And of course my view is that the comparison with Moore reveals a weakness, because it looks as if the problems that Moore has with the relation between reasons and values apply equally to Kagan.

Their overall pictures are more or less identical in structure, despite some differences in substance (e.g. Moore's picture is additive), and the problems we found in Moore's position derive from its structure, not from its additivity. First, no persuasive reason is offered for thinking that there must be something invariant. Second, we face a difficulty that there is no real reason to face, namely that of knitting together invariance and variability. Third, the only way in which this can be done requires us to suppose that the value that something has in a context may be much less than the value it contributes to the relevant whole. Finally, that gives us the now familiar problems with the relation between reasons and values, that we may have more reason to protect a 'factor' than can be explained by appeal to any value that the factor enjoys in the context. Values and reasons have come apart again.

If that is so, one should of course ask why Kagan is so sure that a given genuine factor must always have the same value, and why he is so sure that the governing functions must remain constant. He seems simply to assume that there are universal moral principles, and he infers from this that there must be a set of invariant rules (or perhaps a single invariant rule) governing the interaction of the various moral factors in determining the moral status of an act. But this inference looks invalid. Ross's position has universal moral principles, and it does have the ubiquity assumption (at least for underived prima facie principles), and he does talk in terms of which obligation is the 'most stringent'. But one could perfectly well imagine a version of his view that simply says that the different prima facie obligations may relate to each other in various sorts of way, and that there is no general form to the move from what we find at the contributory level to what we find at the overall level. If we then ask what sense is given to the claim that the principles are universal, the answer can only be that they specify features that always count somehow, and always on the same side.

We could work backwards through Kagan's inferences. Fundamental moral principles are universal; so the role played by genuine factors must be invariant; so the governing function must remain the same from case to case. If these inferences were sound, my position would be the contrapositive of Kagan's. But they are not.

At one point Kagan shows awareness of the position I am preferring to his. Consider the sort of case referred to above, where Moore, as an additivist, would say that a feature with no value cannot affect the value contributed by other features, thinking that $1 + 0 = 1$, while Kagan thinks it possible that the governing function is not additive but multiplicative, giving us $1 \times 0 = 0$. (Both allow that a valueless feature can make a difference to the value of the whole, but Moore supposes that this can only happen where the value of the whole differs from the sum of any values contributed by the parts.) Of the situation above, Kagan notes that it would be possible to say that the value of the 1-rated factor is changed from 1 to 0 by the presence of the 0-rated factor, rather than, as he does, that the 1-rated factor is merely prevented from making a difference commensurate to its value. He comments on this that it is not clear what would turn on this disagreement (1988: 20–1n).

Let us consider how to place disabling conditions in Kagan's picture. A disabling condition comes, let us suppose, with a value of 0, and by its presence prevents another factor from being of value in the way it might otherwise have been. Kagan supposes that what the disabling condition does is to prevent that factor from making the difference it would normally have made, while leaving it as valuable in this context as it is elsewhere. The factor is prevented from contributing a value which it nonetheless retains. This tells us that there needs to be a difference between having no value and contributing a value of zero. Many factors will have no value, and not affect the value of anything else either. A disabling condition has no value, we are supposing, but it contributes that lack of value to a multiplicative function. Suppose, then, that there is a factor which plays both roles. It contributes value of its own, and also acts as a disabler for another factor. If this is possible, we need to be able to think of a factor that has value converting the value of another to zero. Of course there are two ways of doing that: by preventing the second factor from contributing value which it still retains, and by changing its value. But Kagan seems to have ruled out both of these ways. I conclude that his position is not sufficiently flexible to capture the phenomena.

11

Rationality, Value, and Meaning

---

1. COMPETENCE WITH A PRACTICAL CONCEPT

Particularism is officially a doctrine in meta-ethical theory. I have been presenting it as a local consequence of the holistic claim that a feature that is a reason in favour of action in one case may be no reason at all in another, or even a reason against. The holistic claim itself is a view in practical philosophy, in the theory of reasons for action in general, and it doesn't have anything special to say about moral reasons. One might even take it, as I in fact do, as a local consequence of a fully general conception of what are sometimes called 'favouring' reasons; I say 'local' because as well as reasons for action, practical reasons, there are reasons for belief, theoretical reasons, and one could, I suppose, imagine that holism is only true of the practical ones. But I would dispute this contrast, on the grounds that there cannot be so great a difference between the practical and the theoretical. This leaves me saying that particularism is a (very) local consequence of a general conception of favouring reasons, the claim that a feature that is a reason in favour in one case may be no reason at all in another, or even a reason against. All this was laid out in Chapter 5.1.

If particularism is a consequence of a wholly general doctrine in the theory of reasons, we should pay attention to the generalizable aspects of the picture of moral rationality that it expresses. For there is an implicit claim that in the moral case rationality need not amount to what people have often wanted it to amount to. To be rational, to think rationally, to be a competent assessor of reasons, need not be to be a competent rule-handler, nor is it necessary that one should be a competent assessor of the context-independent individual contributions of the reasons present in the case, because there may be no such context-independent contributions to be assessed.

Kitchen-scales conceptions of rationality, or of 'rational weight', make two claims:

1. The weight of a rational element or reason is not affected by the weight, nor indeed even by the presence, of any other rational element.
2. Once one has assessed the separate weight of each element, evaluative judgement consists of adding up the pros and cons to see which side is weightier.

These claims express a sort of atomism in the theory of reasons—an atomistic conception of rationality. Opposed to this will be a sort of holism, of which particularism is a local expression, and which will deny both of them. How extreme a holism will this be? We have seen that we have a choice between two claims, extreme and moderate. The extreme claim is that no feature is a reason except in context, and the status of every reason as a reason is contextually grounded. The moderate claim is that there can be such a thing as the default rational polarity of a feature, though this can be reversed or annulled by other features of the context. For this we do not need to suppose that the default contribution is the most common, of course. We would, I think, need to suppose that one needs to know the default contribution if one is to be a competent assessor of the rational contribution made by this feature case by case. Competence requires knowledge of the default, if there is one. But it also requires an understanding of the sorts of condition that can overturn the default contribution, either by annulling it or reversing it. There would be a sort of explanatory priority enjoyed by the default, which we earlier saw expressed in an asymmetry of explanation. We holists can admit this, for any case where there is a default polarity, without standing back from our commitment to the essential variability of the contributions of which any given feature is capable. For it is not as if a grasp on the default aspect alone would be sufficient for a more general grasp on the range of rational contributions of which a given feature is capable. We could not hope to *infer* the more general aspect of the behaviour of the feature from what we know when we understand the default contribution alone. First, there is not enough in the default contribution to act as a premise in such an inference. Second, and more crucially in the end, that to which we are inferring is not, I think, articulable in the sort of way it would need to be if it is to be capable of standing as the conclusion of an inference.

What, after all, is it that we know when we are competent to judge, in a particular case, the contribution made by a given feature in the light of the entire context? What is the nature of the knowledge that we bring to the new case? It seems to me that the most explicit way of expressing what we know is that we know the *sorts* of difference that the presence of this feature can make in different sorts of situation. What we need to know is the rough limits of a certain range within which the differences actually made from case to case are to fall. But this sort of knowledge seems to me to be essentially inarticulable, since it is not propositional.

Let us change the focus slightly from features to concepts, and ask what is required of a competent user of a practical concept—a thick concept, say, such as 'tasteless', 'charming', 'hasty', or 'lewd'. To be a competent user of such essentially practical concepts is to understand their practical purport, and this is to understand the difference that their applicability can make to the practical shape of the situation and thereby to the nature of the appropriate response. More briefly, we might say that to grasp the practical purport of a concept of this sort is to grasp how its applicability in a given case can affect what one ought to do. But it seems clear that the applicability of concepts of this sort make different differences (different practical contributions) in different contexts. It may be that sometimes a lewd response is appropriate and sometimes not. Certain sorts of humour are out of place at a funeral, though much to be welcomed elsewhere. It seems that a competent grasp of the practical purport of the concept requires that one be able to track these matters, at least to some degree. One needs to know the sort of spread that the concept has, so that one is able to recognize, maybe predict, track, or cope with its behaviour in non-standard contexts. On this picture there will be no such thing as *the* difference made by the presence of the relevant feature (nor by the applicability of the relevant concept), nor even *the* differences that it makes. What then can it be that the competent user knows? It can only be the *sort of* difference that the feature can make (and would make in a suitable context).

The ability to apply this sort of inarticulable knowledge to the varying contexts and cases that pass before us is characteristic of human practical rationality. And of course it is often the case that we need to combine our understanding of two features, both present in the case that confronts us, and interacting with each other in ways that our competence with each should put us into a position to understand. We are faced with several contributing features, and what we know about each enables us to cope somehow with the interfering effects of the context considered as a whole. This gives us a new picture of competence with the sort of contribution that a given feature (or the applicability of a given concept) can make. We don't say, 'This *must* make the same contribution every time, because after all it is the same feature every time—and how on earth are we to work out the way the reasons lie overall (or the overall value) if we cannot in some way hope to work it out from the independent contributions of the parts, conceived of as something that they import into the situation from outside?'. Rather, though the value of the whole must be somehow determined by the contributions of the parts *in that context*, the possibility of rational judgement does not require the parts to make the same contribution every time.

The overall picture, then, begins to look like this. The practical purport of the whole (that is, how one ought to respond to the situation) exists in virtue of, or is determined by, the practical purports of the various relevant features in the case. We are capable of tracking this if we are competent with the various concepts (i.e. familiar with the sorts of difference that each can make), but our ability to do it should not be understood as inferential. There is no possibility of computing (even in a weak sense of that term) the purport of the whole from the independent purports of the parts. In language that comes from a different philosophical field, the compositionality of practical purport does not require that each relevant feature make the same contribution on every occurrence. Knowledge of what we might call the practical meaning (purport) of a concept can get by without that sort of regularity. But it is true that the practical purport of the situation as a whole is constituted by the purports of the contributing parts *as so situated*—just as the value of the whole is the sum of the values of the contributing parts. To parse a situation (if I may be allowed to use a syntactic term in a more semantic sense) is to work out its practical profile and thereby come to see what response it calls for.

2. PARTICULARISM IN THE THEORY OF MEANING

I have been expressing the particularist picture of competence with a moral concept in ways that have been intended to remind readers of a rather similar debate within the theory of meaning. It is, I think, agreed on all hands that the meaning of the whole is determined by the meanings of the parts and the way in which they are there combined. But what is agreed here does little or nothing to tell us how to conceive of the independent contributions of the parts. What I am going to suggest is that there is no essential connection between the agreed view, which I am going to call weak compositionality, and any claim that each linguistic item must make the same contribution in every context (which is what I mean by strong compositionality).[1] Those who make this stronger claim are often driven by the thought that otherwise languages would not be humanly learnable.

I start from the model that emerged in our earlier discussion of Moore. Moore held that each contributing feature had the same practical purport wherever it occurred, but that it might contribute to a whole a purport that it had not got *in that whole*; that is, it might make a difference to the purport of the whole other than the one that we would have predicted from knowing its own independent purport, even though it retains that purport in every case. I suggested, by contrast, that this idea of contributing something other than the purport born in the relevant context was incoherent. Running this debate in terms of the theory of meaning, we see that the analogue of Moore's view would be that though a term retains, in a new and perhaps unusual context, the very same meaning that it has in more ordinary contexts, still the contribution made by that term to the overall meaning of the linguistic context in which it is found might not be identifiable with the meaning it has in that context. My view, by contrast, is that a term that makes a rather different contribution in a strange context must itself bear there as *its* purport the meaning or semantic value that it contributes to the whole *in that case*. This is not at odds with compositionality of the weak sort, since the meaning of the

---

[1] I owe this distinction, though not these terms, to Paul Horwich. For the idea of weak compositionality, see his (1998, ch. 7).

whole is still determined, even in new and unusual contexts, by the meanings of the parts *in that context*. But it does require that one and the same term can make different contributions in different contexts.

But would not this mean that the term is essentially ambiguous? It looks as if terms, on this account, change their meaning as they move from context to context, and this is surely hard to swallow. To answer this, we need to remember that the meaning of the term is what one knows when one is a competent user of that term. If the term is capable of making a range of contributions to differing contexts, this is part of what the competent user must know. To be a competent user, then, is to be in command of the *sorts of* difference that the presence of the term can make to the semantic value of the contexts in which it can appropriately be found. (This is exactly analogous to what we said about thick concepts earlier.) Not only must one know the range of possible semantic contributions of which the term is capable, but one must also be able to tell, to a reasonable degree, which particular contribution the term is in fact making case by case. The meaning of the term, understood in general, is the range of differences that it can make; its meaning in a given context is to be found somewhere in that range (though of course some contexts force an extension or other adaptation of that range). There is a sense, then, in which the term has the same meaning wherever it appears, though it makes different contributions in different contexts, and those different contributions determine what it means there. What determines which of the available possibilities the term in fact contributes *here* can only be other features of the context. One needs, then, to be in a position to understand the sort of difference that the presence of *that* feature makes to the purport of *this* one, in the semantic just as in the practical field. In this sense, one needs to be in command of a fairly wide vocabulary if one is even to get going as a competent language user.

It is compatible with this general approach to allow the possibility of default meanings, that is, a contribution made by a term to the meaning of the sentence in which it appears[2] that does not need any special contextual explanation. There can be such default meanings, so long as we do not expect them to be invariant, nor expect to be able to infer the range of non-default contributions from the default, nor to infer the present non-default contribution from the default contribution together with other features of the context. The role played by defaults in our picture of semantic competence (or semantic rationality) will be strongly analogous to the role they play in our picture of practical rationality.

There is a danger, however, that we will come to think of defaults as core meanings, that is, as a sort of invariant or constant centre that is surrounded by a variant semantic periphery. Some of those who seem to be attracted by

---

[2] The sentence, of course, has its own discursive context which can presumably make its own difference to the semantic purport of the utterances, or sentences, that make it up.

the sort of picture I am proposing (in which I claim no novelty) seem to me to fall into this trap. Stanley Cavell, for instance, in an otherwise exemplary discussion of Wittgenstein's philosophy of language, writes at one point that 'Both the "outer" variance and the "inner" constancy are necessary if a concept is to accomplish its tasks' (1979: 185). An inner constancy sounds very like an invariant core. It is possible, however, that what Cavell means is really that there must be central or paradigm cases if there are to be peripheral or non-standard ones, which is a position with which I would have no official quarrel. More recently, Paul Horwich, though his general drift seems to coincide with the one that I am taking here (especially in his rejection of strong compositionality in favour of its weaker cousin), takes it that every term has what he calls a 'basic use property', and he seems to think that in many cases this constitutes an invariant and specifiable core. For instance, he writes, 'the acceptance property that governs a speaker's overall use of "and" is (roughly) his tendency to accept "p and q" if and only if he accepts both "p" and "q"'; and Horwich gives similar clauses for our use of 'red' and of 'true' (1998: 45). But this is not what I am intending. The idea is not that there is a fixed core meaning, definable and expressible in a specifiable rule, and which governs our use of the relevant term in unusual situations. I see no need to say such a thing even for 'and'. Consider the following uses of 'and':

Jack and Jill lifted the stone.
Two and two make four.
Clapping involves putting left and right hand together sharply.
'And did those feet, in ancient time, walk upon England's pastures green?'[3]
And what do you think you are doing?

The point is that none of these can be understood as expressing conjunction as a fixed core meaning *as well as* something else. The first three cannot be supposed even to entail some conjunction; the last two are instances of a conversational context in which 'and' is the first word, and to think of them as partly conjunctive one would have to suppose a tacit conjunct, which is clearly strained at best.

So even if we are dealing with a term that makes a default contribution, we do not need to conceive of the default aspect of the use of the term in terms of a fixed core meaning. And it would be better if we did not, for to do so is implicitly to suppose that the existence of what we would find ourselves thinking of as a periphery (Cavell's 'outer variance') is inessential to the proper functioning of the term in standard cases. A term, that is, might or might not enjoy a more flexible use in addition to its 'standard' use. But the standard use, the dictionary definition, as it were, can stand alone in its own right.

---

[3] This is the first line of William Blake's 'Jerusalem'; thanks to Michael Dummett for the nice example.

Cavell argues that this is the last gasp of an ultimately distorted approach to language. It is, he wants to say, essential to the terms we use that they can be projected to new and unforeseen contexts. We could not run a language in which we needed to invent a new term for every context which did not exactly match up to the defined limitations of the terms we have already in hand. But when we do project, our projection must not be seen as an arbitrary decision. It will be normatively sensitive to (i.e. able to be assessed as right or wrong by appeal to) what as competent speakers we already know. New contexts invite new applications of an old term in ways that can either be encouraged or discouraged by our existing understanding of the term. That is to say, what one knows when one knows the meaning of the term already contains enough to act as a guide to the applicability of the term in new and unexpected contexts, being capable of inviting or allowing, discouraging or even ruling out a new projection. To know the meaning of the term is, then, already to be a competent judge of how to project it, without this entailing that there be available anything like a core meaning or basic use property of the term by appeal to which such projections are to be assessed, and of which competent users can be said to be implicitly aware.

If that is so, the meaning of the term should not be thought of as a combination of hard core and soft periphery. What is it then that we know when we are competent with the term? It must be something closely analogous to what we found when thinking about competence with a thick concept. To know the meaning of the term is to know the *sorts of* semantic contribution that the term can make to a larger context, and to have a general understanding of what *sorts of* context are those in which it will make this or that *sort of* contribution. There is nothing here that could be captured in a rule. Rules, in the sense with which we are here concerned, must be articulable in principle, even if our competent speaker is incapable of articulating them in practice. But if the meaning of the term consists in an open-ended *range* of available *sorts of* contribution in this way, it is essentially inarticulable. Competence with it will therefore have to consist in a kind of skill rather than a grasp on a specifiable rule; it will have to be conceived as a sort of know-how, for there is nothing of propositional form that, in knowing the meaning of the term, we might be said even vaguely to grasp. A range of possibilities cannot be captured propositionally.

But mustn't there be an articulable core if the 'standard meaning' is to determine the rights and wrongs of any particular projection? To ask this question is to fail to see that normative control over projections does not belong to the single term alone. What determines the rights and wrongs of using this term in that unusual case is at least partly the other features of the case—or the other terms it seems right to use in it. To take Cavell's example, it is because of other features present in relevant cases that it seems right to project the concept of 'feeding' to talk of feeding an electricity meter, of feeding a lawn, and of feeding someone's pride; and if to feed is always to give food, we should not forget the possibility of food for thought. But we will of course tell just the same story about those other features, or those other concepts, as we do about the concept of feeding. For instance, it might be that the notion of feeding is sensitive to those of nourishment, growth, regular demand, and improvement. But growth, to take just one example from that list, is a notion that operates in just the same sort of way as does feeding. The physical growth of a child is different from the economic growth of a company, and both are different from the child's intellectual and emotional growth. But the features that make it right to think of all these different sorts of thing as growth will themselves operate in the same way as does the concept of growth (or the term 'growth') itself. The whole thing whirls on endlessly, without any fixed points.

The picture we are emerging with is one under which our recognition of the meaning of a sentence or utterance cannot be generally understood as inferential or as computational in some weaker sense. On the strong compositionalist picture, we effectively compute the meaning of a whole from the meanings of the parts, and it is held to be vital to the possibility of the sort of linguistic competence that we enjoy that we should be in antecedent command of a finite store of premises, each specifying the regular contribution of an individual feature or of a schema into which features can be fitted (the subject-predicate schema, for instance). Knowing these things, we are in a position to deduce or compute the meaning of sentences built up out of these materials. But on the weak compositionalist account, what we know when we know the meaning of a term is incapable of functioning as a premise, since it is inarticulable. Something that speaks of the sort of contribution that a term can make, and the sort of situation in which it is able to make it, is something from which it is impossible to compute. Nothing like this could be fed into a computer, for instance.

Effectively the same consideration, then, undermines three significant ideas. First, that our understanding of utterances and sentences is inferential. Second, that the normativity of language is a matter of its being governed by rules. Third, that the terms of ordinary language have invariant core meanings. What we have ended up with is effectively a particularist theory of meaning, one in which semantic competence (knowledge of meanings) is strongly analogous to practical competence (knowledge of practical purport)—and all just as particularism sees it. I view the general picture of linguistic competence that I am offering here as essentially Wittgensteinian. It is one under which linguistic competence is not, indeed cannot be, knowledge of a rule. In one sense, indeed, there is nothing wrong with thinking of the meaning of a term as a rule for its use. We only need to remember that the meaning of a term is something normative in style, since it requires us to act in certain ways rather than in others. Only something that is conceived normatively can be misused or misapplied. But it would be a mistake to think that as soon as we are dealing with the normative, we are dealing with rules in any other sense than that. Normativity, according to the particularist, is not a matter of the application of rules, if by rules we mean something articulable, something that is independent of context, but such that knowledge of the rules for all the terms in a sentence and for the structure in which they are here present suffices for knowledge of the meaning of the whole. And this applies as much to linguistic meaning as to moral or other practical purport.

My conclusion here is that the model of rationality suggested by particularist enquiries into our competence with moral reasons is indeed applicable, not only to our competence with other reasons, practical and theoretical, but also to our linguistic competence. We see the same difficulties on both sides of the distinction between practical and semantic purport. There is the challenge to explain how we might be able to work out the purport of a complex if we are not able to take each element in that complex as making the same contribution on every occasion. And there is the challenge to explain how it is that an element retains its independent purport case by case, even though it makes different contributions to different contexts. But these challenges can both be met.[4]

---

[4] See the long footnote on pp. 33–4 of Berlin (1996); also pp. 44–5.

12

Principles of Rational Valuing

In this final chapter I consider the question whether our holism in the theory of value has undesirable consequences. The consequences I have in mind are that we are going to have to abandon certain highly intuitive axioms. These are (where '>' means 'is better than'):

1. $[(A + B) > (A + C)] \rightarrow (B > C)$
2. The indifference of independent alternatives
3. The sure-thing principle
4. Transitivity: $[(A > B) \And (B > C)] \rightarrow (A > C)$

It is often held that if these axioms can be shown to fail, our evaluative practice cannot be rational. Just as the transitivity of weight is essential to the very possibility of weight, and thence to the practice of weighing, so for the transitivity of value.

1. THE ATOMIC PRINCIPLE

Let us start with the first of these, which we will call:

> *The Atomic Principle*: if we value $A + B$ more highly than we value $A + C$, we necessarily value B more highly than we value C.

This principle appears to be incompatible with holism in the theory of value. For the holist claims that a feature (or 'part') can have more value in one context (or 'whole') than it does in another. It may be, then, that in the A-context, B's value is greater than elsewhere; in other contexts we might well value B less than we value C, even though the combination of A and B is more valuable to us (in whatever sense) than that of A and C. And there seem to be innumerable examples of just this phenomenon. I might value salt less than I value sugar, but I value meat with salt much more than I value meat with sugar. I might value friendship more than I value honesty, but I still prefer (that is, value more highly) an honest assessment of my prospects of good health to a friendly one. If this is right, holism is true, and it is at odds with the Atomic Principle.

The Atomic Principle seems to enshrine a general conception about value, which is that the value of one thing cannot be affected by the nature (or the value) of others. If I want to evaluate this object, I should look at it and work out its value, and then do the same for other things, establishing in each case an independent value, and then finally look at the overall result to see how well things have done relative to each other. There is what one might call a sort of 'intrinsicalist' feel to this. By contrast, the holist is an extrinsicalist, holding:

> The Principle of Context-dependent Value: the value of one object can be affected by the nature (or value) of others.

In accepting a doctrine of organic unities (not Moore's, of course), we have committed ourself to this principle. For we hold that a given feature can be more valuable in one context than in another. There is, however, a slightly different version of the Atomic Principle, which we can still accept.

Consider a case where I have a choice between a perfect copy of a book and one that is imperfect, having its first half blank. Prima facie, the view that we prefer a complete book to the one that is half-blank if and only if we prefer the proper first half to the blank pages is just false. I might easily prefer this blank half (intending to use it to write my diary) to the first half of the book, considering them separately, even though I prefer the whole book to the mutilated version. It looks, then, as if the Atomic Principle is incompatible with the existence of organic unities, as we have seen. But this is going too fast. The question in fact depends on which doctrine of organic unity we accept. The view that Moore rejected but which we have accepted was that the parts of an organic unity may acquire increased value as they enter the whole whose value they increase. On this version, the value of the proper first part of the book may be greater in context than the value of the blank pages, because when we consider them separately we are not considering them *as separated*. So there is still room here to say that if we value the common second half equally on either side, we value the proper first half more highly than we value the blank pages iff we value the complete book more highly than we value the mutilated version. And this is very close to the Atomic Principle.

It might seem that this argument is too strong. Haven't we forgotten that the blank pages have significant value in their own right? Perhaps we should rather say that the value of the parts is some function of their value *as separated* and their value as parts of the whole. The blank pages have the same value whether they are parts of the mutilated whole or not; the proper first half has less value than the blank pages, considered as separated, but more value than them when considered separately as a part of the complete whole. This increase in value is not guaranteed to leave the first half more valuable overall than the blank pages. That some shortfall is made up does not tell us how much is made up.

But the Atomic Principle can be defended against this response. Of course, it is possible that the first half acquires increased value when conjoined with its proper continuation, but that the value of the resulting whole is less than the value of second half plus blank pages (given the need for somewhere to write one's diary). But if the value of the whole book is greater than that of the mutilated version, and the value of the second half the same both times, it looks inevitable that the value of the first half in this context should be greater than that of the blank pages, even when we have counted the value of those pages, not only considering them separately but also considering them as separate.

And it certainly *looks* as if there should be room to accept the Atomic Principle in this sense, as an account of the relationships that hold of necessity between one's overall evaluations, once every relevant consideration has been considered, *including* the question what the wholes are of which the elements we are valuing are here present as parts. The Atomic Principle comes in as a constraint *at the end*. The principle that the value of a part may be affected by the nature of other parts, or of the whole of which it is a part, appears at a different point in the evaluative process, and this is a prima facie ground for supposing it to be detachable.

However, even if we did find ourselves accepting the Atomic Principle here, it would be of little practical value. For suppose we admit that if we value the common second half equally on either side, we value the proper first half more highly in its context than we value the blank pages if we value the complete book more highly than we value the mutilated version. This principle will only apply in cases where the increase in value derived from adding the proper first part has no tendency to increase the value of the common second part. But the chances are that anyone persuaded to accept that the value of an element may be altered when it becomes a part of a new whole will also accept that the value of other parts (already present in the whole, as it were) can be changed by the addition of the new part. Though the increase in value is to be attributed to the addition of the new part, that does not necessarily mean that it cannot lead to an increase in value of other parts.

So we have nothing like a complete defence of the Atomic Principle. Even if it remains true, it is probably of limited application. What we have shown here is that the Principle of Context-dependent Value is not at odds with a cautiously formulated version of the Atomic Principle. Naturally, if there are organic unities, value is not always intrinsic. The idea that there can be organic unities is a special case of the application of a notion of extrinsic value, one where the focus is specifically on the relationship between different parts that make up a whole, rather than more generally on the relations between different objects. So we had to assert the Principle of Context-dependent Value in order to get the stronger view of organic unity to work; we had to suppose that the same element could have more value in one context than in another. But if the Atomic Principle can be understood in such a way as to be compatible with both the existence of organic unities and the Principle of Context-dependent Value, this reveals to us that it can be detached from any intrinsicalist ground:

> *Intrinsicalist ground*: the value of one object is necessarily unaffected by the nature (and value) of others.

> *The New Atomic Principle*: if we value $A + B$ more highly than we value $A + C$ (in this context), and value A equally both times, we necessarily value B more highly than we value C (in this context).

What we have seen is that we can accept the second of these without accepting the first. The New Atomic Principle is not at odds with holism in the theory of value.

Note the revision we had to make in the principle. As I originally expressed it, it assumed that the value of A in the context '$A + B$' must be identical with its value in the context '$A + C$'. This assumption is incompatible with holism, and must be dropped—or rather turned into an explicit condition, as above. But once that is done, the Atomic Principle can remain as a constraint on rational preferences.

2. COMPLEMENTARITY

Talk about organic unities is one thing, and talk about complementarity is another. It is more plausible to claim that the value of one part in a whole can be affected by the value of other parts, than it is to claim that the value of one alternative in a choice situation can be affected by the nature of others (or, more correctly, the nature of *the* other). Complementarity is the latter claim; if it is true, we have a further reason in favour of (or, better, a further application of) the Principle of Context-dependent Value.

We might hope that holism does not commit us to complementarity. Suppose that reasons-holism is the truth, and that value-holism is the truth as well. What does this tell us about the possibility of a full ordering, in which everything has its place, and where for each A and each B, A is either better than B, worse than B, or roughly as good as B? Well, so far as what we have yet seen will take us, there might still be a full ordering of that sort, in which everything has its place in the table of values, from best to worst. For all the considerations we have so far adduced concern the way in which the value of a complex is determined from the values of its parts, and the way in which parts may change their values as they move from one complex (context) to another. Once the value of the whole is determined, however, it is not going to vary, and we can enter the whole in its proper place in the great ordering. This would mean, for instance, that transitivity is not threatened by holism. For with everything in its own place, we are never going to get a situation in which *A* is above *B*, *B* above *C*, and *C* above *A* in the Great Order.

This pleasing picture is not as secure as it initially appears. Let us remember that some of the things that have value are actions, and actions (like other things) are chosen out of a set of alternatives available to the agent at the time. Now to adopt the picture I have just described is to suppose that each alternative object of choice has its place in the great ordering of values, a place that is not affected by the place or nature of other alternatives. And this seems to require that the value of an action is never affected by the question what the available alternatives are. Now this is a very attractive doctrine indeed, partly because it enables us to retain a plausible principle of rational choice which is sometimes horribly called the Principle of the Indifference of Independent Alternatives (IIA):

> *IIA*: If in one situation I prefer action *A* to action *B*, it can never be rational for me to prefer *B* to *A* in other situations which differ from the first merely in the fact that further alternatives are available.

In simpler terms, if I choose *A* where my choice is between *A* and *B*, I cannot rationally choose *B* where my choice is between *A*, *B*, and *C*. The availability of *C* may indeed alter my overall choice, but it cannot affect the relative ranking order of *A* and *B* that has already been established.

Though this principle is *very* attractive, I am not convinced that stubborn adherence to it is fully compatible with the broadening holistic perspective that I have been developing. For it is not obvious to me how one can prevent available alternatives from counting as part of the context within which an action is placed. And if one cannot do this, then the general holistic claim that context can make a difference to value seems likely to take us to the view that the value of an action or choice can be affected by the alternatives that are available at the time. This despite the fact that it seems far more plausible to claim that the value of one part in a whole can be affected by the value of other parts than it is to claim that the value of one alternative in a choice situation can be affected by the nature of others. Complementarity is the standard name for the latter claim, the supposedly less plausible one that it looks as if I am going to have to try to defend.

There is a reply to this, however. The argument of the previous paragraph might have been merely that every alternative is an object, though not all objects are alternatives (to each other). Since every object may have its value affected by others, every alternative may have its value affected by other objects, including some that are alternatives to it. There could be no bar against this happening—no bar that ensured that only those objects that are not alternatives to this one are capable of affecting its value. But this, though true, does nothing to establish the controversial doctrine that is really what we are after. That doctrine is that when one object becomes an alternative to another, that change may make a *further* difference to the value of the second—a difference beyond that made by the existence and nature of the first object. And this doctrine does seem very peculiar.[1]

But not as peculiar as all that, perhaps. There may be examples of this phenomenon—of the arrival of a new alternative making a difference to the relative values of two existing alternatives—in ways that are not explained merely by the *existence* or possibility of the thing that becomes an alternative, but rather by its new status as an alternative. Suppose that we have two alternatives A and B, and that we prefer B to A. Our original question was whether we might be rationally led to prefer A to B if there appears a further alternative, C.[2] Any successful example of this must meet certain criteria. It must not be one in which we simply change our minds about our initial ranking of A and B, perhaps for the reason that the appearance of C as an alternative draws our attention to something that we had previously missed. If nothing changes, however, it is hard to see how the ranking of A and B can be reversed by the arrival of C. The question to bear in mind is whether the examples offered contain the right or the wrong sort of change.

To be fully convincing, an example needs to be natural and simple. The best example I know is one that I found in Wilfred Thesiger's *Arabian Sands*. He wrote, about his travels across the desert on camel: 'I would not myself have wished to cross the Empty Quarter in a car. Luckily this was impossible when I did my journeys, for to have done the journey on a camel when I could have done it in a car would have turned the venture into a stunt' (1959: 260). This seems a perfectly rational stance, and what is more there is a potential explanation of what is going on. The concepts of a stunt and a venture are thick concepts. They essentially involve evaluation. Now which alternatives are available can quite easily affect our judgement of someone who takes one rather than the other. And our judgement of the chooser can be explained by a judgement of the choice made, the option chosen. If a third option becomes available, the second one may cease to have a thick property that it had before, and this change may affect our ranking of the first two options. What is more, the change is not a change in the option ranked in any sense that would amount to what I called above a change of information. It is not that our information changes; the facts themselves (the normative, thick facts, that is) change. I think this is a change of the right sort to make

[1] I have expressed this doctrine in terms of a *change*. But that need not be the point. The question could equally well be phrased in terms of the difference between the case where C is not an alternative and the case where it is; can the difference between C's being an alternative and its not being one make a difference to the relative values of A and B? Here there is no talk of change. There is, of course, nothing wrong with examples that do involve change. It is just that one should be careful to avoid supposing that change is essential to the point.

[2] It is not, of course, strictly necessary for us to find an example in which the order of the initial choice is reversed. It would be enough if we found a case in which the relative values are altered, so that the one that we originally preferred we still prefer, but not by so much—or by more, perhaps. Then we could argue that this sort of change in relative preference is bound to lead, on occasion, to a change in ordering. But it is more striking to produce an example in which the ordering is reversed.

a counter-example to IIA. Of course there is some change. But all the change that there is occurs with, first, something's becoming an alternative when it was not before, and, second, changes at the thick level that are consequent on that first change. I suggest that this is sufficient for it to come under the rubric as I originally expressed it. Admittedly my original version does not look promising from this point of view. It was:

> IIA: If in one situation I prefer action A to action B, it can never be rational for me to prefer B to A in other situations which differ from the first merely in the fact that further alternatives are available.

And the Thesiger example is not one of situations which differ merely in the fact that further alternatives are available; they differ also in the normative consequences of that fact (the switch from venture to stunt). But that does not seem very significant to me. No two situations could differ *merely* in the fact that an alternative is available in one that is not in the other. There would be bound to be consequential normative differences of the sort that might affect rational choice, and I claim that these are enough to unsettle IIA.

Bart Streumer offered me a rather different sort of example, in which I choose A rather than B as a way of expressing my disagreement with the unavailability of C, but in which, had C been available, I would have chosen B rather than A or C. Suppose I am terminally ill and I can choose either a very painful death or a somewhat painful death with passive euthanasia, and suppose that the law forbids active euthanasia, which is why it is not available. I might then choose the very painful death as a way of protesting against the unavailability of active euthanasia. But had active euthanasia been available, I might have chosen to have a somewhat painful death with passive euthanasia—perhaps because my parents are opposed to active euthanasia and I want to avoid making my death more difficult for them than it would be if I chose active euthanasia.

So it does look as if there may be examples in which independent alternatives are not indifferent. Maybe, then, even if holism does commit us to the existence of such examples, this is not a disaster. But I raised a question earlier that I have not yet answered. Does holism itself constitute a reason for rejecting IIA? My first attempt to show that it does was a failure. I argued that holists should not be surprised to see the nature of one thing making a difference to the value of another. But this was irrelevant. The real question was whether the rather special feature of 'being an available alternative' can make a difference to the relative values of two things. Holism does not show that this must happen. It is everywhere permissive rather than prescriptive; or perhaps we should say that it forbids some things and prescribes nothing but suspicion, saying that we should be open to the possibility of such a thing and not make a fuss if some crop up. The only reason for supposing that there *cannot* be any examples would be the atomist claim that since the feature of 'being an available alternative' often makes no difference, it makes no difference anywhere.[3]

There remains a difficulty. There appears to be an argument that there could be no counter-example to IIA. If so, the situation is unstable. We would have an example, our holistic position that there could be examples, and an argument that there can't be any. Here is the argument. Sadly, it is one to which there can be no holistic objection *as such*; it does not involve any covert appeal to atomism.

Let us start with a supposed overall ranking, the Great Ordering. Everything has its place in the order. We can compare the values of different objects, and compare different objects in order to establish their relative placing. These activities cannot themselves alter the values of the objects compared or their relative places; otherwise the very notion of relative value would be incoherent. One can compare the values of merely possible objects, e.g. possible courses of action or possible states of affairs. Could there be any difference between the values of merely possible objects and the values of those objects should they become real? No; for otherwise the activity of establishing the relative values of different possibilities would be incoherent. And this would make deliberation before action incoherent, if deliberation is the establishing of relative values of possibilities so as to decide which to make actual. Suppose then that I ask you to rank ownership of each of ten paintings. What you are ranking is a set of possibilities. And suppose that I go on to give you all the paintings, and ask you to rank the ten actual ownings. There can be no conceivable reason for a change in your ranking order. Now: could there be a difference between an order of preference and a ranking order for choice, where what one is dealing with is alternatives? No: there is no possible relevant difference between a preference order and a choice order. Suppose that instead of giving you all the paintings, I give you the money to buy one. You should buy the one that came top in your preference ranking of ownerships. So the feature of 'being an alternative' cannot make a difference.

Matters are more complicated than this. The complications do not make a difference, but they are relevant to what happens later. There is an obvious

---

[3] An interestingly different avenue of approach, which I will not pursue here, starts from something that Derek Parfit is apparently happy to admit, namely an analogous claim concerning not value but 'ought'. Parfit's view seems to be that it is possible that one ought to do *A* if *B* is the only alternative, but that if *C* is also available one ought to do *B*. He denies, however, the claim that the *values* of *A, B,* and *C* can be related in a structurally similar way. He writes: 'Whether I ought to act in one of two ways may depend on whether it would be possible for me to act in some third way. . . . I then ask whether, compared with A +, A would have been better. The relative goodness of these two outcomes cannot depend on whether a third outcome, that will never happen, might have happened' (1984: 429). So in the evaluative realm he is what one might call a choice-atomist but in the deontic realm he is a choice-holist. Now my own view is that this position of Parfit's is unstable. It seems to me that he should deny either both or neither. And my reason is fairly predictable: that if one admits that there are examples of choice-holism in the deontic realm, structurally similar examples will emerge in the evaluative one.

difference between buying just one painting and ranking them all. The difference comes out when we consider a case where I give you the money to buy one painting, then enough to buy another, and so on until you have all ten (though you never knew in advance that I would give you the money for the next). The order in which you buy the paintings need not be the same as your original order of preference. To see this point, it is important to distinguish between two quite different preference orders. The first has ten slots, in each of which one is asked to put one item of the form 'I own picture n'. The second has ten slots, the first of the form 'I own picture n', the second of the form 'I own pictures n and m', the third of the form 'I own pictures n, m, and p', and so on. There is no reason whatever why either of these two orders should be extractable from the other. The point is that if you already have, say, six of the paintings, you might rationally choose to add to those six a painting other than the one that came seventh on the list. To get a true analogue of the original ordering, when it comes to choice, we have to suppose that I give you enough money to buy one, but that just as you try to buy it someone—else gets in first; so you should go for the second on your original list—but the same happens again, and so on down to the tenth. The order of choice should be the order of preference.

What we have, then, is an explanation of why a certain feature, 'being an alternative', cannot make a difference, and therefore of why holism is compatible with a full ordering. In one sense (epistemically, perhaps) it is *possible* that 'being an alternative' can make a difference. But there is an argument (which is not atomistic in any way) that no instance of this could be found. So the situation seems to be that we have on the one side an example in which the feature does make a difference, and a weak general reason derived from our holism to expect this sort of thing to crop up, and an argument on the other side to show that it is impossible. Now this is not one of those situations in which there can be reasons on one side and reasons on the other, and we can just decide where the balance of probability lies, leaving the defeated reasons in place. If we go with the example, we have to show what is wrong with the argument on the other side. I confess that I normally find examples more convincing than arguments.

Luckily this can be done. The property of being an alternative is incapable of making a difference to a ranking order already established because there is no relevant difference between overall preference and overall choice. And just as the ranking preference order may be affected by the list of things to be ranked, so that if we take something off the list, the rankings of the rest may change, so the same is true with the ranking of alternatives. But all that this shows is that *preference is like choice*, and like choice in the crucial respect that it deals with alternatives. Being alternatives is the same as being mutually exclusive. Not all preference rankings are rankings of objects conceived as mutually exclusive, as we have seen. But some are. And the same is true whether we are ranking existing objects or possible ones. So the explanation of why the feature of being an alternative cannot be the cause of a difference between a preference ranking and a choice ranking is that this feature is present on both sides.[4] Our conclusion should be that being an alternative can make a difference to all three rankings: of possible objects, of actual ones, and of objects of choice.

The existence of persuasive examples should then move us without further resistance from value-holism to a sort of choice-holism, which holds that:

1. The value of one alternative can be affected by the nature (or value) of other available alternatives.
2. Assessing the relative merits of different alternatives is not the same as assessing the various alternatives one by one and then comparing the results.

I want to end this passage by comparing what I have said here with something I wrote in *Moral Reasons* (pp. 165–6):

My daughter trod on a sea-urchin on holiday a few years ago, and we caused her considerable pain (not entirely with her consent) in extracting the spines from her heel. Was the pain we caused her something which made our actions worse than they would otherwise have been? Here is a switching argument which says that it was. Had there been available a painless method of getting the spines out, we would and should have adopted it. We would have been wrong to continue digging in her heel with a needle, because of the pain. Surely this shows that as things were our actions were the worse for the pain they caused?

I don't think it does show this. What we should say about cases like these is that a feature which would have made this sort of difference had there been any alternative choice need not necessarily make it if there is no alternative. It seems to me quite consistent to say that as things stood our action was not the worse for the pain it caused, though that pain should have led us to choose another method had one been available.

The idea, expressed in terms of reasons rather than, as above, in terms of values, was that the pain is not a reason against the action if there was no alternative, pain-free course of action available. It is not just that it is not sufficient reason; it is not any reason at all. I presented this thought as an application of a style of what I called a switching argument, whose general form is: if this action were less F, it would be better; so its being F must detract from its overall value. But it can be seen immediately that the example I gave goes further than is required for that purpose. My use of an example that hangs on a point about alternatives was more of a distraction than a help, since the general point I was trying to make was nothing to do with

---

[4] Thanks to Eve Garrard and David McNaughton here. It would be wrong to say, in reply to this argument, that the feature we were originally discussing was that of being an available alternative, not that of being an alternative. The move from an alternative to an available alternative merely takes us from possible choices (preferences) between mutually exclusive options to actual choices.

alternatives. Talk about available alternatives was intended more as an explanation of the supposed fact that, in the example given, the action was not the worse for the pain caused, even if it would have been better with less pain. Since it was not possible to do it with less pain, the pain caused does not make the action worse than it would otherwise have been. In possible world terms: even though, in the nearest world in which there was an available pain-free alternative, the action we did was wrong, wrong because of the pain it caused, and the worse for that pain, the actual action is not the worse for that pain. This is just an application of the holistic thought that a feature can make a difference in one situation that it does not make in another. Where this occurs, holists admit that there must be an explanation of it; the explanation is that in the actual world, there was no alternative.

Perhaps, then, the situation is like this. Holism in the theory of value takes away from us one of our two main reasons for sticking to principles like IIA. If one is a holist, it is going to be hard to think that the question whether something was a real alternative cannot make a difference. If IIA expresses a form of atomism, holists don't have *that* reason to believe it. Perhaps things are slightly worse than this, though, because there were two main potential explanations of how it could be that the feature of 'being an alternative' is incapable of affecting value when other features can do this perfectly well, and both turned out to fail. They were that, with choice of action, we are dealing with comparison of objects only one of which, at most, exists, and that there is a difference between preference and choice. Though we tried to defend IIA by appeal to these two differences, we failed.

There is another reason for wanting to defend IIA, and this is one that can appeal to holists as much as to anyone else. It is that if we lose principles like IIA (and all the rest), we lose what is really the only detailed account of the 'logic' of choice. The loss of IIA seems to be another nail in the coffin of the idea that there is such a logic. One might suggest, however, that the loss of IIA is far worse for atomists than it is for holists. For atomists, the pillars of practical rationality would really be tottering.

With that threat in mind, we need to consider a further attempt to prevent disaster, which involves a distinction between complete and incomplete objects. A complete object is called a 'state of nature'; an incomplete object is anything less than that. Now the idea is that the relevant principles of rational choice apply only to complete objects. We have argued that they do not apply to incomplete objects, such as Wilfred Thesiger's Travels across the desert. But this is nothing to the point. So long as we restrict the domain of the principles of rational choice to entire states of nature, they remain unthreatened.

So let us now turn to the question whether there is a significant difference between ranking states of nature and ranking incomplete objects. If we can show that alternative complementarity and state of nature complementarity stand or fall together, and also that the latter is either false or no more false than true,[5] we will be able to show that alternative complementarity is either false or no more false than true. Equally, however, if we can show that state of nature complementarity is more true than false, and that there is no significant difference between complete and incomplete objects, we have shown that alternative complementarity is more true than false.

Now there appears to be a way of converting any choice between incomplete alternatives (that I be rich, that I be happy) into a choice between complete ones. We simply Cambridge-ize the state of affairs chosen, so that all features of the world appear as features of that state. For example, if I choose that I be rich, my choice is conceived of as being a choice that I be rich and England be part of the UK, and so on for each proposition or its negation. The general idea is to expand an incomplete object into a complete one in a trivial way, and thus show that we can have no substantial reason for saying something about states of nature that we are unwilling to say about alternatives.

This manoeuvre might work if we were dealing with a preference between existing objects. Each object is co-actual, and each can be turned into a world merely by adding to it its relation to every other part of the world. Presumably we hope to be able to continue to rank such expanded objects, even though if all are co-actual, all will be somehow present in each expanded object ranked. But even if a way can be found of doing this, how much sense can be given to the idea that my choice of an incomplete alternative can be expanded into a choice of a complete one, that is, of a state of nature? For there is a relevant difference between the Cambridge-ization of objects and that of alternatives. In the first case there is a criterion determining how we are to proceed in our expansion; this is the actual nature of the rest of the world. But a choice that p cannot without distortion be expanded in that way. For our criterion would be, presumably, that we should expand our description of the choice with true propositions, so far as is compatible with the initial one (that p). But choice has a propositional content, and as such is subject to indeterminacy. In choosing that p, I no doubt choose that the world be in such a way as to enable it to be true that p, but there are many such ways (even working with only one conception of necessity such as physical necessity rather than logical) and the fact of the matter is that I make no choice between them. Possible world accounts of belief attempt to capture this fact by understanding belief as a division of possible worlds into two groups: those in which the belief is true and those in which it is not. Similarly, we can understand choice as a division between worlds (two-way choice is a bipartite division, three-way choice tripartite, and so on) into those 'compatible' with the relevant proposition and the rest. But there is always more than one that is compatible, and, again, the chooser makes no choice between them. Nor can we assume that the chooser opts for that world which is

---

[5] The purpose of this complicated locution will become clear shortly.

nearest the actual one, since there may be no such world to prefer. So it is not easy to turn an incomplete choice into a complete one. Cambridge-ization will not achieve it for us, and there are principled reasons why not.

The upshot of all this is that we cannot collapse the distinction between ranking incomplete states of affairs and ranking complete ones, i.e. states of nature. But this will not tell us whether the distinction between these two is significant, in the sense required. What we are after is whether the value of one alternative may be affected by the nature of another. We have decided that it may, in cases where the choice is between incomplete alternatives. Is this reason to say that it may, where we are choosing between states of nature? I think so. Suppose that we are not thinking of ourselves as choosing which of various possible states of nature is to be actual, but merely ranking those states in order of preference. And let us suppose that none of those states is designated as actual; maybe one is the actual one, but we just don't know or need to know. Here our objects are thought of as merely possible, but why should that make us unable to apply the suggestion made when we were ranking existing objects, that the value of one may be affected by the nature of another? I can see no reason why, and nor can I see why this should alter when we are asked to choose which state of nature shall be real rather than merely to rank them. The distinction between choosing and preferring is just not great enough to justify taking a different view. The point is that the simple fact that we are now dealing with complete rather than incomplete objects is just no bar to one's being made more or less valuable by the nature of another. So the shift to states of nature makes no difference.

I conclude therefore that just as alternatives may vary in their value, according to what other alternatives are available, so may states of nature. But there is a reply to this, of a sort that we have seen before. This is that the nature of any alternative can be pulled into the account of a given state of nature, so that instead of ranking SN1 against SN2, we rank [SN1 when SN2 is the only alternative] against [SN2 when SN1 is the only alternative]. This manoeuvre, which is promoted by John Broome (1991: ch. 5; 1993), would mean that the objects ranked are affected in their nature by the ranking situation. The opposing view is that the objects ranked may be affected in their value by the ranking situation, but not in their nature. Now as a defendant of the principles of rational choice, Broome would, I think, claim not so much that one of these views is preferable to the other, but that both are equally good; our decision between them turns on a matter that is of no significance. That being so, he will obtain the result he wants, namely that complementarity is no more true than false.[6]

How could one adjudicate between these two views? Luckily, there is a reason to insist that the objects one is ranking do not alter their nature

---

[6] And thus that the Sure-Thing Principle (of which more below) is no more false than true. This is the position Broome is really after, so that, no matter how artificial the method of establishing the point, we can end up in a position to use the axioms of expected utility theory. The benefits this brings outweigh the sense of strain involved in any manoeuvres that are necessary along the way.

according to which things they are ranked against. Suppose that we have an entire ranking of states of nature, and then we are asked to rank states SN1, SN2, SN3, SN4, SN5, SN6, and SN7 against each other. We do not achieve the task we have been set if we take the objects ranked to be [SN1 when SN2–7 are the alternatives], etc. These are new objects, not the ones we were originally asked to rank. So the truth we should cling to is that the objects we rank do not change their *nature* according to the things they are ranked against, for otherwise no object can be present unchanged in more than one ranking. But this truth is compatible with the complementarist claim that the objects ranked may change in *value* according to the alternatives.

Even so, one might say, our ranking of the seven states listed above must be identical with our ranking of the admittedly different objects [SN1 when SN2–7 are the alternatives], etc. So the distinction drawn above, though real enough, is of no significance. In reply to this, we can say that there are differences between the two rankings. The first is that we can ask how the ranking of SN1, SN2, etc. would change if we considered SN8 as a further alternative. This question *cannot* be asked of the other ranking, for the alternatives allowed are already specified in the description of each. And this difference is the clue to a more important one. One way in which we approach the relative ranking of alternatives is to ask how things would have been if other alternatives had been available as well as these. For instance, in trying to decide how much difference it makes that this alternative is the only one with feature *F*, we might ask ourselves what the presence of a further alternative which has *F* (but only to a slight degree, perhaps) would have made to the relative ranking. But this sort of question *cannot* be asked if the objects we are ranking are constructed by the choice situation. I conclude that the claim that the objects ranked change their nature according to the choice situation is less true than the rival claim that they only change their value.

The difficulty that I see in this approach is that if it is to avoid the difficulty we have already exposed, that comparison of the value of two objects is relevantly similar to choice, we will have to relativize every item on the full ordering to all other items, first severally and then in pairs and so on up until each is relativized to all others at once. And there will be no way of predicting, from the value of an option that is relativized to degree *n*, what its value will be relativized to other degrees. Given this, the use of the full ordering will be limited indeed. Transitivity, for instance, must fail. For if we rank '*A* when we could have had *B*' above '*B* when we could have had *A*', and '*B* when we could have had *C*' above '*C* when we could have had *B*', it in no way follows that we should rank '*A* when we could have had *C*' above '*C* when we could have had *A*'.[7] It will be perfectly true, that is, that every relativized option occupies one and only one

---

[7] Of course, relative to one and the same three-way comparison, transitivity must be preserved—or at least nothing that I have said gives us any reason to dispute that. If we do dispute it, we will probably do so for quite different reasons, i.e. those stemming from comparisons in which many different criteria are operating at once. For a recent rehearsal of such considerations, see Temkin 1997.

place in the ordering, without this doing anything to preserve the conception of rational choice that the ideal of a full ordering was designed to promote.

There is a further problem. Suppose that we have a full ordering of all relativized options. This locates each option with respect to every other. Suppose now that I ask of item 32 in the list how it compares in value with item 33. It need not be the case that my answer is that item 32 is more valuable than item 33. The option '33 when I could have had 32' is a different option from the simple option '33', no matter how internally complex option 33 may be— and the same goes for option 32. But if my ranking order does not even commit me to claims about the relative values of the items ranked, it is pointless.

We have now come to the conclusion that there is no relevant difference between complete objects such as states of nature and incomplete ones such as alternatives (ordinarily construed), and that state of nature complementarity is more true than false. It turns out that the reasons given in the case of state of nature complementarity are just as good as when the objects ranked are alternatives. It will still be the case that we need to be able to keep the nature of the objects we are ranking constant when we introduce new objects, or when we merely wish to consider what difference that inclusion would have made in order to help us decide how to rank things as they stand.

Our overall conclusion is that complementarity is the truth, whatever the objects of choice, and whether we are ranking objects or alternative courses of action. What then are we to say about the so-called 'Sure-Thing Principle'? This has it that the value of one state of nature cannot be affected by the nature of another. It is the denial of state of nature complementarity. Suppose we have a choice between four prospects (see Figure 1). The Sure-Thing Principle is one of the two main constraints on rational preference or choice (the other is transitivity). In the case above, it generates, among others, the following theorems (where '>' means 'is preferred to'):

1. $A > B$ iff $b > c$
2. $A > C$ iff $a > d$

	States of Nature			States of Nature	
	1	2		1	2
	a	b		a	c
	Prospect A			Prospect B	

	States of Nature			States of Nature	
	1	2		1	2
	d	b		d	c
	Prospect C			Prospect D	

Figure 1 Prospect A, for example, is that one of two states of nature will occur, in the first of which we get a and in the second of which we get b.

3. $B > D$ iff $a > d$
4. $C > D$ iff $b > c$

And from (2) and (3) we can derive

5. $A > C$ iff $B > D$
6. $A > B$ iff $C > D$

The domain of the Sure-Thing Principle is standardly restricted to complete states of nature. This makes it appear that we could still embrace the principle, whatever our views about organic unities or about the mutual behaviour of incomplete objects or states of affairs. But is this true? I have been suggesting that states of nature have two relevant features: they are alternatives, and they are complete. I argued that:

1. Alternative complementarity is more true than false.
2. There is no relevant difference between complete and incomplete objects.
3. So alternative complementarity is true iff state of nature complementarity is true; they stand or fall together.
4. State of nature complementarity is more true than false.

In this process, I tried to show that state of nature complementarity cannot be trivially converted into something compatible with the Sure-Thing Principle. My conclusion is that state of nature complementarity is true, and that the Sure-Thing Principle is therefore false. The move to complete states of nature does not take us from a true complementarity to a false one, nor to one which is no more true than false. Nonetheless, state of nature complementarity is compatible with the revised (though not with the original) Atomic Principle.

Suppose then that we accept a general choice-holism to go with our reasons-holism and our value-holism. Have we now totally lost any possibility of a full ordering? There is one last way in which we could hope to retain anything like a full ordering. This is to say that what we have established is only that the context of real choice (i.e. the actually available alternatives) can affect the value of an option. This result, we might say, is clearly disturbing. But it does not altogether disturb our full ordering. Choice-holism concerns itself with real situations, in which the question what alternatives are available is a serious practical one. As such, it is to be distinguished from any thoughts about the effects of *merely comparing* one option with another. The value of an option will not vary according to what we imagine as the possible alternatives to it; it will only be affected by what actually are the alternatives. And mere comparison is relevantly similar to imaginary choosing, we might say, so long as the purpose of the comparison is to establish relative value. So an object's value is not affected by the mere act of mental comparison with another; it is only able to be affected if the two objects become real alternatives for some agent.

Even this, of course, will do something to upset our full ordering, if we suppose that the very same thing can occur in more than one actual choice situation. But we might deny that possibility, supposing instead that objects of choice are incapable of recurrence. We cannot have the same action again, that is, and we cannot have any other choosable object again either. For the objects of choice are not repeatables. If I offer you a chocolate bar today and you refuse it in favour of a pint of beer, and I offer the very same bar to you tomorrow, the fact that it is the same bar does not show that you have the same choice again. You only have a similar one, and holists allow that objects that are intrinsically similar may yet differ in value because of their context.

Be that as it may, the position that this move is trying to defend is surely another unstable one. It holds that mere comparison of two objects A and B, which we can do at any time at will, is incapable of affecting the values of A and of B; but should they become actual alternatives, their values may be affected. So I may compare A and B and prefer B, and yet when I have to choose between the two, I choose A without irrationality. This distinction between actual and imagined choice, or between the effects of choice and those of comparison, is surely unsustainable. And this means that the dream of a full ordering collapses entirely. For if I cannot compare two objects without being in danger of affecting their relative values by doing so, there is surely no sense left in which objects have their own place in the ranking order. The ranking order must mean that objects have their place on it whether one actually compares them or not; indeed, to compare them is just to establish their relative placings in the order. If one could affect those placings by the act of comparison, the notion of an order would be destroyed.

My conclusions are not very hospitable either to transitivity or to the possibility of a Great Ordering.

BIBLIOGRAPHY

Audi, R. (1996) 'Intuitionism, Pluralism, and the Foundations of Ethics', in Sinnott-Armstrong and Timmons (1996: 101–36).

—— (1998) 'Moderate Intuitionism and the Epistemology of Moral Judgement', *Ethical Theory and Moral Practice*, 1: 15–44, esp. 36–41.

Bakhurst, D. (2000) 'Ethical Particularism in Context', in Hooker and Little (2000: 157–77).

Baldwin, T. (2002) 'Intuitionism and Common Sense', in Stratton-Lake (2002: 92–112).

Belzer, M. (1986) 'Reasoning with Defeasible Principles', *Synthese*, 66: 135–98.

Bennett, J. (1995) *The Act Itself* (Oxford: Clarendon Press).

Berlin, I. (1996) *The Sense of Reality* (Oxford: Oxford University Press), esp. 33–5, 44–5.

Blackburn, S. (1981) 'Rule-Following and Moral Realism', in Holtzman and Leich (1981: 163–87).

—— (1992) 'Through Thick and Thin', *Proceedings of The Aristotelian Society*, suppl. vol. 66: 285–299.

—— (1996) 'Securing the Nots', in Sinnott-Armstrong and Timmons (1996: 82–100, esp. 97–9).

—— (1998) *Ruling Passions* (Oxford: Clarendon Press).

Blum, L. (1994) *Moral Perception and Particularity* (New York: Cambridge University Press).

Bowden, P. (1998) 'Ethical Attention: Accumulating Understandings', *European Journal of Philosophy*, 6: 59–77.

Brandom, R. B. (1994) *Making It Explicit* (Cambridge, Mass.: Harvard University Press).

—— (2000) *Articulating Reasons: An Introduction to Inferentialism* (Cambridge, Mass.: Harvard University Press).

Broad, C. D. (1930) *Five Types of Ethical Theory* (London: Routledge & Kegan Paul).

Broadie, S. W. (1993) *Ethics with Aristotle* (New York: Oxford University Press).

Brody, B. (1979) 'Intuitions and Objective Moral Knowledge', *The Monist*, 62: 446–56.

Broome, J. (1991) *Weighing Goods* (Oxford: Blackwell).

—— (1993) 'Can a Humean be Moderate?', in R. G. Frey and C. Morris (eds.), *Value, Welfare and Morality* (Cambridge: Cambridge University Press), 51–73.

—— (2000) 'Normative Requirements', in J. Dancy (ed.), *Normativity* (Oxford: Blackwell, 2000), 78–99.

Broome, J. (2004) 'Reasons', in Wallace et al. (2004: 28–55).

Burton, S. (1994) 'Particularism, Discretion, and the Rule of Law', *Nomos*, 36: 178–201.

Carritt, E. F. (1930) *The Theory of Morals* (London: Oxford University Press).

Cartwright, N. (1983) *How the Laws of Physics Lie* (Oxford: Clarendon Press).

Cavell, S. (1979) *The Claim of Reason* (Oxford: Clarendon Press).

Chang, R. (ed.) (1998) *Incommensurability, Incomparability and Practical Reason* (Cambridge, Mass.: Harvard University Press).

Chisholm, R. (1976) *Person and Object* (LaSalle, Ill.: Open Court Publishing Co.).

—— (1981) 'Defining Intrinsic Value', *Analysis*, 41: 99–100.

Coetzee, P. (1985) 'Principles and Virtues—or—Principles or Virtues', *South African Journal of Philosophy*, 4: 25–8.

Crisp, R. (1993) 'Motivation, Universality, and the Good', *Ratio*, 6: 181–90.

—— (1996) 'The Dualism of Practical Reason', *Proceedings of the Aristotelian Society*, 96: 53–73.

—— (2000) 'Particularizing Particularism', in Hooker and Little (2000: 23–47).

Cullity, G. (1994) 'International Aid and the Scope of Kindness', *Ethics*, 105: 99–127.

—— (1997) 'Practical Theory', in Cullity and Gaut (1997: 101–24).

—— (2002) 'Particularism and Presumptive Reasons', *Proceedings of the Aristotelian Society*, suppl. vol. 76: 169–90.

—— and Gaut, B. (eds.) (1997) *Ethics and Practical Reason* (Oxford: Clarendon Press).

Dancy, J. (1981) 'On Moral Properties', *Mind*, 90: 367–85.

—— (1982) 'Intuitionism in Meta-epistemology', *Philosophical Studies*, 42: 395–408.

—— (1983) 'Ethical Particularism and Morally Relevant Properties', *Mind*, 92: 530–47.

—— (1985) 'The Role of Imaginary Cases in Ethics', *Pacific Philosophical Quarterly*, 66: 141–53.

—— (1992) 'Caring about Justice', *Philosophy*, 67: 447–66.

—— (1993) *Moral Reasons*, (Oxford: Blackwell).

—— (1995) 'In Defense of Thick Concepts', in P. French, T. E. Uehling, Jr., and H. K. Wettstein (eds.), *Midwest Studies in Philosophy*, vol. 20: *Moral Concepts*, 263–79.

—— (1999*a*) 'Can the Particularist Learn the Difference between Right and Wrong?', in K. Brinkmann (ed.), *The Proceedings of the Twentieth World Congress of Philosophy*, vol. 1: *Ethics* (Bowling Green, OH: Philosophy Documentation Center, 1999), 59–72.

—— (1999*b*) 'Defending Particularism', *Metaphilosophy*, 30: 25–32.

—— (1999*c*) 'Motivation, Dispositions and Aims', *Theoria*, 65: 144–55.

—— (1999*d*) 'On the Logical and Moral Adequacy of Particularism', *Theoria*, 65: 212–24.

—— (2000a) 'The Particularist's Progress', in Hooker and Little (2000: 130–56).

—— (2000b) *Practical Reality* (Oxford: Clarendon Press).

—— (2000c) 'Scanlon's Principles', *Proceedings of the Aristotelian Society*, suppl. vol. 74: 319–38.

—— (2000d) 'Should we Pass the Buck?' in A. O'Hear (ed.), *Philosophy, the Good, the True, and the Beautiful* (Cambridge: Cambridge University Press, 2000), 159–73.

—— (2001) 'Moral Particularism', published online in the Stanford Encyclopedia of Philosophy.

—— (2002) 'La Justesse et ce qui rend-juste', in J.-M. Monnoyer (ed.), *La Structure du Monde: Objets, Propriétés, Etats de Choses. Renouveau de la Métaphysique dans l'école Australienne de Philosophie*, no. hors série de *Recherches sur la Philosophie et le Langage* (Paris: Librairie philosophique J. Vrin, 2002), 443–58.

—— (2003a) 'What do Reasons Do?', *Southern Journal of Philosophy*, 41 (supplement): 95–113; to be reprinted in T. Horgan and M. Timmons (eds.), *Ethics after Moore* (Oxford University Press, forthcoming).

—— (2003b) 'Are there Organic Unities?', *Ethics*, 113: 629–50.

—— (2004a) 'Enticing Reasons', in Wallace et al. (2004: 91–118).

—— (2004b) 'On the Importance of Making Things Right', *Ratio*, 17: 229–37.

Devereux, D. (1986) 'Particular and Universal in Aristotle's Conception of Practical Knowledge', *Review of Metaphysics*, 29: 483–504.

Dretske, F. (1970) 'Epistemic Operators', *Journal of Philosophy*, 67: 1007–23.

Dreyfus, H., and Dreyfus, S. (1986) 'What is Moral Maturity? Towards a Phenomenology of Ethical Expertise', in J. Ogilvy (ed.), *Revisioning Philosophy* (Albany, NY: SUNY Press).

Dworkin, G. (1995) 'Unprincipled Ethics', in P. French, T. E. Uehling, Jr., and H. K. Wettstein (eds.), *Midwest Studies in Philosophy*, vol. 20: *Moral Concepts*, 224–39.

Ewing, A. C. (1928) *The Morality of Punishment* (London: Kegan Paul, Trench, Trubner & Co.).

—— (1947) *The Definition of Good* (London: Macmillan).

Frankena, W. (1963) *Ethics* (Englewood Cliffs, NJ: Prentice Hall), esp. 16–17, 23–5.

Frazier, R. (1995) 'Moral Relevance and Ceteris Paribus Principles', *Ratio*, 8: 113–27.

Friedman, M. (1993) 'Care and Context in Moral Reasoning', in her *What Are Friends For?* (Ithaca, NY: Cornell University Press), 91–116.

Garfield, J. (2000) 'Particularity and Principle: The Structure of Moral Knowledge', in Hooker and Little (2000: 178–204).

Garrard, E., and McNaughton, D. (1998) 'Mapping Moral Motivation', *Ethical Theory and Moral Practice*, 1: 45–59.

Gaut, B. (1993) 'Moral Pluralism', *Philosophical Papers*, 22: 17–40.

Gay, R. (1985) 'Ethical Pluralism: A Reply to Dancy's "Ethical Particularism and Morally Relevant Properties"', *Mind*, 94: 250–62.

Giaquinto, M. (1998) 'Epistemology of the Obvious: A Geometrical Case', *Philosophical Studies*, 92: 181–204.

Gibbard, A. (1990) *Wise Choices, Apt Feelings* (Oxford: Clarendon Press).

Goldstein, I. (1989) 'Pleasure and Pain: Unconditional, Intrinsic Value', *Philosophy and Phenomenological Research*, 50: 255–76.

Hampton, J. E. (1998) *The Authority of Reason* (Cambridge: Cambridge University Press).

Hansson, S. O. (1996) 'What is Ceteris Paribus Preference?', *Journal of Philosophical Logic*, 25: 307–22.

Hare, R. M. (1963) *Freedom and Reason* (Oxford: Clarendon Press).

Herman, B. (1993) *The Practice of Moral Judgement* (Cambridge, Mass.: Harvard University Press).

Holton, R. (2002) 'Principles and Particularisms', *Proceedings of the Aristotelian Society*, suppl. vol. 76: 191–210.

Holtzman, S., and Leich, C. (eds.) (1981) *Wittgenstein: To Follow a Rule* (London: Routledge & Kegan Paul).

Hooker, B. W. (1996) 'Ross-style Pluralism versus Rule-consequentialism', *Mind*, 105: 531–52.

—— (2000) 'Moral Particularism—Wrong and Bad', in Hooker and Little (2000: 1–23).

—— and Little, M. (eds.) (2000) *Moral Particularism* (Oxford: Oxford University Press).

Horwich, P. (1998) *Meaning* (Oxford: Oxford University Press).

Humberstone, I. L. (1990) 'Wanting, Getting, Having', *Philosophical Papers*, 19: 99–118.

—— (1996) 'Intrinsic/Extrinsic', *Synthese*, 108: 205–67.

Hurka, T. (1998) 'Two Kinds of Organic Unity', *Journal of Ethics*, 2: 299–320.

Hurley, S. (1989) *Natural Reasons: Personality and Polity* (Oxford: Oxford University Press).

Hursthouse, R., Lawrence, G., and Quinn, W. (eds.) (1995) *Virtues and Reasons: Essays in Honour of Philippa Foot* (Oxford: Clarendon Press).

Irwin, T. H. (2000) 'Ethics as an Inexact Science: Aristotle's Ambitions for Moral Theory', in Hooker and Little (2000: 100–29).

Jackson, F. (1998) *From Metaphysics to Ethics: A Defence of Conceptual Analysis* (Oxford: Oxford University Press).

—— Pettit, P., and Smith, M. (2000) 'Ethical Particularism and Patterns', in Hooker and Little (2000: 79–99).

Jonsen, A. R., and Toulmin, S. (1988) *The Abuse of Casuistry: A History of Moral Reasoning* (Berkeley: University of California Press).

Kagan, S. (1988) 'The Additive Fallacy', *Ethics*, 99: 5–31.

Keenan, J. F., and Shannon, T. A. (eds.) (1995) *The Context of Casuistry* (Washington, DC: Georgetown University Press).

Korsgaard, C. (1983) 'Two Distinctions in Goodness', *Philosophical Review*, 92: 169–95; reprinted in Korsgaard (1996: 249–74).

—— (1996) *Creating the Kingdom of Ends* (Cambridge: Cambridge University Press).

Kripke, S. (1971) 'Identity and Necessity', in M. Munitz (ed.), *Identity and Individuation* (New York: New York University Press), 135–64.

—— (1982) *Wittgenstein on Rules and Private Language* (Cambridge, Mass.: Harvard University Press).

Lance, M., and Little, M. (forthcoming) 'Mad Dogs and Englishmen: Moral Valence, Defeasibility, and Privileged Conditions'.

Langton, R. (forthcoming) 'Values, Conditioned and Conferred'.

—— and Lewis, D. (1998) 'Defining "Intrinsic"', *Philosophy and Phenomenological Research*, 58: 333–45.

—— —— (2001) 'Marshall and Parsons on "Intrinsic"', *Philosophy and Phenomenological Research*, 63: 353–5.

Larmore, C., *Patterns of Moral Complexity* (Cambridge: Cambridge University Press).

Lemos, N. (1994) *Intrinsic Value: Concept and Warrant* (Cambridge: Cambridge University Press).

Lewis, H. A. (1977) 'Are Generalizations Incomprehensible?', in D. Holdcroft (ed.), *Papers on Logic and Language* (University of Warwick publication), 32–54.

Little, M. (1994) 'Moral Realism: Non-Naturalism', *Philosophical Books*, 35: 225–32.

—— (1995) 'Seeing and Caring: The Role of Affect in Feminist Moral Epistemology', *Hypatia*, 10: 117–37.

—— (1997) 'Virtue as Knowledge: Objections from the Philosophy of Mind', *Nous*, 31: 59–79.

—— (2000) 'Moral Generalities Revisited', in Hooker and Little (2000: 276–304).

—— (2001) 'Wittgensteinian Lessons on Particularism', in C. Elliot (ed.), *Slow Cures and Bad Philosophers: Essays on Wittgenstein, Medicine, and Bioethics* (Durham, NC: Duke University Press), 161–80.

Loudon, R. B. (1991) 'Aristotle's Practical Particularism', in J. P. Anton and A. Preus (eds.), *Essays in Ancient Greek Philosophy*, 4 (Albany, NY: SUNY Press).

—— (1992) *Morality and Moral Theory* (New York: Oxford University Press).

Lucas, J. R. (1955) 'The Lesbian Rule', *Journal of Philosophy*, 30: 195–213.

McDowell, J. (1978) 'Are Moral Requirements Hypothetical Imperatives?', *Proceedings of the Aristotelian Society*, suppl. vol. 52: 13–29; reprinted in McDowell (1998a: 77–94).

—— (1979) 'Virtue and Reason', *The Monist*, 62: 331–50; reprinted in McDowell (1998a: 50–73).

—— (1981) 'Non-cognitivism and Rule-following', in Holtzman and Leich (1981: 141–62); reprinted in McDowell (1998a: 198–218).

McDowell, J. (1982) 'Criteria, Defeasibility, and Knowledge', *Proceedings of the British Academy*, 68: 455–79; reprinted in McDowell (1998*b*: 369–94, esp. p. 378).

——(1998*a*) *Mind, Value, and Reality* (Cambridge, Mass.: Harvard University Press).

——(1998*b*) *Meaning, Knowledge, and Reality* (Cambridge, Mass.: Harvard University Press).

MacIntyre, A. (1984) *After Virtue: A Study in Moral Theory* (London: Duckworth, 2nd edn., revised).

——(1988) *Whose Justice? Which Rationality?* (London: Duckworth).

——(1990) *Three Rival Versions of Moral Inquiry: Encyclopaedia, Genealogy, and Tradition* (Notre Dame, Ind.: University of Notre Dame Press).

McKeever, S., and Ridge, M. (forthcoming) 'What does Holism have to do with Particularism?', *Ratio*.

Mackie, J. L. (1977) *Ethics: Inventing Right and Wrong* (London: Penguin Books).

McNaughton, D. A. (1988) *Moral Vision* (Oxford: Blackwell).

——(1996) 'An Unconnected Heap of Duties?', *Philosophical Quarterly*, 46: 433–47.

——and Rawling, P. (2000) 'Unprincipled Ethics', in Hooker and Little (2000: 256–75).

Mill, J. S. (1861) *Utilitarianism*, ed. R. Crisp (Oxford: Oxford University Press, 1998).

Millgram, E. (2002) 'Murdoch, Practical Reasoning and Particularism', *Notizie di Politeia*, 18: 64–87.

Mitchell, D. (1963) 'Are Moral Principles Really Necessary?', *Australasian Journal of Philosophy*, 41: 163–81.

Moore, G. E. (1903) *Principia Ethica* (Cambridge: Cambridge University Press).

——(1922) 'The Conception of Intrinsic Value', in his *Philosophical Studies* (London: Routledge & Kegan Paul), 253–75.

——(1942) 'A Reply to my Critics', in P. A. Schilpp (ed.), *The Philosophy of G. E. Moore* (New York: Tudor Publishing Co.), 535–687.

Murdoch, I. (1970) *The Sovereignty of Good* (Oxford: Blackwell), esp. 32–3, 44.

——(1992) *Metaphysics as a Guide to Morals* (London: Chatto and Windus), esp. 302, 493.

Nagel, T. (1979) 'Fragmentation of Value', in his *Mortal Questions* (Cambridge: Cambridge University Press), 128–41.

Norman, R. (1997) 'Making Sense of Moral Realism', *Philosophical Investigations*, 20: 117–35.

Nussbaum, M. (1986) *The Fragility of Goodness* (Cambridge: Cambridge University Press).

——(1990) *Love's Knowledge* (New York: Oxford University Press).

——(2000) 'Why Practice Needs Ethical Theory: Particularism, Principle, and Bad Behaviour', in Hooker and Little (2000: 227–55).

O'Neill, O. (1996) *Towards Justice and Virtue: A Reconstructive Account of Practical Reasoning* (Cambridge: Cambridge University Press).

—— (2000) *Bounds of Justice* (Cambridge: Cambridge University Press), esp. 56–7.

Parfit, D. (1984) *Reasons and Persons* (Oxford: Oxford University Press).

—— (1997) 'Reasons and Motivation', *Proceedings of the Aristotelian Society*, suppl. vol. 71: 99–130.

Prichard, H. A. (1912) 'Does Moral Philosophy Rest Upon a Mistake?', *Mind*, 21: 21–37; reprinted in Prichard (1968: 1–17).

—— (1928) 'Duty and Interest', in Prichard (1968: 201–38).

—— (1968) *Moral Obligation*, ed. J. O. Urmson (Oxford: Oxford University Press).

—— (2002) *Moral Writings*, ed. J. MacAdam (Oxford: Clarendon Press).

Quinn, W. (1993*a*) 'Putting Rationality in Its Place', in R. Frey and C. Morris (eds.), *Value, Welfare and Morality* (Cambridge: Cambridge University Press); reprinted in Quinn (1993*b*: 228–55) and in Hursthouse et al. (1995: 181–208).

—— (1993*b*) *Morality and Action* (Cambridge: Cambridge University Press).

Rachels, J. (1993) *The Elements of Moral Philosophy* (New York: Harper Collins).

Rawls, J. (1971) *A Theory of Justice* (Cambridge, Mass.: Harvard University Press).

Raz, J. (1986) *The Morality of Freedom* (Oxford: Clarendon Press).

—— (1998) 'Incommensurability and Agency', in Chang (1998: 110–28).

—— (2000*a*) *Engaging Reason* (Oxford: Oxford University Press, 2000).

—— (2000*b*) 'The Central Conflict: Morality and Self-interest', in Raz (2000*a*: 303–32); reprinted in R. Crisp and B. Hooker (eds.), *Well-Being and Morality: Essays in Honour of James Griffin* (Oxford: Clarendon Press, 2000), 209–38.

—— (2000*c*) 'The Truth in Particularism', in Raz (2000*a*: 218–46); reprinted in Hooker and Little (2000: 48–78). In the text, page references are given to both printings of this paper.

Richardson, H. S. (1990) 'Specifying Norms as a Way to Resolve Concrete Ethical Problems', *Philosophy and Public Affairs*, 19: 279–310.

—— (2000) 'Balancing and Interpreting Bioethical Principles', *Journal of Medicine and Philosophy*, 25: 285–307.

Ross, W. D. (1927) 'The Basis of Objective Judgments in Ethics', *International Journal of Ethics*, 37/2: 113–27.

—— (1930) *The Right and the Good* (Oxford: Clarendon Press).

—— (1939) *Foundations of Ethics* (Oxford: Clarendon Press).

Sandel, M. (1982) *Liberalism and the Limits of Justice* (Cambridge: Cambridge University Press).

Sayre-McCord, G. (1996) 'Coherentist Epistemology and Moral Theory', in Sinnott-Armstrong and Timmons (1996: 137–89).

Scanlon, T. M. (1998) *What We Owe to Each Other* (Cambridge, Mass.: Harvard University Press).

—— (2000) 'Intention and Permissibility', *Proceedings of the Aristotelian Society*, suppl. vol. 74: 301–17.

Schauer, F. (1991) *Playing by the Rules: A Philosophical Examination of Rule-Based Decision-Making in Law and in Life* (Oxford: Clarendon Press).

Scheffler, S. (1987) 'Morality through Thick and Thin', *Philosophical Review*, 96: 411–34; reprinted in his *Boundaries and Allegiances* (Oxford: Oxford University Press, 2001), 197–215.

Schueler, G. F. (2003) *Reasons and Purposes* (Oxford: Clarendon Press).

Sellars, W. (1956) 'Empiricism and the Philosophy of Mind', in H. Feigl and M. Scriven (eds.), *Minnesota Studies in the Philosophy of Science*, vol. 1 (Minneapolis: University of Minnesota Press), 255–329.

Shafer-Landau, R. (1997) 'Moral Rules', *Ethics*, 107: 584–611.

Sherman, N. (1996) *Making a Necessity of Virtue* (Cambridge: Cambridge University Press).

Sidgwick, H. (1907) *The Methods of Ethics*, 7th edn. (London: Macmillan).

Sinnott-Armstrong, W. (1999) 'Some Varieties of Particularism', *Metaphilosophy*, 30: 1–12.

—— and Timmons, M. (eds.) (1996) *Moral Knowledge?* (New York: Oxford University Press).

Smith, Adam (1790) *The Theory of Moral Sentiments*, 6th edn. (London and Edinburgh); esp. Part 3, chs. 4–6.

Smith, M. (1994) *The Moral Problem* (Oxford: Blackwell).

Stocker, M. (1990) *Plural and Conflicting Values* (Oxford: Clarendon Press).

Stoneham, T. (1999) 'Logical Form and Thought Content', *Analysis*, 59: 183–5.

Stratton-Lake, P. J. (1997) 'Can Hooker's Rule-consequentialist Principle Justify Rossian Prima Facie Duties?', *Mind*, 106: 751–8.

—— (2000) *Kant, Duty, and Moral Worth* (London: Routledge).

—— (ed.) (2002) *Re-evaluating Ethical Intuitionism* (Oxford: Oxford University Press).

Tännsjö, T. (1995) 'In Defence of Theory in Ethics', *Canadian Journal of Philosophy*, 25: 571–94.

Temkin, L. (1997) 'Rethinking the Good', in J. Dancy (ed.), *Reading Parfit* (Oxford: Blackwell), 290–345.

Thesiger, W. (1959) *Arabian Sands* (London: Longmans).

Thompson, M. (1995) 'The Representation of Life', in Hursthouse et al. (1995: 247–96).

Timmons, M. (2002) *Moral Theory: An Introduction* (Rowman and Littlefield).

Travis, C. (2000) *Unshadowed Thought* (Cambridge, Mass.: Harvard University Press).

Walker, M. U. (1997) *Moral Understandings* (London: Routledge, 1997).

Wallace, J. D. (1988) *Moral Relevance and Moral Conflict* (Ithaca, NY: Cornell University Press)

—— (1996) *Ethical Norms, Particular Cases* (Ithaca, NY: Cornell University Press).

Wallace, R. J., Pettit, P., Scheffler, S., and Smith, M. (eds.) (2004) *Reason and Value: Themes from the Moral Philosophy of Joseph Raz* (Oxford: Clarendon Press).

White, A. R. (1972) 'What We Believe', in N. Rescher (ed.), *Studies in the Philosophy of Mind*, APQ monograph series no. 6 (Oxford: Blackwell), 69–84.

Wiggins, D. (1976*a*) 'Deliberation and Practical Reason', *Proceedings of the Aristotelian Society*, 76: 29–51; reprinted in Wiggins (1987: 215–37).

—— (1976*b*) 'Truth, Invention and the Meaning of Life', *Proceedings of the British Academy*, 62: 331–78; reprinted in Wiggins (1987: 87–137).

—— (1987) *Needs, Values, Truth* (Oxford, Blackwell).

—— (1997) 'Incommensurability: Four Proposals', in Chang (1998: 52–66).

Williams, B. A. O. (1979) 'Conflicts of Value', in A. Ryan (ed.), *The Idea of Freedom: Essays in Honour of Isaiah Berlin* (Oxford: Oxford University Press), 221–32; reprinted in Williams (1981: 71–82).

—— (1981) *Moral Luck: Philosophical Papers 1973–1980* (Cambridge: Cambridge University Press).

—— (1985) *Ethics and the Limits of Philosophy* (Cambridge, Mass.: Harvard University Press).

—— (1988) 'What Does Intuitionism Imply?', in J. Dancy, J. Moravscik, and C. C. W. Taylor (eds.), *Human Agency: Essays for J. O. Urmson* (Palo Alto, Calif.: Stanford University Press); reprinted in Williams (1995*b*: 182–91).

—— (1995*a*) 'Acts and Omissions, Doing and Not Doing', in R. Hursthouse, G. Lawrence, and W. Quinn (1995: 331–40, esp. 332–3); reprinted in Williams (1995*b*: 56–64, esp. 57).

—— (1995*b*) *Making Sense of Humanity* (Cambridge: Cambridge University Press).

—— (2002) *Truth and Truthfulness* (Princeton: Princeton University Press).

Winch, P. (1965) 'The Universalizability of Moral Judgements', in his *Ethics and Action* (London: Routledge & Kegan Paul, 1972), 151–70.

Wittgenstein, L. (1953) *Philosophical Investigations* (Oxford: Blackwell).

Woods, M. J. (1986) 'Intuition and Perception in Aristotle's Ethics', *Oxford Studies in Ancient Philosophy*, 4: 145–66.

INDEX

Lightning Source UK Ltd.
Milton Keynes UK
20 January 2010

148840UK00004B/4/P